MICRO-PROCESSORS

MICRO-PROCESSORS

An Introduction

PAUL KIMBERLEY

McGraw-Hill Book Company

New York St. Louis San Francisco Bogotá
Guatemala Hamburg Lisbon Madrid Mexico Montreal
Panama Paris San Juan São Paulo Tokyo Toronto

Reprinted by arrangement with Hayes Kennedy Limited, England

First McGraw-Hill Paperback edition, 1982

1 2 3 4 5 6 7 8 9 0 S M S M 8 7 6 5 4 3 2

ISBN 0-07-034548-1

LIBRARY OF CONGRESS CATALOGING IN PUBLICATION DATA

Kimberley, Paul.
Microprocessors.
(McGraw-Hill vocational technical series)
Bibliography: p.
1. Microprocessors. I. Title.
TK7895.M5K55 1982 001.64 82-28
ISBN 0-07-034548-1 (pbk.) AACR2

Contents

Illustrations

Figures:

About this book

This book is for those people who need to inform themselves of the principles and jargon involved in modern microelectronics and computer systems, in particular those systems which are beginning to transform business and industry. The book is aimed at professional laymen, that vast body of engineers, managers, executives, lecturers and professionals from every discipline who, although perfectly competent in their own field, may feel insecure and under-prepared, perhaps even intimidated, when confronted with the microelectronic revolution.

Anyone who has had anything to do with the installation of a conventional computer system will ruefully recall the feeling of being left out of conversations because of an inability to share the secret language of the salesman and other specialists. Anyone contemplating the application of microprocessors to any part of his business will have to deal with such specialists, with systems analysts, microprogrammers, electronic engineers and designers, transducer specialists, not to mention salesmen who will attempt to convince that their system is superior to any other. The manager who has responsibility for the installation and supervision of the system needs to acquire at least a superficial knowledge of a number of disciplines; of computer hardware, mainframe, mini and microcomputers; of programming, the different types of language and methods of programming; of electronics, semiconductors, microprocessors and a host of different types of chip; of memory technology, the different types of memory and its applications; of input and output transducers, the devices that enable computers to extend their range of applications into industrial processes and products; of packaging, switchgear and the necessary environmental controls. This book provides a brief guide to the more important aspects likely to be encountered by the professional layman, together with two generalised case studies, one industrial, one administrative, which show how to approach the problems of applying the new technology.

The book is not meant to be a text book, but rather a book for the brief case, to be dipped into during rail or air trips, or kept on the office bookshelf for reference when required. Beginning with an examination of the development of the technology over the last three decades, it goes on to look at the market trends and the rapidly widening range of applications. Chapter 3 analyses and describes the individual microectronic devices which go to make up a modern microcomputer, so that a non-specialist can at least achieve a broad grasp of the technology involved. Chapter 4 discusses the devices and technologies surrounding the microprocessor, without which it would be of no practical use, and chapter 5 puts it all together in two case studies to suggest how to set about applying the technology to real business situations. Finally, there is a Glossary of over 1000 of the most commonly used terms, without which it is almost impossible to communicate on the subject at all.

The book was planned as a businessman's self-defence kit against the secret language of the 1980's technocrats. Executives of the '80's defend yourselves! You will need to, if your business is to prosper.

1. Introduction

Keeping up to date

For the businessman or practising professional in industry or commerce, time is the enemy. Merely to keep abreast of developments in all the subjects relating to a particular job takes a considerable amount of time. To find time to read books aimed at the top-of-the-pyramid specialist, apart from demanding a starting point of knowledge which may be quite rare, inevitably means something else is left undone. Thus anything that is written to advance knowledge or share experience generally finds a fairly narrow, vertically aligned audience. Due to the remorseless, ever increasing volume of work and what appears to be a diminishing number of able and willing executives, there is an increased dependence upon specialist technical advisers, whom everyone trusts to keep up to date in their own fields.

Experience shows that the publications that are of the most use for the professional layman for most of the time are glossaries, introductions to subjects, dictionaries and the like. This sort of book requires no previous knowledge but presents the reader with a pithy, clear, encapsulated definition or explanation, very quickly. Its object is not to entertain or to educate, but to inform or enlighten. Further it does not seek to impose on the reader the burden of retaining that brief illumination since it can always be referred to again if necessary. In the real world this is by far the most practical approach, since one seldom fixes knowledge in the mind on first acquaintance. If often requires several different explanations of the same topic to acquire a genuine understanding. This then is the rationale behind that which follows.

The knowledge gap

The subject matter contained within the remaining pages is based on strictly practical grounds. The hypothesis is that the first step in any new project is always to assess the level of knowledge and experience of the participants and to begin to create the language that ensures mutual understanding.

There is a surprising phenomenon that reoccurs in every separate project. The combination of the industry and its own unique jargon, the level of understanding of the newer technology and the ability and willingness to adopt its unique language always combine to create a language that is absolutely singular for the life of the project. In-jokes, disasters, personalities and local accents all play a part in producing this hybrid vocabulary.

Whatever the reason and however long it takes, a project will never be totally successful until this verbal shorthand begins to be used, often unconsciously. The danger to the non-specialist or professional layman, is that the use of the special language implies an understanding but can in fact cover up a misunderstanding of the real meaning of the terms used.

An unnerving fact is that this is more likely in the 1980's than it was in the 1970's. By 1970 computers had been in use on a fairly general basis for 10 years and on a much more restricted basis for over 20 years. The large computer companies were investing very heavily in training programmes for users, user management and their own salesmen, analysts and programmers.

For a few years in the later 60's and early 70's some computer companies followed the enlightened path of Industry Marketing education, or vertically integrated marketing as it has come to be known. This process involved the wholesale recruitment of qualified professionals from industry and commerce who were then taught all aspects of computers in a methodical and intense fashion. This group of people were, in turn, used to educate customers from their own industrial background and also to educate computer staff in the problems of the industry concerned.

During this period the computer salesman was the educator par-excellence. He was usually a graduate, professionally experienced and qualified and generally very well spoken and groomed. He was trained in the art and tactics of public speaking, in presentation methods and armed with a whole array of expensive visual aids. At the same time the technical press was in an embryonic stage, seeking to capture and inform a wider and wider circle of readers. Introductory books on every conceivable aspect of computing were published and were often given away free by the computer companies. Indeed, many people claimed of IBM that the company was the world's largest publisher during this time. It was a vital and formative period but now unfortunately the rules have changed completely.

The reason, as ever, is economics. When a salesman had a sales quota of $1 million to $2 million and his products sold for upwards of $100,000, an average easily being $500,000, the economics of meeting targets and being able to spend time on education are fairly obvious. This was transparently the case in the golden days of the mainframe monopoly. Any computer company's branch office could envisage running five or six seminars a year for the benefit of their local business community. Outside the universities, virtually the only way of learning about the technology in the 1970's was through a computer company or its employees, and they did a remarkable job.

It will be seen that the US dollar($) is the unit of currency used throughout this book. This is because the US dollar has become the computer industry's standard measure of performance and pricing. The large computer companies set their targets for all territories, domestic and international, in US dollars. The head offices of the majority of these multinationals are situated in the United States.

Naturally enough in the end technology stole a march on the computer giants and the minicomputer made its breakthrough. This revolution, or apparent revolution, (it was in fact caused by an evolutionary change in solid state physics) literally decimated the price of computer hardware. In some cases it was possible to obtain the same computing power for only one tenth of the purchase price. This process of cost/performance reduction is still continuing, although it will probably end by the mid-80's.

In the heyday of the mainframe, computers were sold direct to the customer, the end user. During this period, in the early 1970's, the end user set up his specialist data processing staff; they had their own computer room, environmentally controlled, their own offices and quite often their own hours of working. In many cases they appeared, and still do today, to be marching to a different drummer than the rest of the working population. In this way the supplier had the responsibility for developing and manufacturing hardware, and for developing the software brains for the computer, such as operating systems and programming languages. The end user (customer) took on the responsibility for the application programming. Thus the supplier provided the means for problem solving, the customer used the computer and his own people for the actual solution.

This had a number of consequences. It meant that only larger organisations could afford to install computers. In general the in-depth education was reserved for that type of customer and quite often, because of immediate DP compartmentalisation, their knowledge was not passed on to the average user. In part this explains the source of that plethora of amusing but generally uninformed stories which blamed the computer for everything except the Second World War.

Although the suppliers' education was broad and generous, for clear commercial reasons it was very specifically directed. There was not then, and is not now, any significant altruistic computer education performed by any bodies except colleges and universities. By virtue of their dependence upon the suppliers for information these academic bodies themselves are, inevitably, always behind what is happening in the field.

The minicomputer has an entirely different rationale, in

design, in its suppliers' marketing and education support and in the creation of a brand new industrial infra structure.

Firstly, the mini was smaller, and had (originally) much less sophistication and capability than the mainframe. Its software varied between 'very limited' and 'non existent'. However it was a computer; it could perform certain jobs perfectly adequately and was, relatively, extremely cheap. Initially the minicomputer manufacturers' marketing problem was largely influenced by their software limitation. It could not hope to expand the numbers of organisations who used computers until there were enough qualified software staff around to support the expansion. It appears that in recognition of this fact they sold to existing computer users, who, because they already possessed the necessary expertise, employed mini computers in other areas of their organisations, generally on separate tasks to those performed by the mainframe. For example, early versions of minicomputers were used for industrial and process control and machine tool control, tasks for which the mainframe was both too expensive and technically inappropriate.

Eventually it was the programmers themselves who solved the marketing problem. A new industry evolved, based on programmers themselves. It became known as the Software Industry and consists of software houses, systems houses and systems integraters. These organisations purchased the hardware from the minicomputer suppliers, occasionally added other peripherals such as printers and video display units from other preferred suppliers and then programmed the machine for an individual customer. This gave the customer the benefits of lower price and a 'turnkey' package where total responsibility was taken by the computing subcontractor. It offered the customer the overwhelming benefit of not necessarily having to set up a DP department. To the equipment supplier it meant he could keep his volume up because he was selling either to major users or a relatively small number of OEMers of system houses. The same factors enabled him to keep his marketing costs down because he only had to sell to a restricted clientele, generally on the same international basis as his mainframe counterpart. This gave the marketing and education responsibility to the new middleman, the systems house.

The reaction from the mainframe suppliers was tardy but predictable. Marketing costs were effectively cut. At best, they did not grow at the previous rates. Inevitably less evident effort was put into educating the market place, except for technical staff. Customer education, until this point either free, or at the worst, inexpensive, now began to be seen as a major item in the purchase of equipment from the mainframe supplier.

Whereas with the mainframe installation all specialist knowledge stopped at the DP department, with the systems house industry it often did not get that far (the past tense is inaccurate; the situation remains the same). Because of the cost competitiveness between local businesses in the systems house industry, marketing costs were, and are, kept to an absolute minimum. Formerly it might have been expected that several copies of full, reasoned and clear proposals would be provided by a mainframe supplier to a prospective client, to enable purchasing decisions to be made. In the Software House industry it is not unknown for the only exchange of information to be a 'gentlemen's agreement', a handshake and an invoice! Thus not only did the numbers of marketing educators decline, so did their quality; and so far nothing has effectively filled the vacuum.

The mainframe and minicomputer now have greater technical similarities. They are still marketed and supported in a different way and still offer differing price/performance characteristics. Whilst the minicomputer has extended the range of applications which were created by the mainframe there has been no resultant revolutionary breakthrough in computer applications. The reason is that the size, price and specifications of both main types of computer have only allowed them to be used in administrative data processing. The lack of contact between users and manufacturers has also had the effect of limiting knowledge to existing users and the immediate circle of prospective customers.

The microcomputer is likely to change this state of affairs but computer users of the future will still need to acquire a fundamental understanding of what a computer is, and is not, in order to take advantage of current technology.

In reality both the mainframe and the minicomputer are sophisticated electromechanical assemblies, containing computer logic, a variety of different types of memory devices, and a variety of transducers. In the case of the mini and mainframe the input transducers referred to could be the keys on the various keyboards and the reading devices for input media. An output transducer could be a disk read head. From the glossary it will be seen that a transducer is a device that converts physical variables, such as heat, pressure and so on, into observable measurement (and vice versa). This defines a keyswitch as the very simplest of pressure transducers, down is on – to a known pressure, and up is off.

It will be instantly recognised by anyone who has even the remotest contact with computers that they are, without exception, extremely rigorous in their demands on the presentation of data. Each piece of information must go into an exact space on a card or a video display unit, etc. It must occupy the whole of that space; it must contain only numeric characters, or an acceptable mix of alphabetic and numeric characters. There are stringent editing and balancing rules. Any commercial computer system only performs as well as the organisation and presentation of data allows.

If that restriction were to be removed, or a way of expanding the range of methods of presenting data could be found, the variety of uses to which the computer could be put would expand correspondingly.

The breakthrough in cost and performance of microprocessors and the range of solid state devices which help create the modern microcomputer, together with increasingly sophisticated and complex transducers have now created a situation where it is possible to install an assembly of sensors, industrial microcomputers and appropriate storage, together with suitable enclosures, cabling, switches and programs to perform a whole range of data processing, word processing, process control, industrial control and robotic tasks for considerably less cost than today's minicomputer.

These latest developments in microelectronics have increased the problems of education. The microprocessor manufacturers, often referred to as fabricators, have an even more distant relationship with the end users. There are very few fabrication plants outside the United States. Thus the product goes from the US plant to their local national importer. The national importer then sells it to one of a number of regional stockists who in turn sell it to the manufacturing concern, where it is to be used within a product. They of course either sell that product direct or through their own distribution system.

Where the microprocessor is to be used to control a process it is generally sold by the stockist to a small electronics firm or systems house. The infra structure to support modern microelectronics is by no means bedded down and established yet.

Thus the education and knowledge dilemma is deeper and wider. Technology is developing in so many new directions at a pace which is impossible for any individual to assimilate. There is now virtually no supplier education apart from lavish brochures and publications, often too specific to a supplier to be of general use. The education that the supplier does provide is once again for specialists; it is not cheap and it is obviously oriented towards his own products.

The vacuum will be filled in time. The seminar, conference and exhibition industries are growing apace. There is evidence that the professional education market will be a force to be reckoned with in the late 80's. Books, magazines, TV and video will all play their part in this process, however random.

Special languages

In his Rede lecture in 1959, C. P. Snow spoke of what he called the 'great divide' between scientists and writers, more generally between Science and the Arts. This gap, occasionally referred to as the 'culture gulf' or 'The Two Cultures', (the title of Snow's lecture) manifested itself in the increasing singularity of language and vocabulary of many of the specialised disciplines. Of course, everyone recognises the need for a code, or shorthand, between two people on the same wavelength; it reduces unnecessary communications. Specialisation has merely extended this process to embrace a whole range of different disciplines.

The boom in education and research has reached such proportions that it is now almost impossible to achieve anything other than a very cursory understanding of another discipline or profession. If a social scientist and a programmer, for example, were to discuss jobs with each other without any prior knowledge, they would need to create a hybrid language before any 'meaningful' communication could take place.

This is particularly true of what have come to be known as 'high technology' topics. Due to a succession of some of the most exciting developments in physics there appears to be an exponential growth in activity and knowledge in almost all aspects of science-based engineering. As a consequence the hardware cost of computing has reduced many times, through the efforts of the specialists. On the other hand, the cost of understanding the effects of the changes in technology and the people costs to make it work have kept pace with inflation, so that a new combination of factors faces today's computer user.

It is clear that no matter how cheap the computer hardware has become it is still dependent upon people to analyse the problem, write programs and operate the equipment. People cost more each year; the actual computer is likely to cost less each year, especially for the next few years.

Technological developements have also changed the rigid rules which previously governed data input, which in turn has led to the potential for a wider application of computers in all businesses. This in turn forces a wider range of people, many of whom are specialists in their own field, to embrace the newer technologies.

So the task of problem identification still remains. Possibly the computer will never be able to help in that area. The challenge presented by microelectronics to the professional layman is to recognise the potential of the new developments and then harness that potential to enhance performance and help him to do a better job.

The principles of the computer

Charles Babbage (1792–1871) is usually regarded as the father of the modern computer. The basic principles he embodied in his designs still define what a computer is, or is not. In 1812 Babbage laid down that if a machine is to perform as a human computer does then it must contain:

Firstly: An arithmetic unit which can perform all normal arithmetic functions. Today we would recognise this as part of the Central Processing Unit. Babbage called it a mill, presumably after the handle and gears needed to operate his machine.

Secondly: A mechanism for retaining all the numerical values which are needed for any calculation and the numbers which represent the instructions for each stage of the calculations. With simple prescience Babbage called this the 'store'.

Thirdly: A power of judgement, or decision making ability. In Babbage's case this did not involve the now commonly accepted principles of Boolean Algebraic Logic, but was mechanically controlled according to strictly defined criteria.

Fourthly: The machine must have a convenient method of feeding numbers into it and a convenient method of extracting results from the machine. Babbage planned to use Jacquard type punch cards for input and actually to set type as well as producing punch cards for output.

Since Babbage's original work on his Difference Engine and

Analytical Engine, which represented the earliest and only partially successful attempts at constructing computers, the research and development effort dedicated to producing devices enbodying Babbage's principles has expanded each year, and shows no sign of diminishing. Succeeding developments are more than adequately covered in many other publications (see Bibliography). This part of the narrative will concentrate upon the developments of the last thirty years.

Mainframes and Minis

From the late 1930's until the early 1950's, universities around the world, particularly in America and Britain, were designing and developing their own unique computing machines. Each had its own acronym; for example there was the A.C.E. or Automatic Computing Engine from the National Physical Laboratory in England. Deuce was the name for the second machine of this design. L.E.O. was the name given to a machine developed by Lyons (the caterers) Electronic Office.

From America came a huge variety, but among the most important were the Harvard Mark I calculator, designed between 1939–1944 by IBM engineers, the Whirlwind from Massachusetts Institute of Technology, and the ENIAC (the Electronic Numerical Integrator And Calculator) from the University of Pennsylvania. This machine incorporated 18,000 valves, 1,500 relays and literally thousands of soldered joints. It was built under the supervision of Professor J. von Neumann and is credited with the first use of the stored program. In this way it was possible, either through direct input switches or paper tape, to talk to the computer in its own binary language and set up all the switches and circuits needed to program a machine.

The ENIAC was completed in 1946. In 1948 IBM introduced their own version containing 23,000 relays and 13,000 valves. Later the Rand Corporation introduced their version, the UNIVAC, and the race to produce the first commercially marketable computer was on. The mainframe industry had begun.

This is a convenient point to review what a computer is, or is not. There are two main types of computers in use, digital and analog. Digital machines are in far more common usage than the analog (or analogue) computer. In fact, due to the advances in solid state physics which will be dealt with later in this section, it is even possible that the digital computer will one day completely replace the analog machine.

In the most basic comparisons, digital machines are used for data processing tasks, administration, accounting and as an aid to management. On the other hand, analog computers are mainly used for scientific research and development (particularly modelling) and in instrumentation and control. A digital computer works on numbers, no matter how far removed from a mathematical type of problem the application may appear to be. All data which is entered into the digital computer or data processing machine is translated by the various input devices into some sort of numerical code (see Glossary for codes and numbering systems). This enables the stored program within the Central Processing Unit to set up the switches and circuits needed to process those numerical inputs along the right path and to translate them on output into a form recognisable by human eyes.

The analog computer normally works on input voltage levels, generated by, for example, mechanical movements. The magnitudes of such voltage levels may fluctuate with time within a known or anticipated range according to mathematical equations. Thus analog machines can be used for such things as continuously modelling expensive scientific experiments, or controlling a complex process or plant. In this type of task the analog machine is measuring voltage levels continuously to give a comprehensive history of readings on what might be a very brief event or phenomenon, for example a satellite launch. Since digital machines operate in a cyclical manner, taking a fixed quantity of data readings within a fixed time, it is unlikely that a digital computer could accommodate this sort of work, especially at the same price level. Analog machines are normally very limited in their range of tasks whereas digital machines are more often general purpose data processing machines. Thus someone buying an analog machine would know precisely the tasks for which he was buying the machine, while someone buying a digital data processing machine is likely to know only what jobs he intends the machine to do in the early stages. He buys the machine as much for its flexibility as for the ability to do a particular job.

The word 'analogy' from which analog is derived means 'agreement' or 'having a similarity to', according to the Concise Oxford Dictionary. It is also taken to mean 'having a parallel meaning', hence analog computing is also referred to as parallel processing.

A good practical illustration of an analog processor is the analog watch. This type of watch displays a value on the watch face which is generated from a set of physical variables, the watch mechanism. The actual time has to be deduced from the watch hands and the scale on the watch face. Thus, although an analog watch will continuously display the exact time, inaccuries are bound to creep in because the observer cannot match the accuracy of the display with his powers of observation. The mechanical movement of mechanisms in the watch can also provide fluctuating inputs which are reflected as inaccuracies on output displays.

Compared to the analog watch the digital watch is only accurate at the exact instant the time value display changes since the whole mechanism is driven by a timed pulse derived from a quartz timer. Nevertheless in practical terms this is a distinction in search of a difference since digital watches appear to be taking over from analog watches, according to the evidence of the last few years.

In the same way technology could make it possible for digital computers to take over the tasks of analog computers. In 1979 the world market for analog computers was stated by one trade magazine to be less than $25,000,000; in fact a very large proportion of the machines this value represents already incorporate a digital processor which stores programs to analyse and print resultant output. This type of machine has come to be known as the hybrid computer, or parallel-digital machine.

It will be necessary to return briefly to the principles of analog signals and analog processing at later points in the narrative. The modern microelectronics manufacturing industry now produces fairly inexpensive Analog to Digital (A to D) and Digital to Analog (D to A) converters which have an impact on the wider applications of computers in the future.

As foreseen in the scientific developments of Babbage and, later, von Neumann, a computer now requires the following essential components.

Input/output: Computers must have the means to conveniently accept data and to conveniently provide data, in an acceptable form to the user (or users). In practice this means the whole range of input and output devices available today, which include such things as:

Paper input; card and tape

Magnetic input; magnetic card, tape, cassettes, floppy disks and conventional hard disks of varying capacities, right up to mass storage units.

Direct input; online keyboards, video display units etc., scanning by optical character recognition methods, optical mark readers, computer to computer transmission and, probably, by voice input in the not too distant future. In almost all cases output can take place on the same or similar devices from which input occurs, with the exception of the invaluable and ubiquitous printer in all of its forms, i.e. impact, thermal, xerographic, ink jet and so on. In order that all these various devices will work on a given computer the particular machine needs a whole range of input/output interfaces for code conversations, bus structures for physical connections, signal conditioning equipment to ensure compatability of signal (voltage/current) levels throughout the system and above all adequate operating systems.

Operating Systems: An operating system is made up of a set of software routines which control the internal operations of a computer. They supervise all input and output operations and control the execution of applications programs. This means that the application programmer can virtually ignore the internal workings of a particular computer when he is writing a program.

The operating system is (metaphorically) that hidden part of the iceberg one hopes is present when one buys a computer. It contains all the supplier-provided software which includes the necessary programming languages, e.g. COBOL, BASIC, FORTRAN, PL/1 etc. It must also include all the necessary utilities, e.g. disk sorts, disk to print, SPOOL programs and so on (refer to the Glossary for definitions). Most importantly it also contains the software devices to initiate jobs, to enable operator intervention, to ensure that all peripherals start and stop in the right sequence and at the right time, to enable the machines to call in programs when it needs them and particularly to use its own resources efficiently in order to service all of its users in the best way.

Operating systems have become the subject of a major sub-industry in publishing and seminar circles and will always be a matter of utmost concern to the user of any standard type of data processing system.

As computer systems become smaller and less data processing oriented other, more directly relevant, operating systems and programming languages will need to be developed.

Storage: Storage is the name that has come to be applied to three elements. The computer's own memory, which itself now has two elements; Random Access Memory and Read Only Memory. Random Access Memory is usable by programmers for programs and data. Read Only Memory is only available to the machine manufacturer, for parts of the operating system or machine control logic. On-line storage generally refers to the disks or tapes actually loaded in the disk or tape drives, capable of direct communications with the processor. Off-line storage is the generic term used for any medium in which data or programs capable of being used by the system are stored.

Manufacturers tend to refer to storage in numerical terms as a comparative unit of measure. For example, a medium to large system might be defined as a 1 megabyte Random Access Memory, 64K Read Only Memory and 300 megabytes of online storage. Refer to the Glossary for definitions.

Logic/Control: The function that separates a computer from all other machines is its 'intelligence' or ability to distinguish between logic states in order to make a decision. Thus this decision-making ability is a result of the ability of the logic circuit (or gate) to direct positive or negative signals (pulses) in a particular direction, thereby obtaining resultant output signals or results (see 'gates' in Glossary). It is this power which enables a program to include the stage of data comparison followed by a decision of the 'YES/NO' variety that makes digital data processing, with all its modern armoury of aids and tools, such a powerful machine.

In this way the modern digital computer realises the concept of all those pioneers involved in the evolutionary steps towards such a machine. The principles have been established for over 150 years; the technology which enables us to achieve the realisation of these principles is less that twenty-five years old.

What becomes clear in any evaluation of computer history is a difference between the forces, or impetus, of pure and applied science and the same forces behind applied technology. Up until the late 1940's or early 1950's it was applied science that determined the developments of computer, in terms of hardware, software and the people who were competent to use the machines. Up until that time the major influences on design were electro-mechanical design engineers, scientists in universities or the research departments of enormous research-based companies, and informed amateurs, possibly regarded as cranks at that time. From the early 1950's on, especially as commercial undertakings began to grasp the economic and business advantages of applying computers to what are now regarded as conventional data processing tasks, a new factor began to emerge.

This factor was the economic pressure on the technological momentum that was gradually being created as a result of more knowledge, more insight and more trained people in the technologies. Thus the engineer took over from the scientist as companies began to apply the conventional productivity and value engineering principles to the design and manufacture of machines. Scientists still have their place in computer and high technology device manufacture but they are tending to become backroom technicians as the solid state physics revolution and productivity improvement techniques exert an increasing influence on function and price of the modern computing elements.

Technological innovation, first energised by the need to compete in the field of data processing, has in fact overtaken the industry itself and is beginning to make its mark in fields well outside conventional data processing. The implications of this expanding and diversifying flood of engineering development and applications are the main reasons behind what remains to be discussed in this and the succeeding chapters.

As more and more manufacturing companies become involved in computer design, development and manufacture, more, rather than fewer, questions remain to be answered. There are fast and slow moving currents in any revolution, as the emphasis in competitive status changes from hardware to software to firmware to qualified people and back and forth between these categories. The decision making processes involved in purchasing remains roughly the same. The decision criteria for anyone involved in purchasing a computing system include cost, relative performance on known tasks, reliability (hardware and software), support facilities in terms of education, hardware and software maintenance, documentation and technical assistance, plus backup in terms of local users, parts and engineers, both in volume and locations, and the availability of sufficient well trained people. In the more technical sense, the criteria include size, power consumption, such things as languages, machine technology, operating systems sophistication and the general willingness of people to install a system. Finally from the marketing point of view, so far a very powerful consideration, it depends on the numbers and quality of salesmen, support staff, documentation, marketing and support facilities, advertising, PR and reputation, brochures and the supply of generally available marketing literature.

All of these factors have a bearing on the decision of what system to buy. The variety of potential for errors in choice is almost infinite. The competitive and economic pressures on the supplier to stay profitable and in the market, and to find new markets, are increasing by the hour, which affects purchasing criteria. Thus the factors to be considered are constantly changing.

In the general industrial environment the computer's potential became apparent somewhat later than in the administrative areas, for a number of reasons. Firstly the suppliers' marketing people, taken as a whole, did not have the depth of knowledge and experience to comprehend the problems, much less the potential computer applications in industry. Of course these people were too fully occupied applying computers to the more easily saleable and understood areas of administration and accounting to need to venture into the more esoteric manufacturing and engineering fields. This also applied to the computer suppliers' development staff so that manufacturing and engineering design, both hardware and software, began to be developed a full ten years after the more conventional administration applications. Added to these factors was the reluctance of engineers themselves to embrace a change in technology and to overcome their own educational and knowledge barriers. For example logic and control circuits have been in use in engineering companies for many years but to date they have generally employed pneumatic and hydraulic principles. So, for example, machine tool controls have been, and still are, strongly influenced by the more established control methods of electro-mechanical, pneumatic and hydraulic industries; much more so than the microelectronics industries. However, things are now changing very rapidly. For computer people it may come as a surprise to realise that all the principles behind conventional computing have been embodied within instrumentation and control engineering circles for over 30 years, without the benefit of digital or analog computers. Both the hydraulic and pneumatic controls industry can supply an enormous range of equipment, including power sources, logic and sensors.

The development of the Micro

Although when one looks back it appears that there was a clear distinction or line which could be drawn between each successive change in computer technology, e.g. mainframe, mini, micro, the real picture is quite different. In many ways it is the mainframe manufacturers themselves who have created the successive breakthroughs in design and technology that have lead to competing types of computers being available. The mainframe manufacturers' need to maintain market share, maintain profit levels and the technological impetus created by their enormous investments in research and development facilities guarantees that the majority of breakthroughs of this sort will still emanate from the dozen or so mainframe manufacturers. Certainly they have all changed from valves to relays to transistors to solid state technologies as soon as they became commercially available. Marketing advantage is still the most important driving force for these companies.

The difference between the major mainframe computers and their minicomputers and microcomputer competitors is that the mainframe manufacturer embraces new technology whereas the minicomputer and the microcomputer industries were created through technological change. The terminology mainframe, mini and micro is now, and probably always has been, inaccurate. Minicomputers often overlap the lower end of mainframes in computing power and cost. Similarly microcomputers can overlap the minicomputer in the same areas. The specialist differentiates between them in terms of computing power, expressed as transaction processing rates or the number of logic gates in a processor. Accepting that there was no precise date of birth of the minicomputer or the microcomputer the next few pages try to piece together what apparently happened.

The earliest computers relied upon the valve and relay for creating the programmable logic circuits necessary for computation. The valve (or vacuum tube) was the product of an industry of the 1920's and 30's. It consumed a great deal of power and generated an immense amount of heat for its size. Naturally a replacement for the valve had to be found. This replacement was the transistor.

The transistor was initially developed around 1947–8. This transistor was a low power amplifier that replaced the vacuum tube. It was small, cheap and could be soldered into position on a circuit board. A whole range of transistors gradually replaced all the previous functions of the older computing elements. Looking back from the perspective of the 80's, it is a rather surprising fact that of the ten leading valve producers in the U.S.A. in 1955 only two are now among the top ten semiconductor manufacturers. Further evidence that a dependence on one technology often inhibits the migration to a new technology.

The early transistor and its allied components were discrete components, cylindrical in form. Later it became the first of the semiconductor devices created from a junction of silicon or germanium. The semiconductor is a device that has a range of characteristics between that of an insulator and a conductor, and is discussed in more detail in Chapter 3.

By the late 1950's the technology to describe the surface

shape of a transistor by means of the developing technique of photolithography and then embedding the necessary impurities into this material (they were fabricated on a wafer of germanium or silicon) which accurately controlled their function had created the integrated circuit industry. Having established the principles it now became a matter of engineering development to fabricate more and more logic gates onto a chip. Now the integrated circuit (chip) is, after fabrication, encapsulated into a protective rectangular plastic cover, its electrodes connected to pin connections which are left exposed for plugging into a socket or soldering into a circuit. This encapsulated chip is called a package.

The present state of the art enables thousands of gates to be integrated on a chip and contained in a single package. The computing power of computers made from these devices is many times greater than that of the earliest computers, for a fraction of the cost. The potential of the semiconductor was grasped by US defence engineers years before computer engineers embraced the change. This came about because of the need to limit the volume and weight occupied in space and defence vehicles due to budgetary constraints on the US space program. These constrains added extra impetus to miniaturisation and packing density, in order to reduce size, improve performance and improve reliability and efficiency; all vital in a space vehicle but obviously slightly less important in an earth based computer with a maintenance engineer on call.

One comparison will provide a useful illustration of the rate of development. In 1980 it is possible to buy a microcomputer, fabricated on a chip, for $300. It has more computing power than ENIAC had; it is perhaps 20 times faster than ENIAC; it is thousands of times more reliable, consumes an insignificant amount of power by comparison (140 kilowatts against 2.5 watts) occupies 1/30,000th the space, is about 1/100,000 the weight, and costs 1/10,000th as much. That is the measure of 30 years progress, brought about largely by improvements in solid state physics techniques.

Improvements in semiconductor technology have been

paralleled by improvements in memory technology. A bewildering variety of different memory types are now fabricated and packaged in the same standard packaging as logic circuits. In fact most fabricators agree that the microprocessor revolution is already over. It is now possible to buy a microprocessor (not a microcomputer, which requires memory, input/output, interfaces, timers and software) for $5. For the manufacturer to reproduce them and then to sell them for $4 would involve him in a doubling of his capital investment for only marginal returns. The work to reduce costs, improve density and performance will continue but is now likely to be increasingly applied to memory technology.

Thus the third type of computer has evolved; the microcomputer. This is a fairly basic and in relative terms, very cheap, computer. It employs high density integrated circuits, perhaps a single printed circuit board microcomputer, contained in a desk or console. At its most basic functional level it requires a video display unit, printer and floppy magnetic disks. This type of microcomputer can now be bought for less than $10,000. There are literally hundreds of suppliers, many of whom do no more than buy all the separate assemblies, package them and add some of their own software; systems integraters, in fact.

The development of the microcomputer came about almost by accident. It began life as what originally came to be known as a programmable controller, essentially very similar in function to those being adopted to control industrial processes today. Three large American Corporations involved in small computer system and 'intelligent' terminal manufacturing (Datapoint, Viatron and Cogar) contracted with the Intel Corporation, one of today's industry leaders of the microprocessor fabrication industry, to implement their computer design on a single chip.

Intel managed to complete the task but the resulting product could not meet the three client companies' specifications in terms of program execution speed. The client companies decided to proceed no further in that particular direction.

Intel then had to decide what to do with their development. Did they scrap it or exploit it? They decided to market it; they called it the Intel 8008 and gave the world its first computer on a chip. A programmable logic controller.

This marks the point at which computers are not only available in different sizes, prices, performance and technology. The computer, or as Intel originally called it the Programmable Logic Controller (PLC), is now capable of being treated as a component in an entirely different end product. Thus it can replace traditional logic or add an element of intelligence where none existed before.

It is at this point that the stringent requirement for the presentation of data rears its ugly head. If it is considered necessary to add intelligence to a washing machine, or a motor car, or a machine tool, or any of the millions of other potential applications, it is clearly impractical to encumber the device by the need to organise data into punch cards, tape or what have you. Similarly it is not always possible to insist that the device to be controlled emits digital signals. Although many of them work on alternating currents the probable nature of the signal to be processed is just as likely to be continuous as intermittent, or analog as digital. Thus it is necessary to perfect signal conditioning techniques, the conversion of analog to digital and digital to analog signals and above all to capture the signals at source. This must be achieved in order to escape the straightjacket that data presentation places on conventional data processing practice.

None of these requirements are new and the solutions are all embodied within an industry that probably existed before Babbage conceived his principles: the transducer industry.

Transducers

Input transducers have gradually become known as sensory perceptors, or sensors, over the years. Together with output transducers they are the vital ingredient in applying the newest microprocessors and memories to the performance improvement of modern industrial products and processes.

Input transducers are devices that translate physical changes of state into engineering variables such as current or voltage. Output transducers perform the reverse function. For example a Platinum Resistance Thermometer can translate a temperature change into a voltage change that a microprocessor can accept as input. The microprocessor could then send a signal to an output transducer to, say, energise a Light Emitting Diode.

Microelectronics components

To make the microelectronics system work – 'microelectronics' being a generic term covering the miniaturised semiconductor chips and memory chips – other devices and products are needed in addition to transducers. They include packaging, switches, programs, – and people!

Packaging is often unique to the end product but a wide variety of shapes and sizes are available and possible from the sculptured office desk for the modern microcomputer, through the whole range of today's domestic appliances, many of which contain the sort of intelligence we have discussed, right up to the industrial control 'black box', the robot and the inherently safe controller and data loggers used, for example, in coal mines.

All have their own requirements and expertise. Like everything else in the computer system the shapes, materials and performance of packaging has developed at a pace parallel to that of semiconductor manufacture.

Switches have also undergone a rapid change in design and function. Once again a spectacular variety are available for any number of special purposes.

Programming

Computer programming is as old as Babbage's original ideas. He needed to input programs and data so that the revolving gears of his Analytical Engine could perform to his instructions. The earliest acronymically named computers had to be talked to at machine level; first by direct input switches and later by paper tape. The first commercial computer users demanded a more usuable and flexible language than machine level, and so the first of the symbolic codes began to be developed. There are now thousands of varieties of computer languages. Each manufacturer has his own version of the commonly used languages. These include COBOL for normal ledger, payroll and analysis applications. BASIC is to some extent superseding COBOL, but each has its own faithful group of adherents. FORTRAN is still widely used for maths and science-based applications. There is a vast choice of easy-to-learn, high level languages, mostly dedicated to writing quick and simple output reports. Then there are languages devoted to time sharing applications and multi-user applications, data communications and so on, *ad infinitum*.

It has been seen that engineering developments have led to improvements in performance and reduction in cost, size and power consumption by every item of hardware in a system. Thirty years of evolutionary development have created a range of software aids from operating systems to programming languages to application packages. But basically people have still not changed.

As has been stated many times already, here and elsewhere, much of the jargon has been absorbed into language without a necessarily concommitant absorption of understanding. There is now a second generation of computer specialists, many of whom have never learned what much of the first generation had to learn. The range of job titles, specialist functions and jargon of computer people has multiplied over the years to the point where quite often a majority of situations vacant advertisements in metropolitan newspapers are for computer specialists, or people from related disciplines.

Computer people comprise the final category to come under the focus of engineering innovation and development. But development is taking place. It is perfectly possible that the most important force in computing over the next decade will be software productivity aids, or tools that will reduce program development time, reduce debugging and documentation time and even allow the user to program his own machine.

Having said that, a great deal more work needs to be done to ensure widespread and early use of current technology by the professional layman and his colleagues. The level of acceptance and knowledge of engineers and programmers needs to improve before the microelectronics product really is treated as a normal component, to be used like any other.

2. The Market: Trends and Applications

So far four broad markets have been referred to: mainframe and mini computers, microelectronics and the amorphous hybrid market of transducers, switches and packaging. This chapter provides a background to the main suppliers, their relative size and market trends. Anticipated end users by market sectors are also briefly described to enable the casual reader at least to identify potential application areas and help promote an awareness of what the industries concerned expect to happen over the next few years.

Suppliers

The conventional data processing marketplace is dominated by IBM. The other major suppliers in this marketplace include Amdahl, Burroughs, Control Data, Digital Equipment (although generally still regarded as a minicomputer manufacturer), Honeywell, N.C.R., Sperry (Univac), I.C.L. and so on. On an international basis, probably twenty to thirty suppliers qualify as mainframe suppliers.

Digital is the doyen of the minis; other important suppliers include Data General, Hewlett Packard, Interdata, Wang, Prime, Harris, G.E.C., Siemens and many more. There are probably two hundred to three hundred suppliers who qualify as minicomputer manufacturers around the world. There is no exclusivity of machine type to manufacturer. Many mainframe suppliers also make minicomputers, and quite often microcomputers too.

The differences between the mainframe and the mini-

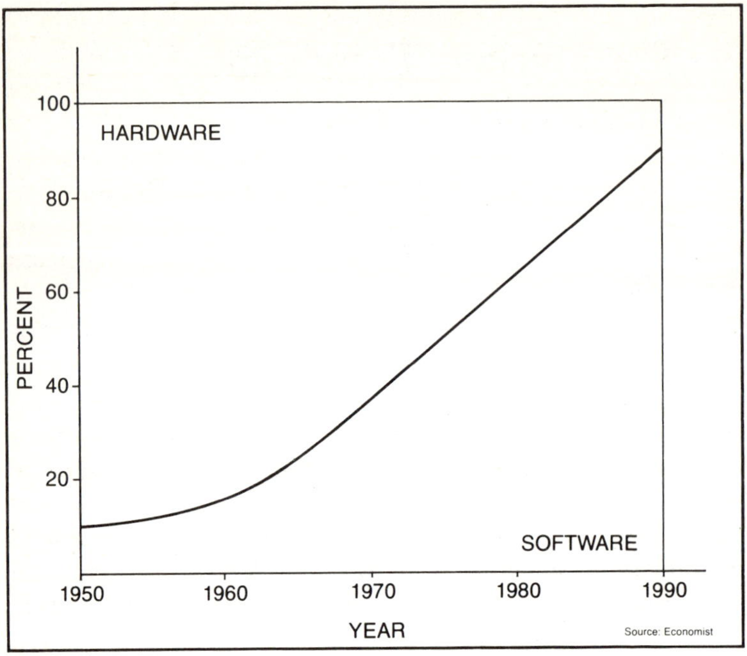

Figure 1 *Changing proportions of computer costs*
A dramatic illustration of the effect that miniaturisation has had on computing costs. It also illustrates the ever increasing people-dependent costs of software and the associated tasks of data entry, file creation, etc.

computer supplier have already been touched on in previous chapters. Generally the minicomputer supplier markets direct or through a network of distributors (stockholders), dealers or agents (independent sales outlets) and OEMers (the misnamed Original Equipment Manufacturer). This network adds value and then sells to the end user, often through his own dealer network.

The purchasers are end users, systems houses (analogous to OEMers), software houses (which add software only) or systems integrators (who assemble the CPU and various peripherals before selling the equipment on to the end user).

Software support comes from those sources already mentioned, from freelance programmers, or by the purchase of complete packages from numerous sources which includes other end users or computer bureaux. Hardware support (maintenance) is normally provided by the manufacturer or distributor but the independent field service company is a new and rapidly growing force to be considered. By now it is reasonable to consider the mini as an extension or subset of the mainframe computer. As a consequence, it is possible to claim that the industry infrastructure which supports both types of supplier is almost twenty years old and quite well established.

The sales dollar volume of the top ten suppliers worldwide in 1979 was of the order of $50,000 million. This ignores all the independent peripheral suppliers, smaller manufacturers, and the whole infrastructure that supports the top of the pyramid supplier: it is obviously a gigantic industry. The applications for these machines would fill several books but it is probably fair to say they are largely dedicated to administrative tasks in the medium to large enterprises around the world. Their growth comes less from new applications than from improved methods of handling existing applications in such areas as data communications, large data base systems and new, improved performance, peripheral and computing devices.

Many of the well known companies are growing more rapidly in the areas of office automation: word processors, photocopying, typewriters, dictation equipment, calculators, facsimile transmission and so on. In time, these will be refined for use with data and telecommunication systems. Although many of the machines and devices produced by the mainframe and minicomputer manufacturers are used for sophisticated production and stock control, relatively few are being used either as a constituent part of, or a component of a product (except in the aerospace and armaments industries), or in direct control of industrial processes. Of course there are exceptional examples of those applications, but by comparison with industrial size, the number of such examples is insignificant.

With only few exceptions, the mainframe and mini computer supplier will be consigned to the background of this book now. The suppliers of the remaining products to be discussed which include integrated circuits and memory devices, transducers, switches, packaging and software, fall into two distinct categories.

The manufacturers of transducers, switches, packaging and software can be numbered by the hundred of thousands. Many of the important suppliers are divisions of major international industrial companies; quoting their names would achieve very little since they are usually recognised only by the cognoscenti. The scene is very local and each major industrial geographical grouping has an indigenous group of suppliers, capable of satisfying all but the most demanding and specific of requirements. On the other hand, the semiconductor industry is characterised by a remarkable concentration of an industry in a single geographic area, sometimes called Silicon Valley (or Chip Gulch). This area of land, literally a sixty kilometre long valley south of San Francisco, California, contains more than five hundred companies, around fifty of whom are right at the forefront of microelectronics development.

There are now facilities located outside this area, one reason being the 'disaster plant' concept. Thus a second plant, well away from the Californian earthquake zone, will ensure continuity of supply even if the worst should happen. Plants are also being located closer to the major consumers. Design and production facilities are tending to be separated, leading to the concept of the chip production unit, or the chip 'foundry'. Nevertheless it is still possible to conclude that approximately 75% of the worlds semiconductor output, measured in value or volume, presently comes from this small area of California.

Within the semiconductor fabrication industry, there are two major types of company. The first does its own design, either for its own products or its client's; it then fabricates, packages, tests and ships. The second is a 'second source'

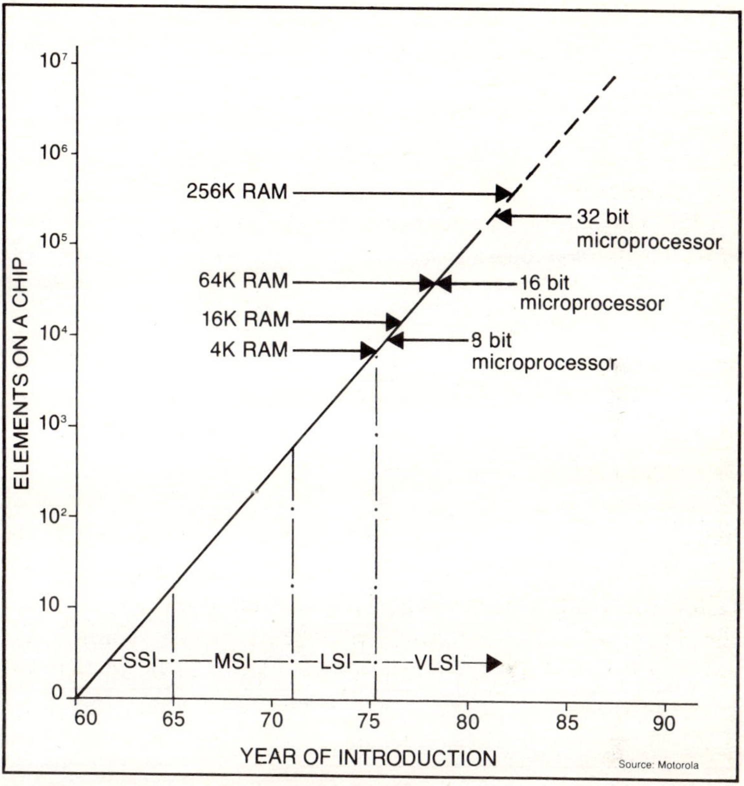

Figure 2 *More and more bits on a chip*
An illustration of the increasing density of packaging from the early 1960's projected through to the late 1980's. The term 'element' describes the basic building block of a circuit, measuring one logic gate or one bit of memory. The chart also illustrates the break points between the scale of integration: SSI, MSI, LSI, VLSI. Significant developments in memory and processor capacity are also charted, showing the remorseless progress of miniaturisation. Note that the left hand scale is exponential while the base is linear.

supplier, manufacturing someone else's design under licence, sometimes referred to as a merchant semiconductor house.

Presently, demand regularly outstrips supply. During 1979 there were delays of up to ten months for the supply of certain

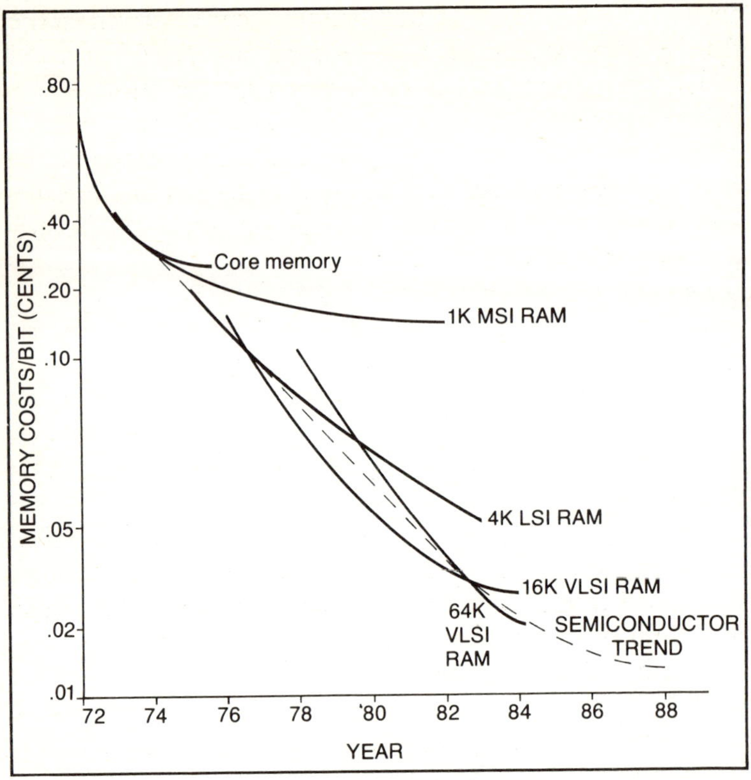

Figure 3 *The effect of miniaturisation on memory costs*
Each improvement in miniaturisation technique has brought about a corresponding reduction in the price of a memory bit and microprocessor element. It will be noted that there is always a period of 1–2 years after the introduction of a new device before it becomes cost-effective compared to the later technology. Note particularly the point at which core memory becomes uncompetitive.

chips. Consistent shortages have led to many governments being forced to recognise the strategic importance of the industry, which in turn is leading to the development of fabrication plants (largely 'second sourcing' at the moment) in Europe and the Far East, including notably, Japan.

The competition to place more and more components on a

single chip has resulted in quantum jumps of integration density from SSI (small scale integration), MSI (medium), LSI (large), VLSI (very large). The reason for the density of packaging will be described in the next chapter, as will the other main technical factor: the progression from four bit microprocessors to eight bit and now to sixteen bit. Presumably the general acceptance of the thirty-two bit microprocessor will follow.

Due to the factors of strategic importance, high competition caused by proximity and the market's unceasing pressure towards more function for lower cost, it is possible that the centre of emphasis of chip development will gradually move away from Silicon Valley to, perhaps, Texas, or even possibly Japan. It will be interesting to observe developments during this decade.

The factors that make this particular industry so volatile, and so important, are clear. The cost of laying down a single fabrication facility for silicon chip production is in the region of $10 million as a minimum. By the mid-80's many experts believe it will cost at least $35 million to lay down the same facility. A technology consultant with the Arthur D. Little Corporation of the United States has said that the capital investment required for a sales increment increase of $100 million is between $70 million and $100 million. Thus the industry, although characterised by many quite new companies, is beginning to run into a period with potential for serious re-structuring. This is a result of the strategic importance of the industry to many nations, not least the United States itself, and the need for increasing levels of capital investment to fund the efforts for competitive improvements in capacity and function. An additional factor is the acquisitive moves of some of the industry's largest customers. Many of these customers do not have their own semiconductor fabrication facilities, but over the years have built a dependence on the product. In the near future they will have to make decisions concerning the safeguarding of their own products and profits. They will have to decide whether to invest in their

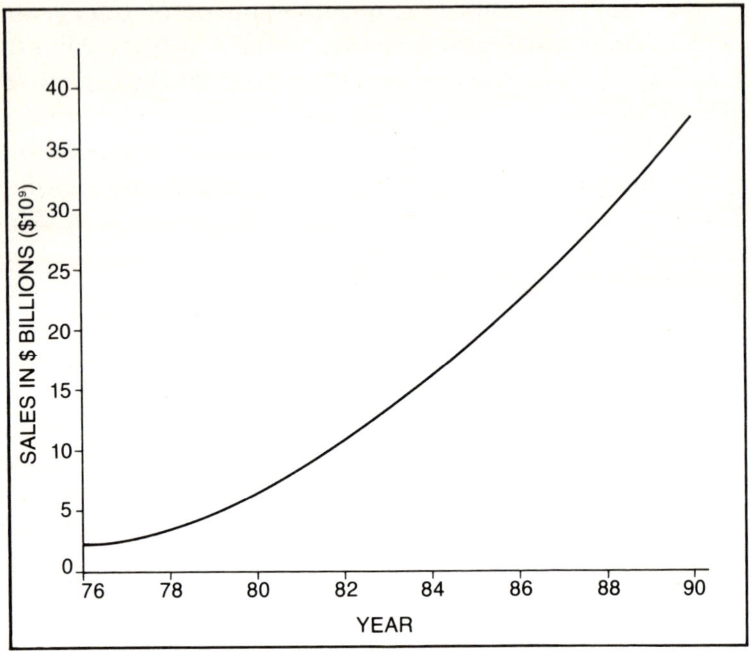

Figure 4 *Growth of the semiconductor market*
An illustration made up of figures from several industry sources and publically available information. It shows that the worldwide market for semiconductor integrated circuits is doubling every 5 years, from a figure of less than $3 billion in 1976 to a projected figure of almost $40 billion by 1990.

own new plant and consequently to hire from a pool of very scarce and expensive expertise, or whether to try and take over an existing facility. Since 1975 there have been fourteen major take-overs, or significant investments in the industry. Those in 1979 totalled almost $800 million in four transactions alone, and one of those was only to acquire a minority shareholding.

Therefore it seems possible that the fledgling industry will be drawn within the sphere of influence of at least the establishment industrial multi-national corporations. Of course, many will continue to remain independent, but some may well be forced to seek new partners.

The market forces that add point to this potential change in ownerships make interesting reading. One important factor is that from a starting point where the semiconductor companies did virtually all the design in the early days in the mid-70's, it seems likely that by the mid-80's at least one third of all integrated circuits will be designed by the end user, not the supplier. This from a consultant for Integrated Circuit Engineering Corporation in December 1979.

An analyst at Dataquest, another U.S. based research corporation, supports this. He points out that the industry is characterised by a small number of customers buying a huge volume of semiconductors. In 1977 the number of these customers buying in excess of $100 million a year increased from one to seven. It will go up to seventeen customers purchasing in excess of $100 million a year by 1981. By 1985, thirty per cent of the industry's production will be used by thirty major customers.

The market

The market size itself is worth a brief look. There is a wide range of contradictory forecasts, but they are all impressive. In 1979, according to *Business Week* the world market was expected to be $10,000 million. By 1985, it is predicted that it will be twice this figure, and by the late 1980's to be $32,000 million (source: Texas Instruments).

These overall figures conceal many different trends for a variety of different semiconductors, but it is clear that most of the world's leading authorities expect the major consumption, hence application, of these devices over the next ten years, to be by American companies; hardly a surprise! What are the most likely application areas? According to two U.S. based research corporations, Dataquest and Gnostic, the following are the important overall trends:

The split and use of semiconductor consumption appears thus:

	1974	1979	1984
Figures in $US billions ($1,000 million)			
Government/Military	0.4	1.1	1.5
Consumer/Automotive	1.2	2.5	5.0
Industrial equipment	2.5	3.5	7.5
Computers	1.3	3.4	7.5
TOTALS	5.4	10.5	21.5

An interesting analysis shows that the percentage of end value represented by semiconductor content increases thus:

	1974	1979	1984
Government/Military	1.5%	3.0%	5%
Consumer/Automotive	0.0%	6.5%	9%
Industrial equipment	0.0%	2.5%	4%
Computers	1.5%	6.5%	12%

Based on figures such as these, it is possible to repeat the semiconductor industry's assertion that the semiconductor is the future 'crude oil' of international industry with some confidence.

'Crude oil' may indeed be a key analogy. The figures quoted here are of such importance to governments and industrial sectors around the world that it is difficult to see the semiconductor industry of thc future being treated much differently to the oil industry of today. All other factors apart, as the IEEE (see glossary) pointed out at the end of 1978, the productivity improvement of the high technology sector of industry was running at 200% more than that of any other sector of industry. The growth of employment opportunity was also growing at a rate of 25% ahead of that of other industry sectors.

So much for the scale, importance, areas of growth and possible strategic – both industrial and national – importance of the industry itself.

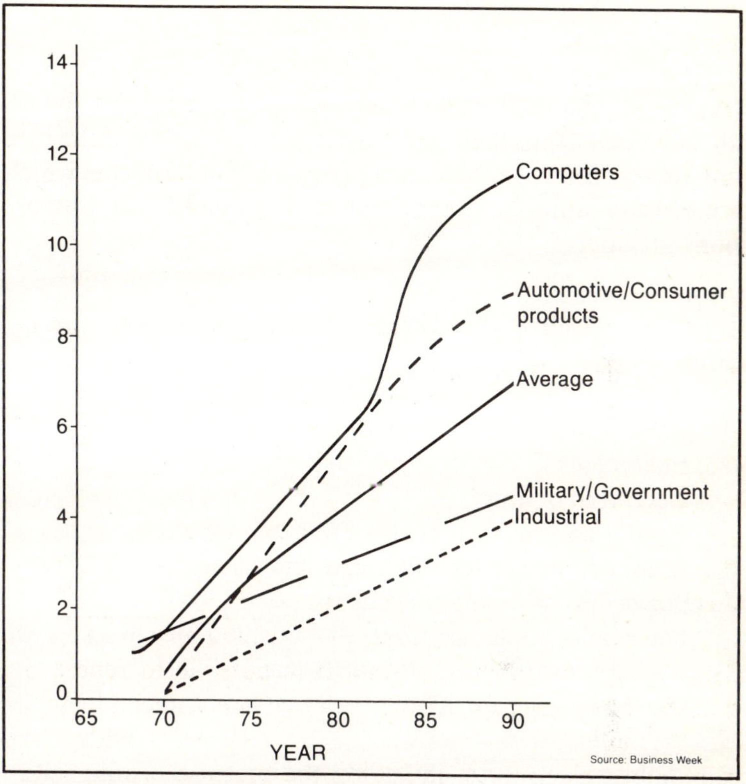

Figure 5 *Semiconductor content of products*
The growing proportion of the end value of a product which the semiconductor represents, broken down into four major groups of products. The average grows from less that 1% in the late 60's to 7% in the late 80's.

At this stage it would probably not be too productive to break down figures in any more detail: many studies exist for those who have an interest. Rather let us look at application areas in terms of industries, products and processes to give a guide as to where the most likely use of micro-electronics and its array of attendant components is likely to be for the reader of this book.

Applications

In general, the high volume users of microelectronics should already be aware of their need to employ them, even if they are not already in use in their own products. The products which are already utilising microelectronics in significant proportions include:

Consumer electronics, where microprocessors are already employed in:

- wrist watches
- radio clocks
- electronic organs
- remote control systems for radio and television
- program storage for radio and television
- television information systems
- household appliance controls (washing machines, dish washers, ovens, infra-red grills, etc.)
- television games machines

Automobile electronics, including the first use of microelectronics in:

- brake control systems
- gasoline and injection control
- safety-belt control
- car clocks
- burglar alarm systems
- seat positioning

In general, these end products already exist; they are merely being enhanced, or cost reduced, by the implementation of a microelectronics element. Products using high volumes of microelectronics components which were virtually created by the capability of new devices, include:

electronic toys
calculators
tape recorders
miniature TV
meters for telephone cost monitoring
and many TV games

This category is still the highest growth area. All high volume use of microelectronics implies an implementation of semiconductor devices within the product, used as a component of that end product. In the case of high volume usage, their consumption is likely to be of such magnitude and value that they can have a series of custom chips designed, leading to lower costs through not having to buy the unnecessary or redundant features contained on a general purpose, standard chip. This will obviously happen more and more as some of the earlier statistics pointed out. The domestic appliance and automobile consumption can be measured in millions of chips a year. More moderate uses, in the hundreds of thousands of chips include:

Data acquisition and data processing, where they are used in:

minicomputers
microcomputers
intelligent data terminals
cash registers
label reading systems
cheque/credit card verification
electronic scales
time clocks
payroll systems
security services
taxi meters
electronic funds transfer
radio phone systems
data communication equipment
remote terminals

and office equipment, where they appear in:

desk calculators
typewriters
word processors
facsimile transmission equipment
programmable photocopiers
touch telephones
programmable telephones
TV information systems

These last two categories will probably employ standard chips or boards and will be integrated with a manufacturer's own software to provide the necessary upgrading of function.

The next chapter discusses some of the important reasons behind a decision to use custom designed or standard chips.

The low-to-medium volume users of micro-electronics, say from the hundreds to the few thousands a year, includes instrumentation, where electronics engineers are accustomed to use them in:

electronic frequency generators
counters/frequency meters
logic analysers
oscilloscopes
development systems
digital voltmeters

These will almost certainly incorporate their own custom designed printed circuit boards using standard chips.

The final category (not definitively final, merely for the purpose of this chapter) sees the microelectronics devices emerge from the system as a programmable controller whereas the other categories of product mentioned previously generally use them as components; basically clever programmable switches in many cases. This category literally controls the product or process. It is by definition a low volume user; the microelectronics element being a relatively low proportion by volume and size but high by addition to function. They can be categorised:

Industrial electronics and industrial control systems:

- machine tool controls
- continuous process monitoring and control
- testing equipment: stress, strain, fatigue, temperature, radiation, power, flow, thickness, etc.
- automatic testing equipment for printed circuit boards and chips
- metrology devices
- control of casting machines
- standard programmable/sequential controllers
- robotics
- quality control
- counting systems
- fill control systems
- automated material handling systems
- medical engineering products
- agricultural engineering products, particularly in control of hydraulic and hydrostatic systems

The list is almost endless. The variety of application is by far the highest in this section. Yet because of the sales value to the microelectronic supplier of a single application, the development of new applications is unlikely to receive the attention in terms of education, publicity and pure marketing support that the importance to the process and business merits.

Thus it is up to the individual manager, or executive, to identify his application area and manage his own project, with the help of the appropriate specialists. The final chapter of this book offers some guidance in this area.

This chapter has discussed, through a few brief statistics, the emerging importance of the semiconductor business to industry around the world. From a starting point less than twenty years ago, by the 1980's the turnover of the industry will be rivalling that of IBM, who in turn is set to become the world's largest manufacturing corporation during the decade of the 80's. The influence of the semiconductor on all products, be they military, consumer, domestic or industrial, is bound to increase over the next decade. The volume of output from the industry is such that every conceivable product or process is bound to be affected to some degree. The challenge to the executive and manager is to ensure its timely and effective incorporation into his product or process, hence the need to understand the semiconductor and related products' capabilities.

3. Microelectronics

Previous chapters have discussed the rapidly diminishing size of computers and the components that make up their processors and memories. The advent of commercially available microelectronic devices such as the microprocessor and solid state memories made it possible to replace conventional central processors with a microprocessor assembly, which resulted in the development of the microcomputer.

The microcomputer does not yet have the speed, capacity or power of a modern minicomputer, but as will be seen during this chapter, it will not be too long before these enhancements are made. Enhancements will generally be based upon the increase of density of packing of components on a chip, and the improved manufacturing yield that the massive research and development expenditure of the semiconductor manufacturers will ultimately achieve.

This development industry, for it has become an industry in its own right, started with the introduction of the transistor, taken together with the need to standardise on packaging sizes and to reduce the space occupied by these packages. The new developments centred upon the realisation by several people, virtually simultaneously, that the elements used for transistor manufacture, silicon and germanium, could be used for a far more revolutionary design of transistor, and thus help complete the range of microelectronic components needed to fabricate complete circuits. These include all the transistor logic components such as resistors, amplifiers and capacitors.

The concept was eventually realised by the use of photolithography techniques, which enabled very small profiles of transistors to be defined in a carefully prepared base material. The process also facilitated the introduction of regulated amounts of impurities in p (positive) and n (negative) regions which, in fact, define the transistor's exact specification and performance. This whole process, described in detail later in this chapter, has, and still is, performed upon the base materials of germanium and silicon.

As the process developed, higher and higher densities of fabrication on a standard 'wafer' of the chosen base material were achieved. However, the transistors produced in this way still had to be laboriously separated, tested and inspected, to have conducting wires attached, to be emplaced in a protective covering and then to be assembled into a circuit with other more conventionally produced electronic components. At this stage circuits were generally constructed of wire wrapped around insulating posts on an insulated base material. At a later stage the photo-etching principles used in the photolithography process were employed to produce printed circuit boards. Components were then simply soldered into place in the printed circuit.

During the period 1959–62, various improvements to the process of photolithography and fabrication techniques enabled insulation layers to be laid down on the wafer and various other circuit elements to be described, such as the pn diode, which allows current to flow only in one direction. By this time the process was producing not only transistors, but integrated circuits themselves. The fabrication process was able to create all the components, or elements, necessary to implement a complete circuit on a small area of silicon or germanium, cut from a wafer. The wafer contained many identical integrated circuits, to take advantage of economies of scale.

By the mid-80's, by the use of VLSI (Very Large Scale Integration) techniques elements will be available with dimensions of 1 micron (one millionth of a metre, or .000039 inches!) VLSI also implies that 5000 logic gates can be emplaced on a single chip. Note that current mainframe computers require something of the order of 100,000 logic gates in order to conform to their need for speed of instruction execution and memory access.

It is likely that the ultimate factor determining minimum size will be discovered by physicists during the next few years. Details of a discovery by a British physicist have recently been reported. His work involves research into techniques to reduce the size of components to achieve an optimum level of miniaturisation. It appears that as his components reduce to their atomic size, their physical properties begin to deviate from their expected norm. Under these conditions their properties vary with their immediate surroundings. The transistors begin to couple in a manner characteristic of human organisms. It is hypothesised that they communicate with each other in a fashion that leads the discoverer to believe they are able, under certain conditions, to make independent intelligent decisions. The level of communication depends on how hard they are driven, or excited, by their power source. Various American agencies have already devoted significant funds to further research into what could be the ultimate chip. Some people are already calling it the superchip.

Today, we have VLSI that can emplace up to 1,000,000 components on a single chip; effectively one circuit. This means that a very powerful processor combining all the components and logic gates on a single chip can be produced for a few dollars, and it is possible because of the economy of scale and the fact that no human intervention is necessary for the operations of soldering joints, testing and packaging. As a consequence, the processor on a chip is much more reliable than any of its predecessors.

The most important production factor in price reduction and performance improvement has been the attention given to yield improvement. As circuits become more complex and densely packed, there is less space available for insulation between components and connections. Thus in the early days of fabrication, there was a very high reject rate. Whole wafers at a time, and sometimes a manufacturer's complete production for weeks at a time were consigned to the scrap pile. A single speck of dust creating a conductor between two conducting tracks is enough to scrap a chip.

Gradually yields were improved by meticulous attention to cleanroom environments and improvements in the photographic and engraving techniques, which are at the heart of the process. Now the limit of normal optical processes has been reached and new processes are emerging based on X-rays and electron beams. While the work to reduce processors in size was continuing, the same aims and techniques were being applied to computer memory development, to the point where a processor and a memory can be fabricated on a single chip. Increasing densities will ensure that today's microcomputers will be like pocket calculators in comparison to the machines which will be produced in a few years time.

To the non-specialist faced with implementing a microprocessor-based system, the choice of memory to be used is probably the most confusing of all the factors to be assimilated. Which of the memory technologies available should be chosen, and why? For example there is CCD (Charge Coupled Device), Bubble Memories, SOS (Silicon On Sapphire), Bipolar and a whole range of MOS (Metal Oxide Silicon) technologies. Thankfully this is a decision that can usually be left to the electronics engineer, or designer, but it might be helpful for the layman to know something about the different types and the pros and cons of each. A section on this topic is included later in this chapter.

Properties of components and elements

This part of the narrative does not set out to be a primer on electronics principles. It attempts to identify the main elements which make up a typical electronic circuit and briefly to describe the function of each, leading up to the fabrication of the various types of logic gates which, when fabricated in the final circuit, make up a processor.

Any microelectronic circuit or device is made up from 'active' elements like transistors, combined with other 'passive' components such as resistors, capacitors and inductors. The function of these devices is exactly the same now as it was twenty years ago; the difference is in their size and methods of manufacture.

Active elements are defined as those which can change their state in response to an external signal. The other components mentioned here, resistors, inductors and capacitors, do not possess that ability.

Any material classified as a conductor contains all the characteristics of a passive device, as indeed virtually any material will conduct electricity to some degree. The difference between the device is merely the degree of specialisation or effectiveness in one particularly property.

Resistors are constructed from materials that disrupt or resist the free flow of electrons in one direction at a particular point or points in a circuit. The more predictable this resistance is, the more valuable the resistor becomes. The materials used to construct resistors and the other components mentioned here are specialised to the extent that further discussion would prove to be of little value to the casual reader of this section although passing reference will be made to certain commonly used materials. Specific ranges of values of passive components are obtained by one of two methods; either by a close control over the manufacturing method or by a selection and testing procedure following manufacture in order to find specific values, when components are produced by mass production methods.

Capacitors are those passive components that exhibit a specific effect when an electromagnetic field is generated in a material due to an electrical charge (or current) being applied to the device. Thus capacitance is the measure of an electric field surrounding a conductor. High values of capacitance are obtained when conductors subject to opposing charges (i.e. positive and negative) are brought into close proximity. Hence capacitors designed to produce high values of capacitance are constructed from metal conductors separated by layers of insulation.

Inductance is a measure of the strength of a magnetic field created by passing a current through a conductor. Inductors comprise a coil wound conductor, sometimes containing a core.

In their discrete form, (i.e. when manufactured as a single component), the transistor, resistor, capacitor and inductor are all employed in TTL (Transistor-Transistor Logic) circuits for a particular function. The methods used for discrete component manufacture are obviously inappropriate for microelectronics fabrication. The silicon used for fabrication is at best a compromise for the passive components. At present there is no practical version of an inductor in microelectronics because of the restrictions posed by the properties of the base material.

However, silicon and the other materials now in use are perfect for the fabrication of transistors. Thus the abundance of active components which, remember, can change states, serves to make up for the relatively poor performance of the passive components in microelectronics.

The immensely valuable property of the transistor that makes it so important to microelectronics is its ability to amplify a signal. Thus, when power consumption is a vital factor in increasing density of circuit fabrication, this ability to create a high value output signal from a low value input signal is vital. When applying a signal to passive elements, no matter how they are combined, the resultant output is always lower than the input.

The influence of Silicon

In an ordinary electrical conductor, say a metal wire, power (current) is carried by electrons that move through the atomic structure of the conductor material in a random passage. In an insulator, all the electrons are bound to atoms or molecules, hence they are captive and not free to carry current. A semiconductor, as discussed earlier, has an intermediate status between that of a conductor and an insulator. In its dormant state, the semiconductor has all the characteristics of an insulator. With the application of a fairly low charge, sufficient current carriers (electrons) are released from their tied positions to convert the device into a conductor.

Silicon itself is a poor conductor of electricity. Therefore, in order to fabricate efficient semiconductor devices, it is necessary to introduce impurities into the silicon crystal which is to be converted into a semiconductor. The process is known as doping and the impurities are called dopants.

The impurities added to the silicon include phosphorus and other elements capable of producing similar results. The semiconductors produced by this method are known as n type semiconductors. Boron can be used and in that case, the resultant device is known as a p type semiconductor; n refers to negative charge of the conducting electrons, p to the positive.

The principle is to add an impurity which creates a known imbalance in the atomic structure of the base element, creating either an extra free electron or a reduction in the number of available electrons. Thus there is either a free and mobile electron capable of carrying a charge, or a 'hole', or absence of an electron. A 'hole' in fact has a positive charge and moves through the atomic structure of the base material in the same way that an extra electron does. The extra electron carries a negative charge.

These then are the basic principles in semiconductor fabrication: the capability of describing a transistor in silicon; the capability of introducing insulation areas on the component; the capability of creating positive and negative charged electrons through the controlled introduction of impurities. A wide range of electronic components can be fabricated within an integrated circuit as a result of these principles and the successive refinements that have followed.

Components

There now follows a catalogue of successive component discoveries. The most important to the implementation of logic gates and memories taken together with the most generally useful, are briefly described here.

The pn *Junction and the Barrier Effect*: A principle used widely in semiconductor devices is known as the barrier effect. It occurs where a p type region and an n type region are brought into contact. There is an infiltration of current carriers from both regions into the opposite region until an area of equilibrium between the two results. Thus at the pn junction a high resistance is created, depleted of charge carriers.

By applying a negative voltage to the p region and a positive voltage to the n region, this depletion area is widened, thus causing a wide barrier. This is known as reverse biasing. It serves to resist any current flow.

By applying a positive voltage to the p region and a negative voltage to the n region, i.e. by reversing previous voltages, the barrier is removed and current is allowed to flow. This is known as forward biasing.

Bipolar Transistor: As previously mentioned, the transistor acts as a switch or a signal amplifier. Many different types of fabricated transistors are now produced. The specific fabrication method depends upon supplier, space and packaging requirements, power consumption requirements and the specific needs imposed by the application for which the transistor is to be used. In the case of the bipolar transistor the range of applications and fabrication methods used is so vast that it will be of more value to concentrate upon the principles of operation only.

The bipolar transistor consists of three regions of different conductivity, arranged as npn or pnp. The term 'bipolar' derives from the fact that charge carriers of both polarities, holes and electrons, are involved in its operation.

The fabrication is so ordered that the one pole is called the collector, the mid-region the base and the other pole the emitter. Thus there are two pn junctions in the design of a bipolar transistor, one between the emitter and base, and the other between the collector and base. The base collector pn

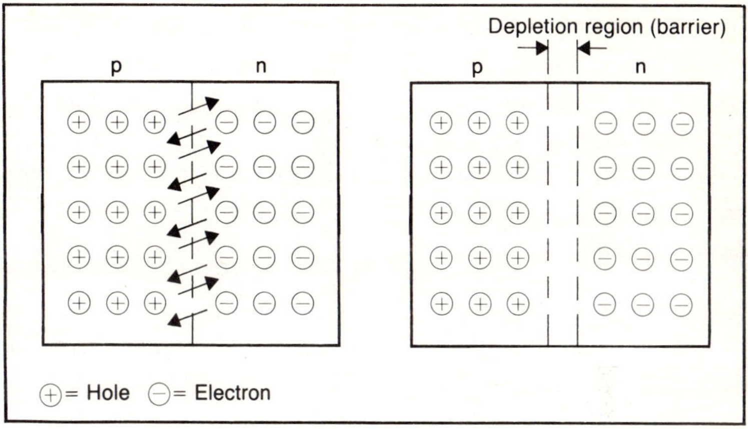

Figure 6 *The pn junction and the barrier effect*
The movement of holes (acceptors) and electrons (donors) to form a high resistance barrier at the pn junction.

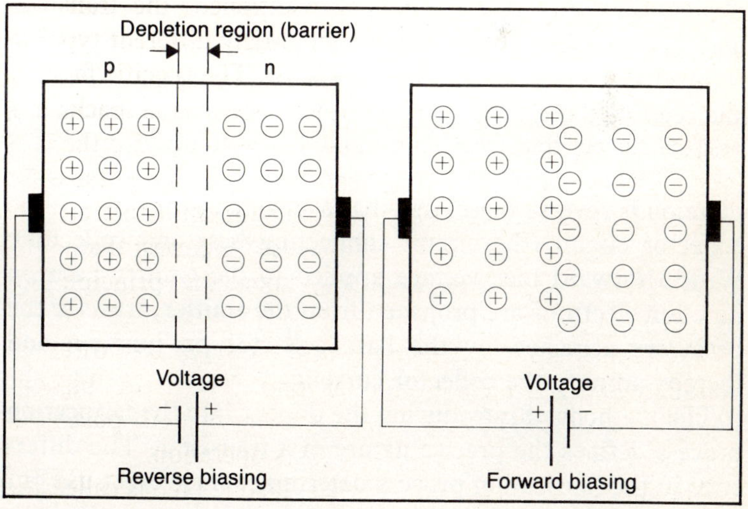

Figure 7 *A pn junction with an external voltage applied*
The movement of holes and electrons to form either a resistive barrier or to produce a conductor, depending on the voltage polarity.

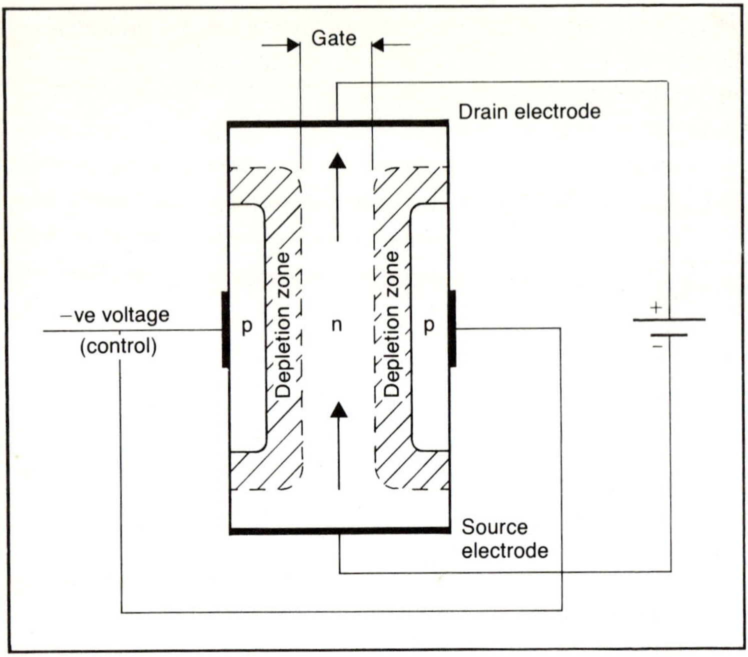

Figure 8 *Junction Field Effect Transistor (JFET)*
The variable size gate which can be achieved by raising or lowering the negative control voltage which results in either an inhibited or assisted current flow from source to drain electrodes.

junction is reverse biased, so that a small current flows in the collector circuit (the circuit connecting base and collector). With a forward bias voltage applied to the emitter base pn junction electrons are projected from the emitter, traverse the base, are attracted by the base collector pn junction and thereby amplify the collector current.

The methods of introducing the dopant into the fabrication process defines the precise nature of a transistor. The difference in the fabrication process determines their exact use but they all confirm to the principles of the bipolar transistor.

The Field Effect Transistor (FET): There are two main types of Field Effect Transistors, the Junction Field Effect Transistor

(JFET) and Metal Oxide Semiconductor FET (MOSFET). The JFET consisting of a silicon crystal, has two p regions diffused sideways into the crystal. A negative voltage applied to these two regions causes the depletion zones of the pn junction to extend further into the n conducting crystal, thus impeding current flow. Therefore by raising or lowering this voltage, it is possible to control the size of 'gate' through which current must flow, hence giving the JFET the potential for being a switch or an amplifier. Note that the use of the word 'gate' in this context is entirely different to that of the logic gate to be discussed a little later on in this chapter.

JFETs are used mainly as amplifiers for analog signals.

The difference between the Bipolar and the Field Effect Transistor is that current controls the former and voltage the latter.

The Metal Oxide Semiconductor Field Effect Transistor (MOSFET): This is the transistor type that is the most significant for Large Scale Integration (LSI) techniques. It comes in various flavours, as will be seen shortly.

At the simplest level necessary to explain its operation a MOSFET comprises a silicon substrate containing two regions of dopants, known as the source and drain. These two regions are connected by an oxide gate, commonly having a second aluminium gate sitting on top of it.

A p channel MOS (pMOS) has a n conducting silicon substrate, with both source and drain p doped. With no voltage applied at the oxide gate the pn junctions around the periphery of the source and drain are blocking current flow. When a negative voltage is supplied to the gate, electrons are repelled into the silicon substrate and holes attracted to the gate. Thus a narrow p conducting layer is formed under the gate.

Consequently, in a pMOS transistor, current flows between the source and drain regions along the channel (or p conduction layer) beneath the surface of the gate.

An n channel MOS (nMOS) has an identical but opposite

performance due to the reversing of polarities of doping regions. pMOS transistors are generally referred to, and employed as, enhancement transistors. Without a voltage applied to the gate the enhancement transistor is a nonconducting device.

nMOS transistors are conversely referred to as depletion transistors where there is a permanent channel, therefore it is always a conducting device unless turned off by applying a gate voltage.

A further refinement of the doping and assembly process has resulted in the most useful transistor type for low power consumption so far, Complementary Metal Oxide Semiconductor (CMOS). A complex arrangement of doped regions, silicon substrate and gates, both aluminium and oxide, have resulted in a device where power dissipation is extremely low. It has a high immunity to electrical noise, very fast operation and is compatible with normal Transistor-Transistor Logic (TTL).

The transistors described here are very complex at the fabrication and design level. In operation, however, they still conform to their basic function of being a semiconductor device capable of being used as a switch or amplifier. The proliferation of fabrication techniques has occurred because designers need to improve the performance of transistors whilst using the same raw materials, in ever diminishing sizes and levels of compaction.

Under the general heading of components, there is one further important group of devices, the diode family.

The Diode (rectifier): A diode is a component with a single pn junction. If an alternating current is applied to the diode current will flow in the forward direction. This results in rectification of an alternating current (AC) wave form into a direct current (DC). In order for current to flow the external voltage has to exceed a design threshold level to overcome resistance set up by the diffusion process. Forward current flows under forward biasing.

FERRANTI ELECTRONICS LIMITED

1. LSI design *An early stage in the design of a Large Scale Integration chip in which an engineer confirms the client's specification and translates it to the fabricator's own configuration.*

FERRANTI ELECTRONICS LIMITED

2. Artwork creation *Very large light screens are used to create the full logic design at scales of up to 500 times full size.*

3. Artwork creation *An automatically draughted version of the design is now created. Some systems record important coordinates as a by-product of this process.*

FERRANTI ELECTRONICS LIMITED

4. Digitising coordinates *Scanning the large scale drawing in order to digitise and record the coordinates of the circuit's interconnection pattern. This data is used at a later stage to control the equipment which creates the mask for chip fabrication.*

FERRANTI ELECTRONICS LIMITED

5. Engineering sample evaluation *Comparing the first engineering samples with the client's original specifications to ensure conformity.*

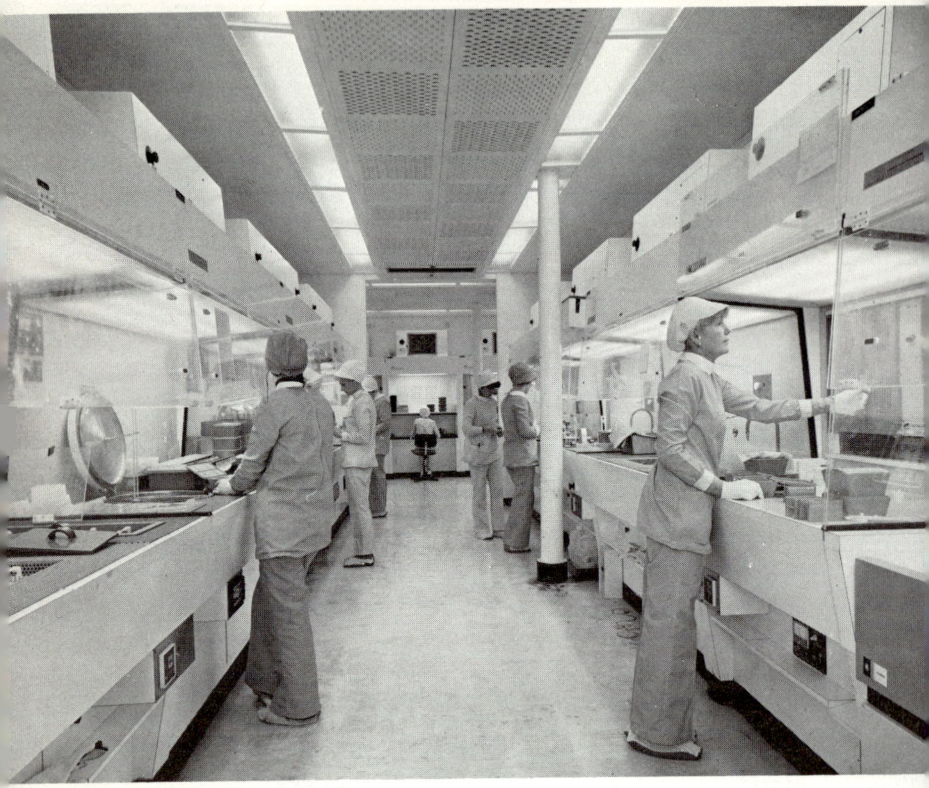

FERRANTI ELECTRONICS LIMITED

6. Wafer fabrication *Wafer fabrication takes place in a sterile, clean room environment. The specific details of a particular fabricator's process are kept a closely guarded secret since the productivity of this process represents the most fruitful area for commercial advantage.*

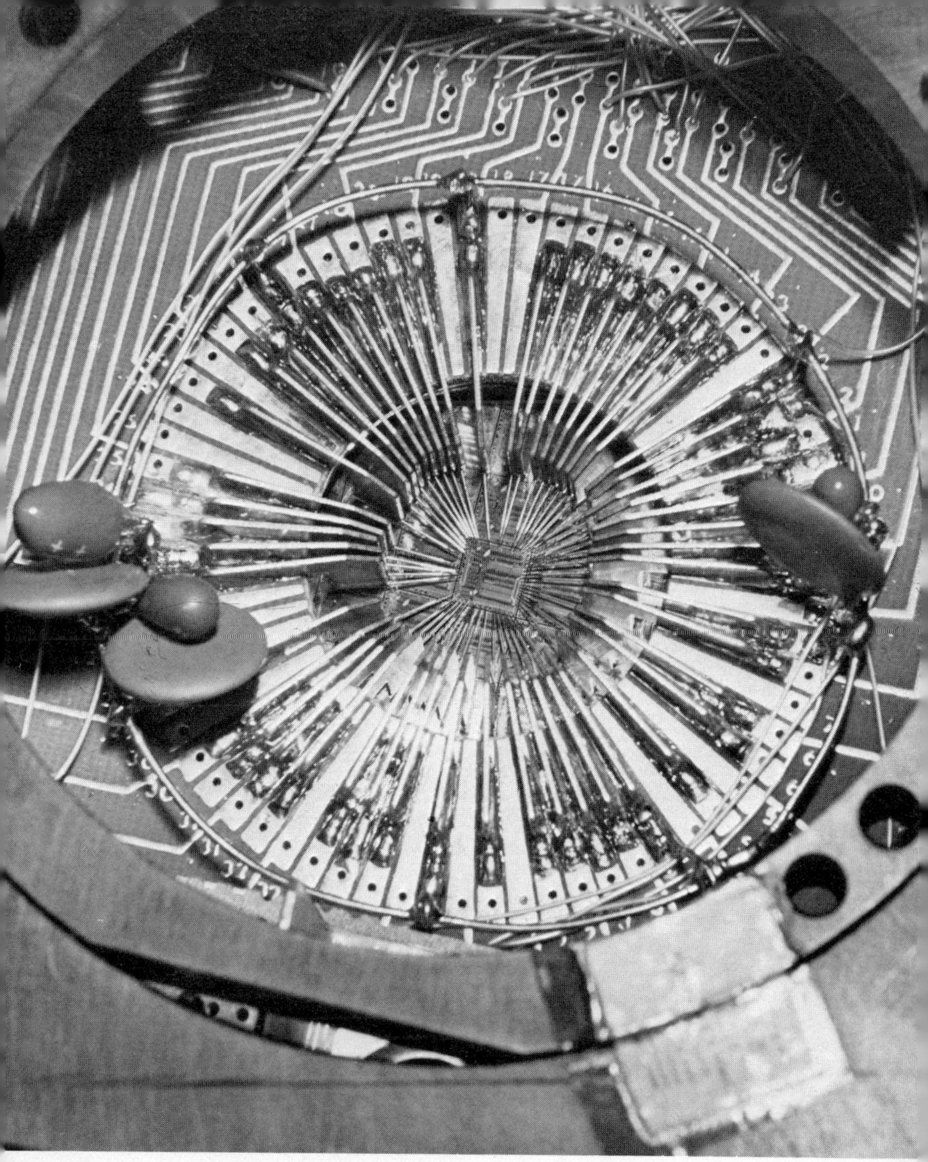

FERRANTI ELECTRONICS LIMITED

7. 100% testing *Before dicing the wafer up into all the separate chips contained on the slice of silicon all the junctions of each die are tested for function. The wafer is then diced up, bonded to its external connections and encapsulated before final product testing.*

FERRANTI ELECTRONICS LIMITED

8. LSI microprocessor *An enlargement of a microprocessor produced by this process. Actual size is ¼ inch square.*

Under reverse biasing the reverse current may be of the order of 10^7 smaller than the forward current, although never actually reaching zero. When changing from forward to reverse direction of current a switching delay occurs, but this switching delay may be as low as 10^{-8} seconds.

These general principles can apply to rectification of very high reverse voltages, up to several kilovolts.

Other special purpose diodes are used for particular applications. For example the Zener diode is used for stabilising voltages or for placing pre-defined limits on signals. The capacitance diode is used to 'tune' resonant circuits and the Shottky diode as a fast switch and for rectification of very high frequencies (microwave) rectifiers.

Logic

Having looked at the basic building-blocks of microelectronic circuits they can now be combined in various ways to make up the principal devices used for logic, universally known as gates. There is a small section on the main types of gates employed by logic circuits in the Glossary but basically each type of gate accepts signals at its input terminal (or wire) and transforms those signals according to rules (logic) contained within its own internal circuit to produce a transformed output signal. In this way desired conditions which match the logic of a particular gate produce a known output signal (or signals). Signal patterns which do not match the gate logic do not produce the desired output. Output signals only occur if the exact code of the gate's internal logic has been matched by the input signals. Note that the use of the word 'gate' is entirely different to the gate used in semiconductor fabrication.

Modern computers require thousands of gates to implement their logic requirements. Thus decision gates are arranged in a variety of configurations to implement a particular software instruction, or line of programmer's code. Current integrated circuit production embodies all the types of components, passive and active, that were discussed earlier. They are organised in thousands of alternative ways in order to produce the required configurations which make up a logic gate, all conforming to the principles of Boolean algebra laid down by George Boole in the nineteenth century.

It was possible to produce logic gates long before the advent of the transistor. Any Control and Instrumentation engineering is well aware of this. Many people used mechanical, electro-mechanical and more popularly, hydraulic and pneumatic circuits to obtain a logical output, well before the Second World War. So the principles of logic gates are not new to, or even first used by, computers.

Early computer logic included Transistor Resistor Logic (TRL). Gates were made up on circuit boards from discrete components. Many more resistors than transistors were used at this time (early to mid 1950's) since the resistor was then so cheap by comparison with the transistor. As diodes became cheap enough to use in circuits, Diode Transistor Logic (DTL) became fashionable, still using discrete components up until the early 1960's. The first microelectronic circuits using the more plentiful and cheaper transistor became known as Resistor Transistor Logic (RTL).

The most commonly used logic today is Transistor Transistor Logic (TTL) since the transistor is the cheapest and most flexible of the microelectronic components available today. TTL evolution has produced the gates and gate arrays that are more efficient and reliable, consume less power, occupy less space and cost less than ever before. However, each of the previously mentioned conventions (TRL, DTL, RTL) may still have its place at a certain stage of product designs. Successive innovation tends to produce new application possibilities and not necessarily replace more established principles.

One further bipolar technology is making headway now. Known as Integrated Injection Logic (I^2L), it consists of a pair of transistors formed in the silicon substrate. Due to the physical arrangement of this pair of transistors, no insulating areas are necessary between the various doped regions, thus dense packaging is achieved together with very high operational speeds.

Semiconductor transducers

A group of transducers has evolved through semiconductor technology. A transducer, as mentioned earlier, is a device which converts physical changes into electrical changes. Their wider use as sensors will be discussed later. The particular implications within integrated circuits for both logic and memory is of more immediate concern.

Photo-Receivers: These are a group of devices which convert light signals into electrical current and voltage signals. The photodiode allows light to pass through the semiconductor material and approach the pn junction. As it does so, it frees electrons and creates holes, thus extending the depletion region. The reverse current (photocurrent) is increased in direct proportion to the light intensity.

The Photovoltaic Cell: In this case no current is applied to the pn junctions. However as the freed electrons and holes approach the pn junction they are separated by the depletion region which causes a resultant voltage to be created (photovoltage) which develops currents in an external field. In this way energy from light is converted into electrical energy.

The Phototransistor: This is a transistor which behaves like a photodiode containing a built-in amplifier. The base collector pn junction is the light-sensitive diode. The photocurrent generated at this junction also passes through the emitter. The emitter current amplifies the original photocurrent by as much as 500 : 1.

The Light Emitting Diode (LED): This has a reverse action to the phototransistor. It exploits the collisions of electrons and holes to convert the current generated into visible light or infra-red radiations. Different colours of LEDs can be obtained by using different types of crystal and dopant. Colours in common use include red, yellow and green.

Charge Coupled Devices (CCD): A child of the semiconductor revolution, these have no counterpart in discrete logic. Essentially CCD are semiconductor circuits similar to MOS except that their operation is based on a chain-type transfer of electrical charges underneath the surface of the crystal. As a consequence it does not produce a charged channel, but a chain of packets of charge, held and transferred sequentially. The interesting feature to this device is that charge can be injected photo-electrically as well as by an applied external voltage, giving rise to a range of TV camera, scanning and digitising applications.

Memories

To the user and specifier of a system, the memory technology is usually of less importance than the way it is to be used. The usual memory types associated with computers (of any size) are Random Access Memory (RAM) used for program storage, data storage and working, and 'scratchpad' areas. Peripheral devices serve the same purpose in general purpose computing. Devices such as floppy disks, hard disks, magnetic tape, magnetic cassette – and even paper tape and card, all store data and programs and may be regarded as memory devices. However this section concerns itself with the main memory technologies of RAM and Read Only Memory (ROM).

RAM allows a user to write into and read from its contents. It can also be overwritten. The peripherals, central processor and programming languages perform the physical operations of reading and writing into the memory, specifically RAM. ROM is a memory type which can only be written into by a special programming device. This is usually a microprocessor development system, which is a microcomputer especially designed for electronic engineers. It contains a ROM programmer, which enables it to load data or programs into a ROM chip. The chip is then loaded on to a memory board in the computer. It can only be read by the processor. Normally no one can overwrite ROM without the use of a development system.

ROM is used in conventional computing for elements of operating systems, in order to speed up certain aspects of a machine's operation or performance. ROM is almost always used in industrial systems for program storage where the risks posed by the loss of the program override the cost considerations of ROM as against RAM, since ROM is considerably more expensive than RAM.

There are two types of RAM; dynamic and static. The dynamic variety is the cheapest to buy but involves creating-systems and writing programs to continuously rewrite the contents of memory since dynamic RAM will not hold a charge for any length of time. Static RAM, as its name implies, will hold the contents of memory as long as power is maintained. For critical applications of RAM a version backed up by battery can be obtained. Actually, it is a printed circuit board on which RAM is mounted with a battery permanently connected into the circuit. At present these batteries are fairly bulky devices but some of the new technologies emerging are producing smaller batteries capable of thirty years shelf life and then performing adequately. CMOS memories are capable of being operated from very low power sources and are often used in critical applications or where the application is battery powered.

ROM is actually of no use until it is programmed, hence it is usually known as Programmable Read Only Memory (PROM). Several different types exist, for varying purposes. Until recently the most commonly used PROM (for storing the dot matrix pattern of characters to be represented on a video display for example) were memories where the pattern was permanently created by fusible links. These are literally a series of fuses which can be blown (or not) in order to create a bit (binary digit) pattern which the device could interpret as a character when the appropriate key on the keyboard was depressed.

A device commonly referred to as a PROM 'blower' (more formally called a PROM programmer) is used to program this type of PROM under the control of a program held in the development system.

Another type of PROM is based on an ultra-violet (UV) ray technique, which imprints an optical image on the memory cell to expose a pattern. This is known as an Erasable Programmable Read Only Memory (EPROM). It is useful because it can be erased and re-used by the PROM programmer. In the past EPROM has occasionally been prone to a partial or full loss (corruption), of its contents, due to static electricity developing in a carpet or the frame of a computer. However, that was a relatively rare event and today's equipment is usually designed to eliminate that possibility.

One further type of PROM is in use, which at present is a proprietary type from a single supplier. It is called Electrically Alterable Read Only Memory (EAROM). By using this memory technology, it is not only possible to re-use the chip but also to address and alter only certain selected parts of the memory, which saves time and helps avoid errors.

Memory assemblies are just a series of chips loaded on to a printed circuit board. Densities are continuing to increase, and the 64K bit chip is already available. Some suppliers are talking about the million bit memory, based on bubble memory technology.

For the ordinary industrial user however, memory is usually bought in 1K to 4K blocks, often already mounted on a printed circuit board. The 1K memory is usually made up of chips which are of 128 byte (1000 bit) or 128 characters capacity. It will still be some time before the massive capacity memory chips are available in quantity and in a price range suitable for the ordinary user. A great deal more development needs to be done before memories are as cheap, as plentiful and as small as the microprocessor.

Memory technology

In the 1950's and 60's memories were made up of tiny circular doughnuts (cores) of ferrite. These cores were less than $\frac{1}{4}$ inch in diameter and they were strung together in a great matrix of wires which were used to carry current in one direction or the other. A third wire was used to 'read' the direction of magnetism of each individual core, which represented a single binary digit of information. In those days memory was usually referred to as core, and often still is.

Core was expensive and tedious to assemble, and consumed a great deal of power. It was obvious that semiconductor memories (solid state memories) would be a major break-through when they became economically feasible.

Memory is addressed by the processor in the system either by the individual bit or groupings of bits known as 'bytes' or 'half bytes', (8 bits or 4 bits), or 'words' which can vary from 12 bits to 64 bits depending entirely on the architecture of the computer and the capabilities of its low level programming languages. This means that the Basic Assembler Language (BAL), which is the lowest level a programmer can use, defines the smallest portion of memory it can address. The smaller the portion of memory that the program can talk to, the more efficient the usage of memory by the machine becomes. This is one reason for the various manufacturers' claims concerning their instruction sets, which are codes available to the programmer. Generally speaking, the more instructions in Basic Assembler Language that are available to the programmer, the more precise his use of memory becomes, since it enables him to get at smaller and smaller blocks of memory, sometimes down to an individual bit.

The most common memory technologies in use today employ the various semiconductor technologies already discussed, using the transistor as a switching device. Different technologies are selected for different applications. For example CMOS is widely used for watch memories and pocket calculator memories, since it requires a very low voltage power

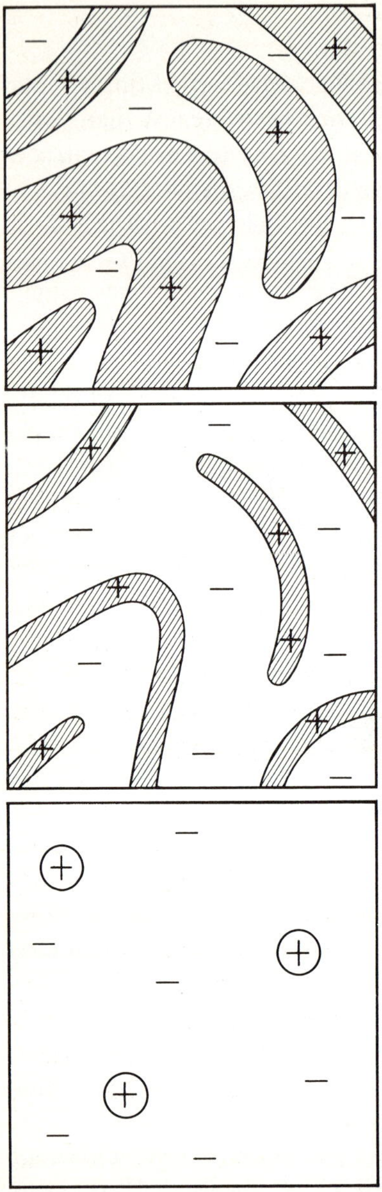

9A: *No applied magnetic field*
The positive and negative domain structures are equal in surface area under these conditions.

9B: *A small applied magnetic field*
The positive domain begins to shrink in surface area.

9C: *Critical applied magnetic field*
At the correct magnetic strength the domains reform into circular (bubble) formations.

Figure 9 *Bubble Memory*

source to sustain it. However, CMOS is relatively expensive and therefore the bipolar technologies are in more common usuage for memories in general purpose applications.

Lower cost, but slightly inferior performance memories in terms of speed, are becoming available in the form of CCD and bubble memories. Magnetic bubble memories have the potential to provide high density, solid state, reliable storage devices. They are expected to be quite cheap, but probably not as cheap as bipolar RAM.

The principle of bubble memory is based on the discovery that if a single crystal of a ferro-magnetic material is cut into a thin film, such that the surface of the film is exactly at right angles (perpendicular) to the preferred axis of magnetism of the material, the surface (or domain) structure is observed to consist of wavy strips. These strips have alternating directions of magnetism in the same direction of the material from which the film was cut, i.e. perpendicular to the film surface. The strips can actually be observed as light and dark areas when subjected to polarised light.

In the absence of an externally applied magnetic field, the surface volume of strips magnetised in one direction equals the surface volume of strips magnetised in the other. Thus the film surface is in a state of magnetic equilibrium when no external magnetic field exists.

When a magnetic field is applied perpendicular to the film surface, the strips magnetised in the same direction as that field increase in size at the expense of those having the reverse magnetisation. As the field's strength is increased the strips continue to shrink until suddenly the strips (or domains) reform into compact cylinders. If the magnetic field is further increased, there is a continuing reduction in cylinder diameter until a critical point is reached where the cylinders collapse and saturate the surface of the film.

A known range of field strengths exists for given materials to create the cylindrical shapes on film surfaces. When viewed end on, the cylinders look like bubbles. Hence the Bell Telephone Laboratory people who discovered the phenomena

christened them 'bubble memories'. The result of this discovery is that by placing films of appropriate materials in magnetic fields, the presence or absence of a bubble may be interpreted as a 1 or 0 (a binary digit). The condition may be changed by altering the strength of the magnetic field.
This technology is still young, but it does hold out the hope of large scale, stable, reliable and cheap memories, perhaps even the elusive megabit memory chip.

The final memory to be mentioned, perhaps the ultimate development, is based on the 'superconductor'. It employs the principle of the Josephson Junction (see Glossary) and requires a temperature very close to absolute zero for operation. If and when they become commercially feasible, the density of memory will be increased by a huge order of magnitude over today's highest density; they will operate up to 100 times faster because of virtually non-existent resistances within the circuits, and for the same reason consume a minimum of power. However, the so-called cryoelectronic memory has a lot more development in front of it before it becomes a practical proposition for normal use.

This chapter has, so far, discussed the individual elements that comprise an integrated circuit, from transistors to gates. It has looked at the arrays that enable these gates to answer YES/NO questions; in fact all the separate elements of a microprocessor. By looking at memory types, the survey of the semiconductor devices that make up today's microcomputers is now complete.

Before ending the chapter, it may be of interest to take a brief look at the integrated circuit fabrication process itself to gain an understanding of the complexity and expense involved in manufacturing these devices.

Fabrication of the integrated circuit:

The objectives behind the fabrication of integrated circuits include the lowest product cost, the best possible price/performance ratio, and the highest reliability possible; all the goals of normal manufacturing, in fact. However to these should probably be added the best uses of very expensive resources including capital equipment, the use of very expensive people and highly refined and costly raw materials.

The factors that make such objectives difficult to achieve and in some cases mutually exclusive, are probably no different in the microelectronics fabrication industry to any other manufacturing operation. However the financial gearing in the fabrication industry is much higher than most; the technical risks also are higher than most other industries.

Circuit design

The following description traces the design stage through to the beginning of the fabrication process. In practice this design work is increasingly being done by consultant design companies, independent of the fabricator himself. The major purchaser, the fabricator's customer, is also taking on much more responsibility for his own designs.

The customer who needs a purpose designed circuit is very rare. The tooling costs, as can be interpreted from what follows, are of necessity very high. Thus a company requiring a custom designed circuit needs a very good technical and business case to justify its decision. This becomes even more true as a wider range of standard circuits becomes available and practical. Universal general purpose circuits like the Uncommitted Logic Array (ULA) find an increasing level of acceptance. The ULA is a circuit containing a predefined number of gates, and sometimes logic circuits, that the customer himself can connect together in a variety of different circuit arrangements. This combines the flexibility of discrete components with the packaging density and economics of integrated circuits.

Obviously the people who find themselves in these areas are specialists likely to know which factors to take into account but it is interesting to observe that even with today's devices, the decision on which to use, or which route to travel, is at least as complex as any other 'make or buy' decision.

The first stage in custom circuit design is to produce logic drawings, which employ electronic engineering symbols to represent function, circuits and power requirements. This has to be done in strict accordance with the integrated circuit manufacturer's design rules. Generally, the customer will have to sign a non-disclosure agreement with his supplier to protect their design conventions. Also he will quite possibly have to make a production commitment since process and assembly capacities are scheduled well ahead of time.

The logic drawing, once approved by the supplier, is then converted into an integrated circuit (chip) layout. This stage can be performed by either a consultant, the customer or the supplier. Normally a first prototype, called a breadboard, is created at this stage. It is constructed from printed circuit board, discrete components and solid state circuits and is used to verify function and performance of the circuit's logic. It can also be used for demonstration purposes, enabling marketing and customer clientele to provide their input before final design approval is given.

A circuit test program is written in parallel with this activity. The program is used in an automatic circuit testing machine in order to check every single component value and the logic of the integrated circuit. The breadboard can be used to validate the test program so that the potential for error is minimised at an early stage, before the expensive commitments are made.

Chip layout is carried out using Computer Aided Design (CAD) techniques. These techniques optimise circuit layouts and help to avoid the drawing errors and miscalculations inherent in manual circuit layout. However it is possible that this computer generated layout will be altered by hand in order to produce a design improvement outside the capability of the CAD's own design logic.

At this stage the final layout is scanned by a machine which converts the drawing to digital signals. It is stored magnetically, extremely accurately edited and then plotted out on a large scale plotter from the digitised version. The process of digitisation is a vital precursor to size reduction from the drawing scale to the miniature chip scale. The equipment used to scan, digitise and miniaturise is also used to magnify the scale chip up to 500 times its actual size for the plotting of output and editing processes. Circuit changes can then be made using co-ordinates keyed in on a VDU.

At each stage of editing and checking, plots (print-outs) are produced to confirm the effect of that change. When final approval for a design is given, the computer holding the digitised description of the chip produces output from which a set of plates, called photomasks, are produced.

As may be recalled from an earlier description, the different types of Large Scale Integration of circuits actually involves many layers of material to be fabricated, etched and doped. Thus each mask contains a single layer. The pattern for each mask, approximately five inches in size, contains a great many repeats of the same design, in order to optimise the production process.

The plates which become masks start life as photographic plates. The image is created by a computer controlled spot light source from the digitised data held on file. The pattern initially produced is checked, reduced in size once more and then employs a photographic 'step and repeat' process to create the mask for all the hundreds of other outlines called for on that particular wafer. The image may be etched in photographic emulsion or permanently etched into a Chrome film bound to a glass base, depending on the process used by the fabricator. The whole design and mask making process takes place under spotless conditions. When produced these masks are the culmination of the design process.

A typical critical path from the commencement of specification to mask completion will take at least six months, assuming no delays are introduced into the process. Since the decision to go ahead with a custom designed chip, as opposed to a ULA or standard design, may take many months to reach and the fabrication process itself takes time after the design is completed, even assuming availability of fabrication capacity, the whole process is lengthy, costly and not without risk.

Wafer fabrication

The wafer fabrication processing plant must be of the highest order of cleanliness. The air inside the plant is washed, filtered and regulated to a state hundreds of times cleaner than a hospital's operating theatre.

The raw materials used by the process are silicon wafers, often ready prepared for use. The process employs a variety of chemicals, very expensive capital equipment, the masks themselves and an absolute minimum of people. A wafer fabrication plant, like its design facilities, is highly capital intensive and derives the maximum benefit possible from economies of scale.

The silicon goes through many subsidiary conditioning processes before it reaches the fabrication plant. It is highly refined from its oxide and chemically purified to a very high degree. A batch of this processed material, say approximately 20 pounds (10 kilograms) is then placed into a crucible and heated to melting point (1420°C). Dopants are then added, all the while the silicon being kept free of all other impurities. A silicon crystal is 'grown' from the resulting melt by the insertion of a single perfect crystal seed which is subsequently slowly withdrawn from the melt. In this way crystals several feet long and up to 4 inches in diameter can be grown.

The crystal is then cylindrically ground, usually to either a 3 inches or a 100 mm diameter. Wafers of about $\frac{1}{2}$ mm thick are then sawn off and finished (polished) to a very high specification. The final, and critical step, prior to circuit etching, is the growth on the surface of the silicon crystal wafer of a film of silicon dioxide. This is produced by a series of very complex, computer controlled, chemical processes.

The fabrication steps then commence, beginning with the coating of the wafer with a layer of photoresistant material.

Conventional photolithography methods are then used, although to incredibly high tolerances, and the strictest standards of cleanliness and control.

The photoresistant material, after suitable chemical treatment, is exposed to ultra-violet light through the photomask. In the newer methods, due to the level of miniaturision required in VLSI, electron beams, which are controlled by computer co-ordinates, are steadily replacing the mask method.

The photoresistant area which has been exposed to the ultra-violet light is then removed by an acid solvent. Then follows a diffusion process to introduce selected dopants. Once again many different methods exist to introduce these dopants, each separate method predetermining the ultimate use of the integrated circuit.

The process is repeated until the appropriate number of layers and their constituent dopants have been completed.

The end of the chemical part of fabrication is now complete: what is left is known as a multi-layer die. Each die on the wafer is checked to confirm that it performs to specification: defective dice being marked with ink to ensure that they do not reach the final product packaging stage. This process is once again computer controlled, stepping and repeating and testing each circuit as in the production of the mask.The test machines also maintain accurate statistics of rejects. These records form an important part of research into improved fabrication techniques.

The completed circuit now has to be placed in its own package. The wafer is sectioned off to separate out the individual chips; those circuits that have passed inspection are bonded into plastic packaging, or the actual rectangular 'chip' that is generally associated with the microprocessor. Their wires are then connected to the pins through which they are ultimately plugged or soldered to a printed circuit board. Then follows a comprehensive testing process which eliminates all but the most perfect.

A great deal of production development work continues in

order to further reduce the cost and size of fabrication. Of particular interest is the work going on in the photolithography area of fabrication, since this is the key element in the accurate and cheap production of integrated circuits. Emphasis is being placed on the electron beam and X-ray methods of etching circuits into the silicon dioxide coating.

Once again the evolutionary nature of developments in microelectronics is apparent. When looking back, all the products now available seem to have gone through a magical transformation compared to the earlier discrete devices. The facts are that each one has been refined and improved through a countless series of small evolutionary changes. Exactly the same principles apply to the design and production of integrated circuits, and will continue to apply until the insurmountable physical limits are met. It is the processes that have evolved.

Development

An intriguing illustration of the cross fertilisation of ideas between different technologies is now emerging in the field of materials development. Scientists researching into new plastic materials at the University of Texas are experimenting with a polymer made from acetylene. Their investigations reveal that by adding a small amount of iodine to this particular polymer a new material is produced which has electrical conducting properties of the order of 100 billion times greater than the normal polymer. A further development of the application of dopant techniques to plastics technology suggests that the plastic semiconductor will soon be feasible. It appears possible that a new era of integrated circuit fabrication is dawning.

Another aspect of using dopants to enhance the properties of certain materials is also gradually being revealed. Ion implantation techniques are now being used in metallurgy to create very hard surfaces for cutting tools and the like. At first glance this may seem to be merely a newer method of surface hardening. In fact it has provided the stimulus for a new branch of materials technology. By bombarding the surface of a metal with ions the 'grain' of the metal, or crystals, are so disrupted that the metal develops an amorphous surface, free from crystals, like glass in fact. Not only do these surfaces become very hard, but they lose the tendency to fracture that is present in many traditional hard metals.

This new area of research has led to the 'glassy' metal. In principle, if a metal (presently expensive gold-silicon alloys) is cooled at a rate of 1 million degrees per second it progresses straight to this 'glassy' state. The resultant material is a very fine wire, around two or three thousandths of an inch in gauge.

The physical properties of a glassy metal would suggest it to be ideal for the base material for bubble memories. It is easily magnetisable due to the random distribution of its atoms. It may be possible to fabricate bubble memories with a density over twenty times greater than that of any other material yet discovered. It is also possible that it could be used as the superconductor material, thus helping to bring the Josephson Junction (see Glossary) one step closer to commercial reality.

4. The Other Hardware

The intention of this chapter is to take a look at some of the other devices and technologies that, of necessity, surround the microprocessor in order for it to be used in any practical sense. No matter what the type of system is, be it used in the office, the factory, the home, in entertainment, transport or defence applications, the microprocessor is powerless without its attendant connectors, cables, switches, transducers and packaging.

Packaging

Like all other industries the electronic packaging industry has created its own phraseology. The electronic device which does not have a box, case or enclosure surrounding it is referred to as a 'naked' device. Naked products are sold to users who intend to mount the assembly into their own case, for example mounting the assembly inside an existing control panel.

One of the most basic forms of packaging is called a card frame. This is literally a framework into which printed circuit boards can be slotted or pushed along guide rails. This enables the boards to be positioned such that interconnections can be made between the boards or along a backplane, which is an interconnecting conductive rail or bus which connects each board together in the correct sequence or circuit. Versions of this card frame can also be referred to as a chassis. The frame or chassis is the basic physical building block for an electronic system.

Usually these frames, together with their printed circuit board contents, need to be loaded into another box, the outer package, in order to satisfy legislative requirements or to meet aesthetic demands. For example, a device to be used in a mine would need to meet very strict environmental requirements; the whole package would need to be flameproof. The device would need to be inherently safe and to satisfy a most stringent set of regulations concerning hostile or hazardous environments. On the other hand, for an office automation project the outer case would need to be attractively shaped and coloured to blend in with the immediate surroundings.

Such outer packaging is known by a plethora of names which to some extent depend upon its ultimate use. These names include: enclosure, cabinet, console, desk, box, panel, mounting case, racking system, housing and so on.

Conventions which concern dimensions, interfacing standards, environmental requirements and electrical performance include IEA, IEEE, BSI, DIN and many others more specific to a particular country or industry.

A typical package will also need to contain fans positioned for heat dissipation and appropriate handles, flashing lights and hinged panels for access.

Materials used for the outer packaging generally depend upon the application and are obviously subject to all of the previously mentioned conventions. They range from the various plastics for office use through to aluminium or steel for more robust purposes.

A visit to an electronics trade show or exhibition or a look at an electronics trade magazine will demonstrate the range of standard shapes and materials now available. The industry is characterised by local suppliers. There are a few multinational suppliers but they are easily outnumbered by indigenous manufacturers.

Switches

A genuinely bewildering variety of electrical switches is available. As with packaging the choice is normally made by a draughtsman or designer.

The switch industry is less local than the packaging business. The sheer bulk of packaging inhibits exports; lack of bulk encourages switch exports.

As the range of applications increases the industry is tending to become more specialised. As a consequence there are thousands of switch suppliers around the world. An example of the sort of specialisation it is possible to encounter is that a particular supplier might specialise in the miniature, subminiature and micro-miniature range. Designs within this category include push button, illuminated push button, slider switch, rocker switch, toggle switch, paddle switch, thumbwheel and rotary switches. They can be panel mounted or printed circuit board mounted; they can be simple on/off switches or multiposition (pole) switches. They can be decimal input and BCD output.

Switches can be to industry standard designs, custom built for special applications; they can be built for either purpose from standard components. They can be designed to meet any of the previously mentioned legislative requirements for millions of operations (called high repeatability), for medium or for only occasional use.

Consequently switch selection is very much a field for the person with specialist knowledge; not from the technical standpoint alone, but more from the aspect of knowing sources of supply for particular types of switch. To keep up to date in this field requires a fair amount of reading and talking to suppliers' representatives, fairly frequent attendance at trade shows and a good up-to-date library of product literature.

Cables and connections

Whilst an executive who is tempted to glance through these pages may on occasion conceivably be involved in the selection of appropriate packaging for a product or system, it is less likely that he will be deeply involved in switch selection, although naturally there are occasions when this can be of extreme importance; it is distinctly improbable that his advice will be sought on connections or cables. In fact there is less variety in the latter items than the former. It should still be perfectly reasonable to leave their selection to the specialist and only to seek assurance that they conform to all relevant standards and are not over-specified for the task in hand.

Over-specifying can be expensive; since the materials vary from precious to non-ferrous the cost implications should always be borne in mind. This admonition does not just refer to cables and connections but also to swtiches and packaging of all types. It is not too difficult to conceive of products where the cost of the packaging and attendant switches, etc. far exceed the cost of the intelligence it is designed to support! In fact, this state of affairs is all too common.

Transducers

As a reminder, transducers consist of that group of devices which convert physical energy or movement into electrical energy. There are two types; input transducers, which convert a physical movement or change into electrical energy in order to transmit appropriate signals to the processor at the heart of the system, and output transducers. Output transducers, known by many alternative names, take signals from the processor and convert them into physical movement. As an example the reading element on a punch card reader in a computer could be regarded as an input transducer. It converts changes of state into electrical signals, which the processor receives, performs logical operations upon them with the help of programs, files and memory, and concludes with output signals. These output signals may request a write operation on a disk or a printer. The device which converts that request into physical movement, e.g. the disk write head or the printer mechanism, either is or contains an output transducer.

There are literally hundreds of thousands of both types of transducer but the basic underlying principles are much more limited.

Transducers are widely used in the instrumentation and control industries. Quite often the instruments in which they are employed do not contain any intelligence at all, they merely decode the input signals and display them. Example of a non-intelligent tranducer instrument include the temperature and humidity recorder contained in the controlled environment computer room, or the fuel gauge in a car and the display on a filling station petrol pump, although the micro is having an affect on all of these applications now.

Since the object of this book is to promote awareness and understanding of what is possible, the remainder of this chapter will be given over to a review of those devices commonly known as sensors, or the transducers which, when forming part of a microprocessor based system will influence almost every product and process that modern man regards as essential. Already there are hundreds of well publicised applications, ranging from computers themselves, to motor car applications, domestic appliances and the rapidly expanding industry of robotics. Robotics is a particularly important area for the study of sensors because, without highly refined sensory and feedback systems, the required accuracy of their control would be impossible to achieve. Todays robots need to know angular positions of all moving components within the robot assembly; to have very sensitive pressure transducers to control their materials handling functions and to have comprehensive intelligence to assimulate and control the information coming in from those sensors. In the general sense this can be said to be the same for all devices employing microelectronics and transducers.

Bearing in mind that an input transducer is designed to measure physical variables by converting that variable into electrical energy, the reverse is true of an output transducer, which is required to react in a predictable, physical fashion in response to signals controlled by the central processor.

The physical variables which are capable of being transduced include force, weight, torque, velocity, flow and fluid pressure.

Measureable variables which affect the composition of elements rather than size, shape, or movement include temperature, moisture measurement, hardness, viscosity, density and composition of materials.

The final category concerns the measurement of magnetic field, strength, electrical quantities, radiation and pollution.

Many of the applications of these principles are esoteric and would not have a direct relevance to an executives' day to day business life. Most of the principles are embodied in the instruments referred to previously or are embraced by the data logging industry.

Data logging is, broadly speaking, another term for data acquisition or data recording. Data loggers are a range of devices that accept input from transducers and record the data in the normal range of computer storage media. Some models have limited intelligence but very few have large storage capacity. However, they can be regarded as a simple form of the microelectronics system which employs microprocessors and transducers.

Rather than reviewing the whole range of transducers it is probably of greater use to concentrate on the more general applications and refer readers who require a more detailed description to one of the vast library of textbooks on the subject.

Size and displacement

Firstly, it is important to recognise that all transducers will introduce errors into a system of measurement. It is inevitable when converting from a non-electrical measurement to an electrical signal. The point to be aware of is that the transducer itself must be calibrated (measured and normalised) from time to time, and that the scale of introduced errors should be recognised and compensated. In practice this error is cumulative; the higher the reading, the greater the error. Therefore if the error cannot be compensated the computing system must at least know the scale and be able to rely on the repeatability of the error. Random errors are impossible to compute; predictable errors are an acceptable second best to perfect accuracy.

Some of the most common applications require the sensing of physical size. The device most commonly used in this case is the displacement transducer. In one case two electrodes are placed on the material to be measured, one on either side. An electrical charge is passed through the circuit connecting these two electrodes, from which the measured resistance in the material being gauged can be compared with a known resistance for that type of material. The measured size will be computed from a formula in which size is proportional to resistance for a known material.

There is a wide variety of variations on this technique as can be imagined. Other methods are chosen to suit specific application. These include current measurement, capacitance, magnetic flux, ultrasonic waves and nuclear radiation using either alpha, beta, gamma, or X ray sensing methods.

The choice of methods depends upon materials to be measured and the accuracy required amongst other factors. These methods can be used to sense the thickest materials right down to less than one thousandth of an inch and within an accuracy (repeatability) of 1% where necessary.

The simplest form of physical size measurement, or displacement measurement, is obtained by a potentiometer. The basic potentiometer ('pot') consists of a wire with a sliding contact ('wiper'). The sliding contact is moved by the measurement process; as the resistance between the two contacts varies with distance the size (displacement) can be computed. A rotary potentiometer is a variation of the basic type. This has two static contacts, one at either end of a coil of wound wire and a sliding contact. The rotary potentiometer is often used to measure angular movement. For example, the throttle pedal assembly on an electric milk van contains a rotary potentiometer which feeds back throttle position (hence demand) to the electrical power source.

The strain gauge is another example of a device which

measures size and movement. This type of transducer is based on the principle that fine wires will change their electrical resistance when mechanically strained. Thus if a measuring head is connected to a tightly wound wire such that any movement of its measuring head introduces strain into the wire, its resistance can be measured and converted into physical measurement.

The Hall Effect, employed in the proximity switch, is widely used to measure displacement. This measuring device can in fact be defined as a solid state device. In essence, a magnetic field is set up by the Hall Effect device. Movement of a material through that magnetic field modifies the measured strength of the field, from which displacement may be derived.

A further popular type of transducer for displacement sensing involves encoding a scale, either with special optical marks (e.g. graticules) or magnetic codes (similar to magnetic tape). Movement of the scale results in the transducer observing a change in the code; it is then decoded and compared to the scale for displacement measurement.

All of these general principles are embodied in thousands of different types of transducers, many of them specially designed for one particular application. It is sufficient for the purposes of this chapter to know what is possible in order to illustrate the point that any system which needs to recognise physical size or change of size or position can be accommodated by employing some of the principles mentioned here.

Angular movement

A popular, robust and cheap method of measuring angular displacement has already been mentioned: the rotary potentiometer, which employes the measurement of resistance or variation of resistance. Other types of transducer for angular measurement include those devices that employ an encoded plate or graticule. Angular movement causes displacement of the coded plate with respect to a datum. This displacement is interpreted and converted to an input signal from which the exact displacement can be calculated.

There are many other methods used with increasing degrees of sophistication. However, the more sensitive and sophisticated devices lend themselves much more to laboratory work than for commercial microelectronics system.

Tilt and level

Once again there are a large number of laboratory type instruments available, including transducers which use pendulums, fine balances, optical devices and the popular digitally encoded disk method. All have their uses but for the types of systems under general consideration here it may be possible to avoid the use of such sophisticated devices by using simple variants of the potentiometer and allowing the intelligence at the heart of the system to resolve the angular position, proportional to resistance. In fact a moon landing vehicle used just such a technique for positioning the legs of the vehicle as it landed on the uneven surface of the moon.

Velocity

Linear and angular velocity can be resolved by measuring movement with respect to time. Some of the techniques already discussed are clearly of practical use here, such as a linear potentiometer or Hall Effect device. Once again the intelligence would need to perform the mathematical operations to convert this movement into signals that a program could then resolve into a value.

The methods employed include digital encoding, doppler methods and laser beams. In each case the difference from a known start point is interpreted to give the required value.

Force, weight and torque

The resistance method is used in several devices in much the same way as for linear displacement. The calculation for force and weight has to take into account the force necessary to displace the measuring head or probe. One technique used for measurement in this category takes advantage of piezo-electric principle. Certain materials display this phenomenon, in which an electric potential can be measured across the surface of a crystal if its dimensions are altered as a result of physical change, be it force, weight or torque. An element which exhibits piezo-electric properties is also known as an electro-restrictive element.

More sophisticated transducers can be constructed which include two different piezo-electric crystals bonded together which 'twist' in a predictable fashion under known conditions. This enables even more accurate measurements to be made.

Not surprisingly certain semiconductors have been discovered to have piezo-electric qualities and they are increasingly being used in the newer transducers.

The potentiometer is widely used in pressure transducer applications.

Flow, pressure, heat and moisture

Each of these variables has its own unique range of transducers. By now it will be apparent that although the basic principles are roughly similar to other types of transducers the variety of methods will be unique to those physical variables being sensed, especially where the sensing is to take place on less easily observable phenomena.

The basic method is still the resistive technique although electro magnetic, encoding and ultrasonic systems are also used, in addition to several others. However, this is less likely to be a typical problem for the average executive. It will be clear that established methods do exist, and that much development is taking place to improve and extend the range. Any transducer manufacturer will be able to advise on specific requirements for these and the more specialised variables that can be sensed.

Output transducers

Output transducers generally have simpler jobs to perform than input transducers. They can take the form of Chart recorders, disk write heads, valves, switches, linear actuators, solenoids, stepper motors or anything that will execute a physical movement in response to signal, or trigger, from another device.

Many output transducers can only operate in the binary mode. For example, a simple switch, a relay or a solenoid are either on or off. There is no intermediate state. For systems requiring a measure of proportional control, for example in hydraulic or pneumatic circuits, linear actuators (proportionally controlled devices), stepper motors or geared motors offer a better solution.

At the movement this seems to be the area of least development and most need. It is probable that the dramatic expansion of the robotics industry will force rapid development of a much more diverse range of output transducers over the next few years.

Terminal

Terminal is a name given to a connection at the end of a current carrying cable or conductor. In this case the terminal is the end of the line of discussion of microelectronics hardware.

The first part of this book has discussed the various types of hardware which any computer system – mainframe to micro – needs to use. It may seem to some readers, perhaps those with a traditional computer background, that the text has dwelt overmuch on hardware and not enough on such topics as software or system analysis or the computer professional.

This is the result of a deliberate decision, taken to reinforce the contention that as the microprocessor and its associated chips, and the other products mentioned in this book, move into all facets of business and personal life the skills necessary to cope with its challenge, to use it to benefit the business or organisation will not come from computer departments alone. Nor will they come from engineering departments alone, nor any other single source. In time the specialists will take over, as they have in other new technologies but in the meantime the state of the art is such that in order to make best use of the micro it has to be appreciated at the hardware level.

The microelectronics revolution has not just produced a cheaper computer; it merely looks as though it has. What the revolution is doing is providing devices which offer opportunities for a fundamental re-evaluation and redesign of products and processes. This time there are very few experts around to help management; managers have to come to terms with the technology if they are not to abdicate total responsibility in favour of the new specialists.

5. Putting it all together

The first four chapters followed an 'explosion' process, taking a general broad look at the subject and then looking at the separate elements in greater detail, culminating in an examination of integrated circuits and transducers.

The object of this section is to reverse the process and to take a look at what is involved in creating a computing system, using the elements discussed earlier. With any type of computing system, the purchaser has inescapable duties and responsibilities. Later sections of this chapter address the topic of project management and allocation of responsibilities. The earlier sections look at what is involved in putting together the separate elements of a computer system, be it part of the product, controlling a process, or performing a business administrative function.

Two examples have been chosen. The first is used to illustrate how microelectronics can be applied to an industrial project in a demanding environment. The second takes a fairly typical business data processing project. Both examples follow the project through from first ideas to installation.

An industrial project

A manufacturer of agricultural implements has a range of mechanical hedge trimmers of the type that can be mounted onto a tractor. Generally these are hydraulically driven and positioned, by as many as five different hydraulic cylinders in order to extend the cutting arm and to obtain the correct angle on the cutting head (flail, or flail mower). At present the operator of one of these machines has to control all the hydraulic rams separately, each having its own control lever.

In addition, he has to drive the tractor forward whilst looking over his shoulder to make sure the mower is cutting straight and level. The operator's job is clearly difficult and demands skill and experience. Nor is his job without danger.

If the separate control of all these rams could be combined into a single controlling device, such as an aeroplane type of joystick, some of the hazards and some of the need for skill and experience might be removed from the job. Assuming this is the project to be tackled, what are the individual steps involved? An initial impression can be formed by just looking at the headings of the activities:

Compile a business case
Compile a requirements specification
Decide whether to make or buy
Choose a supplier
Draw up a product specification
Draw up a project plan
Undertake hardware design
Undertake software design
Undertake test gear design
Compile the documentation
Complete training
Complete testing
Complete trials
Adopt as standard

Looking at each of these headings in a little more detail:

Business case

Most manufacturers have their own philosophy on the incorporation of new ideas for products or components. In this case it is assumed that a decision has been made on the basis of market protection: the assumption that if company 'A' do not incorporate this sort of innovation their competitor, company 'B', will and thereby obtain a competitive advantage in the market. So it is important for them to improve this particular aspect of their product design. In general terms they now have to decide which route to take. Do they improve control by creating extra hydraulic circuitry, by extra mechanical devices, by a complete product redesign or by the application of microelectronics?

Typically, a manufacturer in this category will have no expertise in electronics, since all of their previous experience has been mechanical and production engineering, coupled with fairly basic electrical competence for such things as lighting and ignition.

Thus the first, and almost certainly, the most difficult set of decisions revolves around the choice of technology. In this case the manufacturer makes the decision: if it can be done for the same price or less than the technologies we know and will provide the same function or more than the technologies we know, we will try a microelectronics solution.

This decision would normally be taken in parallel with a knowledge of the impact of a resultant price increase (if any) on the market, bearing in mind the enhancement of the product, the timing of the new product and knowledge of any competitive activity in this area.

This exercise can take months; it usually happens, at the present time at least, because someone within the company suggests the idea. It is unlikely that any single supplier to the company would actually market and present the idea to them, bearing in mind the current state of knowledge and experience.

Requirements

In a project like this it is vital that objectives for the project are agreed and written down before any work takes place. The first requirements must include the objectives implicit within the business case, including price, timing and the function the product is expected to perform. Additionally, industrial standards on safety and any other relevant points (for example noise) must be written into the specification. It is not necessary to go into any detail on design; the chosen supplier should be equipped to handle that aspect of the job.

Such things as reassurance should be considered. For example, it should be possible to visually reassure the average operator by some sort of display that the 'black box' is actually working and doing what he expects it to do. Remember, in a mechanical device, every action stimulates a reaction, which the operator is used to and can see and feel. This will not always be the case when independent machine intelligence is applied to the job.

The positioning of these displays should also be stipulated by the specifier. It is unfair to expect an outside supplier to know a product as well as the user or the manufacturer.

Safety warnings should also be specified. For example, if a known combination of angles of all the hydraulically controlled arms can produce an unstable vehicle attitude then *both* visual and audible warnings should be specified. Such things as flashing lights and sirens could be appropriate. Remember they need to be seen and heard under conditions which can occasionally be described as hazardous. They must also be capable of being seen easily from the normal operator position. These alarms should be capable of being switched off, but deliberately and with difficulty. In no circumstances should the operator be able to 'lock out' the warning function of the system, as so many people did with car safety belt alarms.

A 'get you home' facility needs to be considered. The sophistication of microelectronics will be of no use to the operator if it fails in an inaccessible spot, and as a result he is not only unable to use the device, but also unable to set it to a position which allows him to get the vehicle or implement back to a repair site. At times it will fail, have no doubt. And when it does fail Murphy's law will prevail. For example, in the case of the flail mower, it could be possible that if the 'black box' malfunctions, the hydraulic rams could be locked in position, making it impossible to move the tractor through a farm gate without a major stripping down job. Therefore, it is important to specify the need for an alternate, emergency only, method of control.

Finally in this section, serviceability. It is highly unlikely that the end user will have electronic technicians on his staff, nor will he intend to employ any in the future if he can avoid it. The same is less likely to be true of the manufacturer, but even so, his maintenance people will not be retrained overnight. Therefore the product specification needs careful thought in the area of maintenance skills. It is likely that the specification will conclude that the product must be totally replaceable by a technician with traditional skills. This would mean a sealed, black box type of product capable of being fitted and removed by the auto mechanic or similar technician. However, he will need to assess whether, under certain circumstances, it is the black box or the other associated components that have failed, or whether it is something else he can repair himself. Thus the device will need to provide diagnostic facilities. For example, it might be decided to request a facility to test each input and output position to establish that they are working. Simple push buttons and LED displays could be appropriate for this task.

These are the sort of factors to be considered in drawing up a requirements specification for applying microelectronics to an engineering product. In fact this sort of product was chosen as an example to illustrate that it is perfectly feasible to apply the newer microelectronics technologies, with all their apparent fragility and undoubted sophistication, to the demanding world of normal mechanical engineered products. Agricultural engineering is a particularly good example since it is traditionally regarded as being imprecise and intolerant of fragility, operating as it does in all weathers and under all conditions, generally miles away from a conventional electrical power service.

In summary, the requirements specification for such a product as this flail mower must include:

Business objectives

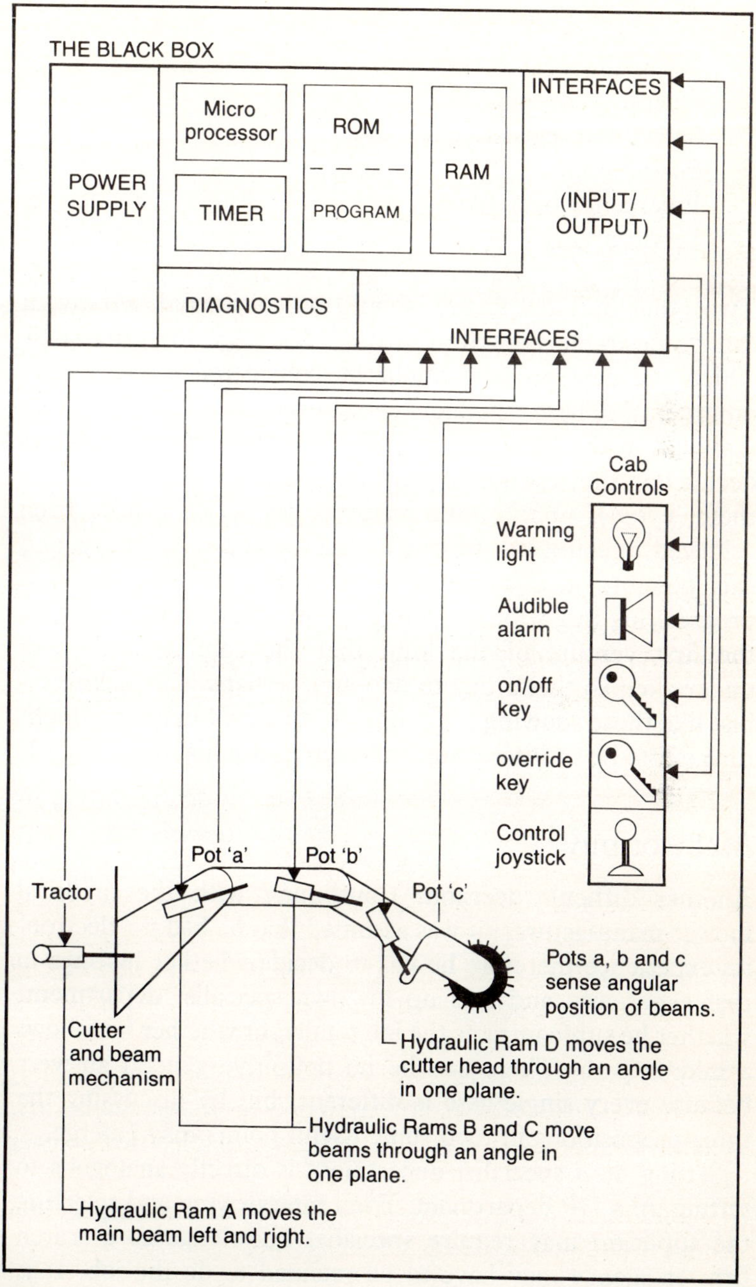

Figure 10 *The 'mythical mower' schematic*

Price, timing and function
Operator reassurance
Safety and legislative aspects
Positioning
Emergency override
Serviceability

Two other optional factors should be considered. Firstly, it can be desirable to write down at this stage the criteria by which the new product might be considered a success (or otherwise). These are not necessarily the same as those included in the business case. For example, if the operators decide that they cannot live without these new aids after using them, even if none of the business case criteria have been achieved, it could still be considered a success. Secondly, and this possibly just for academic interest, the keeping of a progress log might be considered. This could conceivably be the first venture of the kind that the company has ever undertaken so that a day to day log, perhaps with pictures – just like those showing the progress of a new building – might turn out to be an interesting and even useful historical record.

Make or buy?

Another difficult decision. Continuing with the mythical mower manufacturer; it was assumed that he had no electronics experience therefore he has to decide whether he buys in that experience and sets up his own specialist department, whether he sub-contracts the job totally, or whether he follows a middle path. There can be no definitive general answers because every single case is different, but by discussing the three propositions in turn some useful points may emerge.

Setting up a specialist department is directly analogous to setting up a DP department. Even interviewing and selecting the applicant may require specialist knowledge so a search firm or agency may have to be retained to do the job. It is possibly unsafe to rely on just one specialist since he may walk away half way through a project and thereby waste most of the work that has been done up to that point. On the other hand, two extra people, especially relatively expensive specialists, could be an embarrassing luxury in the early days. Therefore the decision to set up an in-house electronics engineering department is likely to be reflection of the board's determination to employ the new technology.

In the strictest sense, it would be an investment decision. For not only will people be required, together with their attendant overheads, but also capital equipment. This equipment will include power supplies, oscilloscopes, development systems and various other items of electronic equipment. At 1980 prices, for one engineer, this could cost up to $100,000 after making allowances for benches, working and office space, component supply and allowances for trade magazines and suppliers' literature (which often has to be purchased these days). Since a development system (the programming device) and various other items of equipment can be shared between two or three people, the second engineer is only likely to require about $20,000 of capital equipment initially. However, after the second engineer has been employed for a while the work generated by the two engineers will probably require an electronics technician to perform some of the laboratory testing and to build test gear. It will also be necessary to have the services of an engineering draughtsman with special experience in laying out electronic designs, printed circuit board layouts and a knowledge of the industries' suppliers.

In practice, this represents a minimum electronic engineering facility, possessing the capability of designing and building a product through to prototype stage.

A point should be made here on the skills required: the electronic engineers will need an appreciation of mechanical engineering and the principles of hydraulics. This will take time to acquire. They will also need to have a good appreciation of transducer technology in addition to their own professional skills in microelectronics.

At least one of them will need to be a competent Assembler

level programmer. The draughtsman can normally be relied upon to research and select the packaging, switches, connections, cabling and so on.

So apart from the difficulties of recruiting the right people and the cost of recruiting, there are other important factors to consider. Capital equipment, possibly a minimum of $150,000 as a guide. Staff costs, based on U.S. and U.K. rates are likely to amount to $80,000 a year in addition to the cost of facilities, employee benefits and the like.

All in all, the decision to set up a new department could well involve an investment decision of $300,000 in the first full year.

It is possible to identify the direct costs in this exercise but it is much more difficult to evaluate the intangible costs, which include the cost of managing this department. Grafting on the new technology to an existing business offers a demanding management challenge, to say the least.

The cost and effort involved in setting up a new department may seem to be exaggerated, and perhaps they are when compared to certain known cases. To place that exercise in its proper perspective, it is necessary to look at what is involved in totally sub-contracting the work. This will initially involve research into the industrial infrastructure which is available to support a project such as the electronic controller for our mower.

One of the main considerations to be borne in mind is the need for security, in fact, security from two aspects. The chosen supplier needs to be financially stable with a good track record over a reasonable period. Apart from having all the right facilities, preferably being local and appearing capable of being able to do the job, he must give appropriate assurances on confidentiality of design and software. Since competitive edge is the most likely attribute the new product will offer, it is essential that the chosen supplier makes firm commitments on this aspect of his work. This may present particular difficulties if it is considered beneficial to patent the design or copyright the drawings and software, since under patent law, it may be considered that in employing a sub-contractor at some stage 'publication' may have taken place before the patent has been approved, which may provide patent offices with a reason to turn down the application. If this is a particular issue, the appropriate professional advice needs to be taken.

There are two main types of supplier qualified to do this sort of work. There is the supplier who already produces his own range of electronic products and as a consequence possesses all of the necessary equipment and staff to develop and manufacture them. Then there is the sub-contractor, without any products of his own. The first type will probably not be interested since they are likely to be concentrating exclusively on their own products. The more likely supplier is the electronics sub-contractor who does not have any products of his own but acts as a merchant 'build and test' house. There are a wide variety of companies within this definition but large numbers of them can be eliminated. Most of them prefer to specialise, quite naturally, in high volume, rapid turnaround work for such people as domestic appliance manufacturers. Since the mower job is at best small batch work, say no more than 1000 a year, they probably would not be interested. Also many of them do not have their own design and development departments, so that group can be eliminated. Therefore it is likely to be a smaller, more flexible electronics supplier who will ultimately do the job. It should be fairly easy to select a short list from this category by asking the right questions on confidentiality, volume and facilities. This, taken together with locality, track record and references, should enable a short list to be drawn up.

There are other sources of supply. For example, there are many companies specialising in design and prototyping. The problem is that this creates a dependence on two suppliers: the prototyper and the volume supplier. This is also true of almost all other sources of supply, which include industrial control systems houses (a new phenomenon), consultants, either independent or one of the major consultancies, or colleges and universities. There are many different ways of getting the job done, but supplier selection at this stage of industrial development is still rather chancy and, to have the best chance of success, requires detailed attention from management.

The middle course between totally sub-contracting and setting up a new department may appear to be the most attractive in this case. Ideally, this would not involve establishing any lavish facilities but would necessitate hiring, or retraining a technician; preferably someone who already works in the company. This has the merit of having a person who knows the products and who can gradually assimilate the new technology. He can act as the link man, probably on a part time basis, and will one day form the basis for an in-house electronics department when the time is right. However, this technician should not be regarded as a surrogate manager: management still have the responsibility for meeting objectives.

Whichever way is chosen the decision will not be easy even if taken professionally and rationally and based upon all the available facts. It will always be possible to see a different way of doing things later on, but like all purchasing decisions, the earlier the decision is made the sooner the benefits show themselves.

Before moving on to the next topic, a word on pricing. Assuming the decision to sub-contract has been made, the method the supplier uses to charge his customers varies with the type of supplier. For example, if a contract designer is employed for the development up to prototype stage, the price paid is likely to be a fixed price or cost plus. The volume supplier may require a tooling or test equipment lump sum payment, but apart from that the price paid should be to the normal unit or bulk pricing formula. If one supplier is chosen to do all design and manufacture he may require a separate development contract. This means that during the prototyping stage both companies share the development costs, probably to ratios or figures agreed in advance. At the same time it may be necessary to give him formal assurances on volume supply. The supplier might consider it unfair if he were used for development solely, since he is being only partially reimbursed for his development work where he normally earns his income by bulk manufacturing. There are no firm rules for supplier negotiations in this field, but it is only fair to make an effort to understand how the supplier earns his living and to be prepared to compromise on the way business is normally done in the traditional manufacturing business.

Product specification

The chosen supplier will probably submit some sort of proposal during your negotiations. After that the next step is to take the initial requirements specification, together with the supplier's proposal, and between the two companies to turn it into a full, formal product specification.

One way of approaching this task is to form a small committee, including people from product design and marketing, and ask each person to draw up his own 'wish list'. Even to get to this stage may involve sending one or two people on courses or to seminars so that they develop an instinct for what might be possible. It does no harm to ask for things that are not possible; it is unfortunate – and often happens – that people do not ask for certain features because they do not realise what is possible. At this stage both management and supplier need to be at their creative best to ensure that all parties have an opportunity to provide input to the design and to try and ensure that everyone knows what is possible, what is not possible and what the areas of risk are.

Certain requirements may not be able to be met in practice because until the prototype is built, the behaviour of the device cannot be accurately predicted. For example, in the case of the mower, it probably would not be possible to tell whether an analog or digital output signal will be best to energise the hydraulic rams. An analog output could be more expensive to develop; a digital signal might set up too great a vibration in the device due to 'pulsing' of the hydraulic fluid.

Hence a 'model' stage might need to be introduced into the development cycle.

The 'wish' list needs to be given an order of priority. For example, when listing the features of the required system it might be possible to list them under:

must have: absolutely vital to the function of the device (e.g. safety features)

desirable: features that are not absolutely necessary but are considered important enough to include if technically feasible or not too expensive (e.g. try and fit it into the existing control panel rather than create a special black box).

would be nice: a chance to include the flight-of-fancy sort of requirement. For example, in the case of the mower, to create a self levelling program so that no matter what angular position the wheel of the tractor happened to be in, the cutters are always maintained level, a little like the self levelling gun in a tank turret.

Ultimately, the wish list is refined to a formally documented set of requirements which, after due consultation, are agreed and form the basis of all the work that follows.

Project planning

Specification completion can be considered as the project start date. An appendix to the specification should be a formal project plan. This should identify every single definable step in the project and allocate a start date, a finish date and responsibility. Carrying on with the mower example, a typical project plan could be outlined as in the table on page 100.

A number of points about this plan. Firstly, it is only hypothetical; it could take more or less time in real life. The reason for including it here is to identify some of the main jobs to be considered. Secondly, plans can appear in any number of guises such as Gantt charts, bar charts and PERT diagrams for example, depending on the conventions people are familiar with.

Thirdly, a system of review must be set up at the same time as the plan is agreed. It is not sufficient to let the technicians make all the decisions, many of which may have wider, business implications. It is most important to hold regular review meetings, usually monthly, at which the management of both companies is represented, in addition to the technicians. This does not prevent the technicians talking to each other as often as they wish. It merely provides a regular platform for the exchange of information on progress, or the lack of progress. This in turn enables the manager to keep his colleagues informed and to reschedule as appropriate.

The supplier has a rather odd role in these meetings. By now the technicians will be speaking their own special language. Suppliers' management will understand it, and because it is a job going through his factory, he will be familiar with progress and the technical status of the work on a day-to-day basis. However, his counterpart from the manufacturing company, his customer, is relatively isolated from both the technical details and the exact status of the work in relation to the plan. Invariably these meetings turn into a re-education session; the job evolves, the language evolves but the customer's manager is submerged in the daily realities of running his own business. This aspect of progress meetings is inevitable, and it is as well to recognise it in advance and to plan for it. The more comprehensive the minutes of such meetings are, the easier is the re-education task at each meeting.

Hardware design/software design

Probably the single most important technical decision that the mower company have to make is their selection of the control lever, or joystick. Their aim in selecting this lever is to replace several hydraulic ram control levers so the joystick must have several switches built into it. There are ranges of appropriate

Activity	Responsibility		Time into project (weeks)
	Mower manufacturing company	*Sub-contractor*	
Agree specification	X	X	0
Select hardware	X	X	0–4
Hardware design		X	0–8
Software design		X	2–10
Test gear design		X	2–10
PCB layout		X	0–4
PCB manufacture		X	4–8
PCB assembly		X	8–10
PCB test		X	10–14
Package designs	X	X	0–4
Complete parts lists		X	14
Finalise engineering drawings		X	14
Code programs		X	10–16
Desk check		X	16
Assemble programs		X	16–18
Correct		X	18–20
Program test		X	20–22
Debug		X	22–26
System test		X	26–30
Debug		X	30–32
Complete test gear assembly		X	32
Prototype completion		X	32
Laboratory test		X	32–34
Factory test	X	X	34–40
Field test	X		40–52
Documentation:			
Design manual		X	34–40
Maintenance manual		X	34–40
Training/education:			
Management	X	X	40
Design/development staff	X	X	40–42
Operators	X		40–52
Customers	X		52–70
Life trials	X		52–70
Modifications	X	X	52–70
Adopt as standard	X		75

standard joysticks made by a few manufacturers now. One variety has four built-in pairs of contacts, one in each of the North, East, West and South lever positions. It would also be possible to fit a button switch into the top of the lever, giving five sets of contacts from a single control lever.

After choosing the control lever, by working to the product specification, the technicians can decide upon the positioning of the controller enclosure, its diagnostic and warning features and all the necessary input and output devices.

Starting with the 'intelligence' at the heart of the system and then working out progressively to each input and output point: the principal steps involved in this sort of industrial microelectronics application are as follows (Note: these steps are common to most microelectronic applications, from word processors and business data processing microcomputers to industrial control systems).

The first decision the electronic engineer has to make is whether he uses a commercially available microcomputer board or whether he constructs his own. The advantages of buying an off-the-shelf board are that it has a known cost and performance and no development or design work is necessary. Hence, by using a standard product (often ex-stock) it is possible to speed up the project.

There are some disadvantages; these boards are not usually of industrial quality; they are not usually manufactured to tolerances and performance standards that the industrial working environment requires. Quite often these standard boards are designed for the hobbyist computer market; consequently they will not possess such features as optical isolation, for protection against power surges. This is not necessary in a domestic, clean mains power environment, but it is vital in a battery powered circuit. They do not generally perform outside a quite narrow operating temperature range. For industrial work, the tolerance range might need to be somewhere around $-30°$ to $+50°C$. Also the normal off-the-shelf board, although it may contain a sufficiently powerful processor and abundant RAM and ROM together with adequate input and output connections, is unlikely to have CMOS memory. CMOS would be too expensive and unnecessary for the hobbyist because the home computer runs off mains power and therefore power consumption is not a problem. However, for an on-board application, running off 12 V or 24 V batteries, low power consumption is vital.

Finally, it is fairly unusual to find off-the-shelf microcomputer boards with battery backed up RAM. Battery back up enables RAM to function even when the principal power source is disconnected for a while. This could be most important for an industrial application but is seldom seen to be critical to the hobbyist. For these reasons, a standard microcomputer board is unlikely to fill the bill. Incidentally, standard computer boards are sometimes called 'naked' when they are supplied without an enclosure or appropriate packaging.

However, industrial grade microcomputer boards are beginning to be seen more frequently at the bigger distributors. The problem here is that they are considerably more expensive than hobbyist type boards and are, of course, made to a standard size, which may not fit into the space available to the designer, especially if he has to provide another board for extra memory, signal conditioning, special interfaces and the like.

The reasons for the price disparity between the normal hobbyist type of board and the industrial grade is due to the much more stringent design requirements and particularly the expense involved in testing the industrial product. It is assumed that if a domestic grade board fails the owner will attempt to repair it himself or take it in for repair. It is not normally used in critical applications. When it is, it often turns out to be a case of 'penny wise, pound foolish'. Industrial systems on the other hand must be as reliable as it is possible to make them. Even if the mythical mower does have a 'get you home' procedure, the driver only expects to have to use it during an exceptional emergency. Frequent breakdowns would have a dramatic impact on sales of the product with many other side effects. So each industrial grade board is tested for function, each component on the board is inspected and tested for performance and, as far as possible, each track on the circuit is tested and inspected. Very sophisticated production equipment is necessary to ensure a minimum of rejects and expensive environmental testing is carried out prior to shipping. The costs involved in these procedures are obviously reflected in the cost of the boards.

The electronic engineer, therefore, has to make a careful evaluation of what is available as standard, and obviously their costs. For any given task it is quite possible that a standard board would have to be supplemented by a second printed circuit board containing such things as extra memory and special interfacing requirements. If this proves to be the case, he may have to make a decision on size. For example, a standard enclosure (box or case) may be available for one board but not two, after due allowance for mounting and connections have been made. It might also be impossible to actually mount a larger enclosure in the desired position on the mower.

For the purposes of illustration it is assumed that the engineer decides to design a special board rather than use a standard product, for reasons of space and cost. That being the case, what are the main steps involved in designing a microcomputer system?

Firstly, the designer produces an overall schematic diagram showing where the transducers have to be mounted (to measure the angles of the mower and all the assemblies controlled by the hydraulic rams). Then he positions the warning devices, the joystick and the controller itself. From this schematic he is able to confirm all the inputs and outputs that need to be interfaced to the microprocessor. Note that any single input or output device may require several connections to the microprocessor system, causing a need for many more inputs and outputs than would seem to be necessary on first impressions.

At the same time that the joystick is being chosen the device to energise the hydraulic rams also has to be chosen. This device can be regarded as an output transducer and could, for example, be a solenoid or a special valve. The input transducers could all be of the rotary potentiometer variety, where the resistance varies with angular movement.

Other decisions need to be made. Since a 12 V or 24 V battery is to be the main power source, a constant power supply for the circuit has to be designed. Any digital to analog or analog to digital conversion must be catered for; optical isolation needs to be considered for filtering out the inevitable spikes and numerous other electrical considerations need to be taken into account. All these decisions must be made before the designer chooses his microprocessor. He will also need some sort of timing device (clock) for timing signal samples and output. He will need to provide battery backed up RAM, together with ROM, for the program. Finally, he needs the processor itself.

Before he can decide on which processor, he needs to be sure that his development system is capable of programming the microprocessor of his choice; they are often only capable of programming one type of processor. A universal development system, although quite expensive by comparison, can be made to program any type by the use of software emulators.

Finally, before the engineer makes a decision on how much ROM and RAM he must provide, he needs a fair idea of program logic and size. ROM will be needed for permanent storage of the program; RAM will be used to temporarily store data coming in through the sensor interfaces and for a program scratchpad area.

This underlines the need to perform hardware and software design in unison, something that has patently not been done too well or too often with conventional data processing systems.

So in order to calculate the amount of ROM and RAM he needs he has to 'size' the program. This can be done in a number of ways, from the suck-it-and-see approach on the one hand, right up to writing a mock program approximating to the final program, on the other. In a system of this sort the program is usually not too complex, and since it is normally written in a low level language there is not too much redundant program code contained in memory. A typical program size range for this application is likely to be from 1 K up to 3 K or 4 K. It will certainly be very small compared to business data processing applications.

The program will be reading digital signals into RAM. These signals are provided by the sensors (input transducers) mounted around the assembly. They will be providing information on angular positions of the assemblies which support the cutting head. The program will also be reading signals from the joystick as the operator demands movement in one direction or another by moving the joystick against one of the sets of contacts built into its assembly. All input signals are modified to the right level of digital input by an interface the designer has to provide for the system. The clock times the rate at which these samples are taken.

When input signals have been processed by the program permanently stored in ROM, if a change in output signals is required, the calculated signals are sent out, through the interface, to the appropriate output transducer. This could be, for example, a valve, a solenoid, a stepper motor or linear actuator. The most likely choice in this case would be an electro-hydraulic valve which is able to convert an electrical impulse into a hydraulic movement.

Thus the system converts a joystick 'demand' into a hydraulic movement, achieving it with one control level instead of four or five. But it might have been possible to achieve this result hydraulically, so what is the advantage of a microelectronic system? The answer is in the intelligence that the microprocessor provides, through the program. Typical examples of the sort of logic that a program could employ are:

> To move each ram in a predetermined sequence, or in an organised pattern.

To allocate a priority to particular input signals, for either safety or speed of movement.

To vary the rate of movement of the ram in either a linear or a polynomial relationship, so that the operator can move the cutter into approximate position very quickly and then move the final 5% or so very carefully.

To limit the amount of travel of certain rams in certain directions, as a safety and stability feature.

To exclude certain combinations of angles for the same reason.

To provide an auto-home facility, where perhaps the push button on the joystick would cause the whole assembly to return automatically to the normal road travelling position.

These are examples of functions that could be built into the software. These functions need to be specified unambiguously and in detail when the initial requirements specification is made.

So the hardware designer has now completed this schematic of hardware and also probably has a block diagram illustrating the logic of the software. This has forced him to choose the input and output transducers and to design the interface and power supply. He has also had to choose his processor, ROM and RAM – and to calculate how much of each.

His logic design is now complete. These diagrams would ideally be drawn up on standard sheets by a draughtsman as a preliminary to laying out the printed circuit board design proper. Either the engineer or the draughtsman lays out the design; after checking it is then re-drawn, at many times full scale, often using proprietary drawing office aids such as special tape and the like, to identify positions where the circuit tracks run. Hole positions are also marked for the discrete components (for example, power transistors for output signals) and chips (memory, the processor, the clock, etc.). This is known as the PCB layout stage. Then the large scale drawing is subjected to a photographic process (often subcontracted) to produce an accurate full scale negative, after which a chemical etching process is used to create a printed circuit. This process is similar to, but is a much simpler and cheaper process than, the integrated circuit fabrication described in an earlier chapter.

Probably only one or two prototype boards will be made. Components are then positioned on the PCB and soldered into position. In the case of the chips, a plug-in base is soldered into position allowing the chips to be removed from their sockets by simply pulling them out. This is obviously necessary for PROM (Programmable Read Only Memory), since the chip will not be placed into position before the program is loaded into it.

The next logical step in the design process is that the PROM chip is programmed. As mentioned earlier, a development system is used for this purpose. The development system is a specially designed microcomputer, normally with floppy disks for program storage, a printer for hard copy output, and a V.D.U. and keyboard for input. The program is typed in at the keyboard and displayed on the V.D.U. When the program has been completely keyed in, the programmer instructs the computer to compile the program, or convert it into the binary code that the processor on the PCB will recognise. Depending on the programming language and the type of development system, the compilation process will also inform the programmer of syntax errors, or mistakes in the way the program was keyed in and misuses of program conventions. Syntax errors are errors in the grammar of the programming language, not of the sense or logic. Logical program errors can only be discovered by testing the program in a simulated real life situation. Syntax errors can be reduced by the use of supplier provided Editor programs.

Once the syntax errors are corrected and a clean compilation is obtained, the program is loaded on to a floppy disk for storage and also printed out for the files. If the programmer is confident of his logic, he now has to test the programs. In conventional data processing, this is generally much easier to do since test data can be input on punched cards or from a file of some sort and the results of the test compared to a known result for validation. Testing a microprocessor system for signal processing as opposed to data processing is not quite as straightforward as that. The programmer needs to be sure that his program works before he loads it into ROM prior to placing that memory chip (or chips) into position on the board.

One way this is done is to use an emulation facility which is available on several development systems. This makes it possible to connect the development system (and hence the program to be tested) into the otherwise complete printed circuit board. Then the board is connected to a test rig designed to simulate the end product, the mythical mower.

Thus by building a test rig containing perhaps only a single input sensor and a single output transducer, it is possible to complete a circuit under laboratory conditions to test the reaction of the program to variation in sensor input signals, once power is applied. This process of testing and modification is crucial if the program is to perform to specification before the product reaches the customers' premises. This whole testing process is interactive with the development system. It not only enables program logic errors to be detected; variations of the process enable the circuit logic to be tested as well.

When all is satisfactorily completed, the program is copied from the floppy disk and, via a PROM programming device connected into the development system, the program's binary code is transferred into the correct memory positions in the chip. The chip is then assembled into position on the board.

The first prototype printed circuit board is now ready for assembly into its packaging. For some applications it may be necessary to encapsulate the board completely within an appropriate plastic material (epoxy resin), perhaps to resist environmental conditions. In the example being considered here, the more likely enclosure will be a fabricated steel or cast iron case, consistent with the environment in which it must operate and its position on the mower assembly. Wiring connections are provided, in this case, probably of the auto tag type. They will be connected *in situ* in the factory assembly shop.

The sensors must also be 'armoured' probably by a plastic encapsulation. They will then be mounted in a position where they will be least exposed to damage. Similarly, alarm systems need to be placed in position. Finally, wiring will be run from each input and output to the controller tags and the final connections made. Once again, the wiring will need to be of a rugged industrial quality and protected from damage as far as possible.

During the trial period for this sort of product, two more items are necessary. Firstly, a calibrator is needed. Since some sensor values vary with age and environment, the potentiometer being a good example, a device needs to be made available to establish the new, changed values and to let the processor know what the new values are. Thus a plug needs to be provided so that the calibrator can read off sensor values and then be able to plug the device into the processor and to read them into memory, by key or dial or any convenient mechanism.

Secondly, in order to be able to change certain program values (parameters) in the field, a portable programming device needs to be employed. Both calibrators and hand held programmers are now in common use for these sorts of tasks.

Several more prototypes are likely to be developed before the final, approved version is completed and incorporated as a standard component in the mythical mower. The remaining stages in the project are common to many development programs: documentation and training.

Documentation

Documentation of a microelectronics product is more important than most since the product hardware and software bears the designer's own fingerprints: the design is unique to that man. If it is not accurately and comprehensively explained in manuals, drawings, circuits and schematics, it could be difficult for another engineer to pick the job up and modify the designs at a later stage if that proved to be necessary.

Product test procedures, test rigs and manufacturing drawings all need to be of a high standard. Too often a company which has developed a product which it then manufactures relies upon the local knowledge of the designer. A product must be capable of being changed and manufactured independently of the original designer: that is the test of adequate documentation.

Training and education

The stage normally reserved until last, or even completely overlooked, is education and training. Obviously technician training needs to take place, otherwise the product is sure to be a failure. Management and marketing education should also be considered. Management education is necessary so that managers can be informed of the results of their decisions, any important lessons may be learned and input can be derived for policy making. Marketing education is necessary so that the marketing department can fully understand the new system, and as a result, creatively sell the benefits to their customers.

The final education stage is often the process that lets the whole project down. The results of developments of this nature need to be communicated to every level of concerned executive and employee, particularly in view of the increasing publicity being given to the sociological impact of the microprocessor.

Summing up the industrial project

The process of developing a microelectronics signal processing system described here is obviously an idealised and academic view. There are many more activities that take place; many parts of the job overlap; mistakes are made, people change jobs, prices change, markets change, suppliers fail to supply, and so on, *ad infinitum*. Nevertheless it does provide a general overall framework to check on before taking on a real life project. This framework is common to a very wide range of applications. The project management disciplines are common to all.

The administration project

The previous example was deliberately chosen as an illustration of the versatility of current technology. The second example is more an illustration of the need for versatility in management.

The price of a microcomputer now makes it possible for virtually any small business to install a system to help run the business. The business may be a small independent concern, a department of a larger company, a school, a laboratory, a shop or any other operation with administrative problems.

Previous chapters have discussed the shortage and expense of specialists. More than ever the business professional is on his own. He is unlikely to have access to his own specialist and will have to live with the consequences of his own decisions.

Any small business that is currently using a mix of clerical labour and mechanised accounting for the purposes of sales accounting, purchase ledger, stock control and payroll will need to replace machines from time to time. People with a detailed knowledge of procedures may leave or come up for retirement, or possibly a change of premises is imminent or there may be pressure on office space. Whatever the reason the time will come when a small business will look to replace present systems with a computer based system.

For the sake of illustration it is assumed that the applications to be run on the computer are those previously listed: sales accounting, (invoicing, statement preparation and sales ledger), purchase ledger, stock control, payroll and accounts to monthly trial balance (nominal or general ledger).

Obviously every case will vary to some degree but it will be of value to follow this case study through as a check list for any similar situation.

The project will involve gradually phasing out accounting machines, building up files and programs on the computer and at a given date switching over to the new system.

The challenge is often daunting. It involves making the right choice, meeting expense budgets, meeting the timetable and avoiding adversely affecting customers, suppliers or employees.

Typical activity headings required to try and meet these often conflicting objectives include:

Compile a business case
Compile a requirements specification
Decision: Turnkey/package/program in house?
Choose supplier (or suppliers)
Draw up a systems specification
Draw up a project plan
Site preparation
Order stationery
Write software
Write documentation
Program test
Systems test
Parallel run
Go live
Systems audit

The project will have many points in common with the previous example but will contain sufficient differences to make it worthwhile examining each heading in turn.

Business case

Although it is unlikely that the small business being considered possesses an expert in computers the general level of knowledge concerning the computer's capability is bound to be higher than in the previous example. By now all adults are used to coping with some aspect of computer input or output and virtually everyone is used to pocket or desk calculators, which are in effect small computers. Therefore the benefits of precision, space saving, speed and versatility are unlikely to be challenged in the first instance. The important task is to document exactly what the new system has to achieve in order to pay for itself. For example, it might be to complete invoicing one day earlier than present systems, which will give rise to a one time saving of one day's debtors plus a perpetual saving on servicing those debtors. It might be to reduce stock, to identify redundant stock, to reduce debtors to a given number of days, to avoid hiring new staff to cope with an increased workload, or any of a number of situations which can be measured in financial terms. This will give an overall value to the system destined to achieve these benefits. By making normal business assumptions concerning write off periods, HP or leasing, a fairly simple equation can be deduced.

It is important to include all elements in the equation. The equation will need to include hardware, software, training and documentation costs; costs of hardware maintenance and software maintenance; delivery charges; insurance and duty where appropriate; site preparation charges, air conditioning (if needed); costs of supplies; costs of any extra ancillary equipment; the costs of extra space and the costs involved in back up facilities. To do a thorough job it might be prudent to make a cost allowance for the time taken by management in education, research, negotiation and planning and parallel running.

For the complete equation, apart from direct savings resulting from a successful installation, such things as space savings and reductions in labour costs, consumables and the income from the sale of any mechanised accounting equipment also needs to be included.

Drawing up a business case for an administrative project is generally a fairly straightforward task and should give a reasonable guideline to the level of expense that can legitimately be incurred against the project. In practice a change of system is normally the signal for other reforms, often delayed for years for one reason or another. Anything from the installation of a vending machine to the wholesale reconstruction of offices can be triggered by the installation of a new computer system.

One set of aims which cannot be quantified with any certainty are often referred to as 'intangibles'.

Intangibles are those benefits that cannot be measured in financial or numerical terms but are nevertheless very desirable aims. For example, one aim might be to offer customers a more comprehensive statement or a better level of service. Another intangible benefit might be an improvement of the employees lot by, for example, smoothing out the work load.

Intangible benefits cannot be directly quantified but they can show a financial return. One technique that is occasionally used in order to add a cash value into the financial justification is the 'how much would it be worth' question. For example, 'how much would it be worth to the company (or you) if the accounts could be balanced by, say the third of the month rather than the 10th of the month?' Any manager would be able to place an approximate value on that facility.

Requirements specification

More often than not this task is not attempted by the intending first time computer user. Experienced computer users have developed the technique as a result of having made enough errors or omissions in the past to justify a first time user spending money for advice to ensure that the same mistake will not reoccur.

Typically the requirement specification will contain details of each application, file sizes and numbers and types of each transaction. For example, the sales accounting system is likely to specify the number of invoices to be processed per month, and daily peak loads. It should contain a typical invoice illustrating names and addresses, layout, and details of average and maximum detail lines on the invoice.

File sizes will include the maximum number of name and address lines, account details, number of months to be covered, credit details and various other data currently provided or required of the new system.

Volumes of data, peak loads, file sizes and report or forms layout are of prime importance. They will determine the processor type, the memory size for programs and the amount of backing storage. They will also determine the number of input devices and the speed and type of printer.

A requirements specification should also contain minimum requirements of devices. For example, although input volumes may not justify it, extra input devices may be a particular requirement since input may need to take place at more than one desk simultaneously.

This example assumes that the computer being specified is a microcomputer and, by definition, almost, is to cost less than $40,000. In this case the choice of hardware is restricted by software. For example very few available operating systems currently support more than one video display unit. If two are required a multiuser operating system must be included as part of the specification.

If peak volumes are a problem a minimum speed for the printer must be specified. It should be noted that a microcomputer of the type being discussed would be hard pressed to take advantage of a 300 character per second printer, unless the printer itself is programmable to take advantage of space skipping to avoid the print head running to the end of each line before moving to the next. Certain redesign of forms may be necessary to comply with the currently available technology if the printer speed appears to be a problem.

Generally there is a choice of intelligent or dumb terminals. Intelligent terminals contain programmable keys which can, for example, insert the date by a single key depression. They will also have separate keys for each cursor control movement (the cursor on a video display, analogous to the printing position on a typewriter). On a dumb terminal it is often necessary to press two keys simultaneously to obtain the correct cursor control movement.

Storage needs to be calculated by multiplying file sizes by the maximum anticipated number of records (e.g. account names) on a file. Floppy disks on conventional microcomputers can now go to around two million characters of storage. It is now possible to obtain a microcomputer with a 16–20 million character capacity hard disk, but care must be taken to ensure that the operating system is proven to support a disk of this size and more than one terminal since a single terminal installation is unlikely to need such storage capacity.

System specifications on applications currently being run by other methods should be relatively straightforward. Hardware specifications are more difficult and are bound to be complicated by the claims of aggressive salesmen, confusing trade papers and bewildering demonstrations at exhibitions. However, there is one simple rule for this type of equipment. Ask a couple of potential suppliers to run a similar program to those being specified on his demonstration system and use experienced staff from the business to operate the equipment, or at least to observe the demonstration.

This specification cannot be drawn up in isolation. It needs the advice and help of suppliers, users of other installations or consultants. If the specification is drawn up correctly it can form part of the contract with the supplier and thus go a long way towards ensuring a successful installation.

Turnkey/package/in-house programming

The requirements specification should have specified the anticipated hardware configuration; it should also have specified the input documents and the output documents required by the system, which determines the program logic. The business case should have defined the level of expense, timescale and expected benefits, both tangible and intangible. The next phase is the last of the planning phases; all that follows is operational.

The decision to be taken here is basically whether to write the programs in-house or whether to buy, or to lease a pre-programmed package. Over the years a great many articles and publications have been devoted to this topic, therefore this section will review only the major points to be considered.

The decision revolves around cost and convenience. If it is possible to recruit a programmer in-house and then for him to specify and write all the necessary programs to exact requirements for the same cost as an outside contractor then it can be a worthwhile exercise. In this case the programmer is likely to know the business well and will therefore not require a period of familiarisation. However, it will need to be ascertained that the person selected is likely to remain with the company for a reasonable period after the installation for maintenance purposes. The programmer's original job is likely to need to be filled by an extra person; he is also likely to need leave of absence for training. In effect the decision to follow this route for the first time user of relatively low microcomputer systems is unusual and should only be taken if the cost savings are virtually guaranteed and continuity is assured: a family business could conceivably decide on this approach.

More typically competing suppliers have a range of pre-programmed application packages available for sale or for use under license. Often these will cost a small proportion of what it would cost to develop brand new systems in-house. In practice it is generally an impressive demonstration of a package that prompts the installation of a computer system. At this level of expenditure people tend to buy a computer solution to a problem rather than buy hardware to do a job. If it is the package that initially started the exercise then the requirements specification is made slightly easier because it almost certainly means that a supplier short list has already been created. It also means that much of the risk has been eliminated since other sites already running the system are likely to be available for visits and discussions.

The real difficulty arises if no appropriate package exists, which is still perfectly possible at this end of the market. Programming rates around the world in 1980 are in the range of $25–$50 an hour. Thus even the very simplest program will cost several hundred dollars to write. The best that can be done here is to negotiate a fixed price contract for a working system, hardware and software. This is generally known as a turnkey system, one where a single supplier supplies all the hardware and all of the software, which may include some packages, and all the appropriate support to ensure satisfactory performance of the system.

Turnkey systems may appear to be slightly more expensive than other methods of installing a system but they do have the merit of a single supplier having the contractual responsibility for performance, price and delivery.

Supplier selection

The infra-structure behind the selling and support of small business computer systems is complex; it varies with geographical area, even within cities. Certain suppliers have national coverage with their own sales forces. However, with only a few exceptions they no longer sell to the end user. They sell to the OEMer, who has a contract with the supplier to buy equipment at around 25% discount and then must add value in the form of programs before selling it on to the end user. In fact the OEMer, in one guise or another, is likely to be the type of organisation selling microcomputers. In their turn they may employ software houses to help them write programs, to develop new application packages and to improve operating systems but the OEMer is the normal sales outlet for this sort of equipment.

In some parts of the world OEMers have contracts with several suppliers, thereby offering a better selection to the end user. OEMers generally make their profit from multiple sales of packages; they are in business to sell software therefore any hardware vehicle which helps them sell their software is useful. As a result there is competition among OEMers for the best hardware, which in turn illustrates the survival of the fittest principle once more. Generally speaking the best hardware is offered by the OEMer with the best track record, which in turn attracts more customers.

Thus the first step in selecting a supplier is to find out who are, locally, the best known and the biggest. Obviously trade papers, Chambers of Commerce, trade shows and advertisements in the press help to inform most people but personal contacts are still the most reliable source of information.

Having drawn up a short list, the selection of a supplier should be no different to selecting a supplier for any other item of capital equipment, except perhaps that the microcomputer suppliers are likely to be relatively unknown and new to the prospective purchaser. The initial short list should be refined down to three contenders before serious negotiations start. It is perfectly possible to compile a 'short list' of twenty prospective suppliers so it is important to have a check list which will help eliminate the weaker contenders. The following is a general guide to the questions which could be asked of all prospective suppliers. Incidentally it is of much greater benefit to ask these questions of a supplier direct rather than through a questionnaire or a third party. The local salesman should be a sufficiently reliable source of information for this purpose.

In no particular order, the questions should seek to determine:

Size: Number of countries in which the supplier operates; the number of cities; the specific size for this country in terms of numbers of offices, numbers of personnel (broken down if possible into sales staff, operations staff and administrative staff).

Credibility: The length of time in business, financial resources, financial performance, names and background of directors.

Installations: The number of installations locally and nationally. The number of installations running the applications under consideration.

Reference sites: Names and addresses of reference sites, where it is possible to talk to the user privately.

Type of business: Is the supplier a manufacturer, an OEMer, a Systems Integrator or a Software House – or even a freelance salesman?

Specialist areas: Is the potential supplier's area of specialisation in the same field as the system under consideration.

Reputation: What sort of reputation does the supplier have; is his response to calls for information adequate, does he inspire trust and confidence?

Ultimately it is this factor of reputation and trust that is likely to weed out the final short list. The factors which then enable a decision to be made are basically performance, price, contract and delivery.

Unless a supplier can demonstrate either a reasonable system which is sufficiently close to the specification and/or a competence to meet the specification he should not be on the short list. To select the final vendor from three is now merely a question of degree of competence.

Price is seldom a simple comparison. The rule is: 'compare apples with apples'. OEMers in particular 'bundle' their prices. They tend to quote a single price to include hardware and software. Normally hardware and software maintenance is quoted separately as an annual figure. It is a reasonable business stance from the OEMers point of view since he knows what tasks he must perform for the price. However, for the prospective purchaser there is an area for negotiation here, especially if the supplier is offering a package program with only a few days of installation effort to install the programs. Also it will be reasonably certain that the OEMer will be marking up the hardware by at least 25%.

The OEMer's argument is that he has to pay all of his fixed overheads out of profits made on the packages and hardware mark up. The decision on how far to press on price discounts must be left to the judgement of the man on the spot; it benefits no one if suppliers are forced out of business through unwise deals. On the other hand it is no secret that packages can make phenomenal profits for their developers. There are no rules for package prices except what the market will bear.

There are further important points on price to consider. Establish the level of support, i.e. man-days, price of support, the cost of manuals, extra copies of manuals, the cost of training, further training for new staff. Does the price charged for support include the time spent in travelling? Establish that the hardware supplier has a local spares depot and local maintenance engineers and that the price in their maintenance contract does not contain hidden extras.

To a certain extent the questions concerning price overlap with the questions on contracts. Since there is such a wide selection of potential suppliers the range of contract type is almost infinite. Quite often the OEMer will proffer a single page letter as a contract. At the other extreme a multinational may demand signature of an eight page, small print document, governed by the laws of Delaware or Massachusetts!

The more common occurrence is somewhere in the middle and it might help a prospective purchaser to remind himself of what both parties are trying to achieve and in so doing identify the possible areas for amendment, if it is seen to be important.

The supplier is attempting to obtain a known price for a well defined product, with a nominated level of support.

Generally his contract is only an offer to sell until he has countersigned it. He is trying to ensure that his price is proof against inflation, that his support and product offering is not open ended and that he does not run into unforeseen financial obligations resulting from poor product performance. In order to help clarify these items he often includes a definitions section to describe what he calls hardware and software and so on. A supplier very rarely guarantees that his product will perform the task for which it is purchased. He will rarely accept a penalty bond or clause. He should always include a warranty on hardware and software. Generally the supplier requires a deposit and may ask for stage payments.

The supplier will include clauses in his contract designed to protect his patents, copyrights and effort in developing systems. Quite often the use of software is limited to a license to use the software for a period of up to 15 years. Unless the end user has paid for the software development the title to that software will not pass to the end user; in rare cases there may be a case for shared title to software.

The purchaser is attempting to obtain a guaranteed system performance, at a known price, with a guaranteed level of support. This system is to meet his own specification, to contain no hidden extras and to be installed in a known time.

Both parties want to conclude the deal in good faith and both intend to stay in business and probably intend to do business with each other again.

Therefore the contract needs to be a document that is seen to be reasonable by both parties and one that reaffirms and supports the trust and good faith that has developed between the negotiators.

Unfortunately this is not always the case, especially when dealing with a parent company at arm's length. In practice the larger the supplier the less chance there is to amend the contract they offer. There is every chance to renegotiate with a very small company.

Nevertheless negotiation is possible; apparently punitive clauses can be deleted, clauses that limit rights under common law and consumer law must be deleted and terms like 'best efforts' can be clarified and quantified.

Ultimately the best area for negotiation is on price, since that is generally a local decision. So the result that must be achieved is the balance between the best price and financial terms for a required system performance against the most tolerable contract.

Systems specification

From this stage onwards the project is 'real life', as opposed to planning. This phase involves a detailed layout of all print forms, input video screen layouts and disk file layouts. In fact the systems specification is an expansion of the requirements specification carried out at an earlier phase, this time, however, by the supplier.

The system specification will include details of all volumes and file sizes and the supplier's description of how the programs will run (their logic) and details on error procedures, error messages by the system, back up procedures, system start and restart procedures and normal operating procedures.

It is particularly important to ensure to plan for a 'crisis' operation. In other words, to write down procedures to cope with every sort of emergency, from any sort of hardware failure, to power failure to software malfunction (where predictable). As a point of interest once the system is operational management should introduce unannounced 'fire drills' to test all of these various contingency plans.

Project planning

This chart on page 125 like the industrial example, is merely an illustration of activity headings, responsibilities and timescale. Project managers from the customer and the supplier must have the responsibility for monitoring the plan. Project review meetings should take place at regular intervals and should continue for several months after the successful installation, to ensure that all the bugs are out of the system and that future developments are planned in a professional manner.

For the purposes of this example it is assumed that the hardware has been chosen, that the majority of the software is provided by packages and that a small amount of custom programming is undertaken.

The remainder of this section discusses the most important aspects of each of these headings, following contract signature.

Site preparation

Any hardware supplier, even if he is supplying equipment through an OEM agreement, is likely to have allowed for an installation planning call by their specialist. If the call is not offered it is as well to request that the supplier sends a representative along to take a look at possible sites for the equipment. Delivery is normally free to an accessible ground floor site. If the site chosen involves moving the equipment up stairs or through windows the cost of scaffolding, extra labour and possibly time are likely to be added to the cost of the equipment.

The site chosen must have sufficient space to allow an all round clearance of at least one metre. It must be reasonably well ventilated otherwise the heat generated can cause very uncomfortable working conditions. It may, on advice, be necessary to install appropriate air conditioning, especially if the office chosen is small and well insulated.

Care should be taken to locate the machine where the noise of the cooling fans do not cause an unnecessary inconvenience to people in other departments.

Space for supplies, for example stationery and floppy disks, should be provided in the immediate vicinity of the machine.

As a general rule it is better to locate the microcomputer in a convenient position in a general office rather than in a special enclosed office. The one encourages familarity and engenders the attitude that the computer is just another piece of office

Activity	Responsibility		Time into project (weeks)
	Customer	*Supplier*	
Select supplier	X		0
Negotiate contract	X	X	4
Nominate project managers	X	X	1
Agree hardware configuration	X	X	4
Agree systems specification:			
packages	X	X	4
custom programs	X	X	4
Agree implementation plan	X	X	4
Sign contract	X	X	4
Site preparation	X		4–20
Software design		X	4–8
Code software		X	8–10
Desk check		X	10
Compile programs		X	10
Debug programs		X	10–12
Program test		X	12
Debug		X	12–14
Initial operator training	X	X	14
Order stationery	X		10
Set up files	X		14–20
Audit files	X		20–22
Correct files	X		22–24
Final operator training	X	X	24
Systems test at supplier's premises	X	X	25
Install equipment	X	X	26
Systems test *in situ*	X	X	26–28
Complete documentation		X	28
Educate non-computer staff	X		28
Inform customers	X		28
Parallel run	X	X	28–36
Go live	X		36
Systems audit	X	X	36----

equipment: the other tends to create a 'computer department', by definition for specialists.

Apart from these considerations any light, clean and convenient office having an available floor area of 10–20 square metres should be appropriate. The floor does not generally need to be load bearing although it is as well to check on the floor load bearing capacity.

Software design: programming

Having agreed the systems specifications for both packages and custom built programs the end user is not involved again until systems testing time. As with the previous example the program is coded onto special program coding sheets; it should be checked by a senior technician (the chief programmer, for example) for overall logic and any obvious errors. The program is then assembled (if written in Basic Assembler), compiled (if written in a higher level language) or interpreted (if written in a high level language for the more commonly used commercial microcomputers). The resulting output is then checked for syntax errors, corrected and rerun, and then debugged after successive iterations until a 'clean' program is produced. Programs are then tested against data produced by the programmer. This test data is meant to test all practical variables and conditions. In practice it is never possible to check all combinations and permutations in this way. The detailed system testing is largely the responsibility of the end user since he is much more likely to appreciate the pecularities of his own system.

Initial operator training

An introductory stage of operator training can be extremely valuable if it is possible to obtain use of the machine to be installed prior to its installation on the user's site. If this facility can be arranged it can save weeks. This phase is therefore an intermediate training program and need only take a few hours.

File set up in any system requires that people who have a good knowledge of current systems help transfer the data over from one system to another. In the example of the sales ledger it will mean taking the clerically or machine maintained ledger cards and entering all that information into the new system.

In order to perform this task the operators involved in file set up will need to be taught enough about the operation of the system to understand what they are doing. The supplier will normally provide an introductory manual, file and display screen layouts and a few hours of operator training for the express purpose of setting up the files of data on the computer.

File creation

This is the first direct involvement of operational staff with the new system. After a brief initial training in the use of their video display screen, the disks and the printer, they will be engaged upon keying in the data that comprises the files, or the data base, for the microcomputer sales ledger system, and so on.

Before file set up is started it is important to validate the file sizes and volumes originally assessed during the system specification phase. This is an opportunity to discard redundant records and to create new records, as appropriate. The time taken to find and key in this information must not be underestimated. Many computer people will quote data entry figures of up to 20,000 keystrokes an hour by proficient operators. The people employed to set up files are not normally proficient operators; they are trainees. They will also have to search out a lot of the information required. They may have to ask questions to supply missing information. Most non-computer systems rely upon local knowledge. A computer requires this knowledge to be quantified.

The net effect of this type of file set up is that operator input keying speeds are often no more than 1,000–2,000 keystrokes an hour. Of course, it is possible to introduce an intermediate stage and to transcribe all the relevant information onto standard keying-in forms. This may offer benefits but is likely to take at least as long as the direct method. Either way the experienced people will be needed to sort out any problems, which means overtime and weekend working or temporary staff to help fill the gap.

As files are set up print-outs should be taken so that other staff can make a separate clerical check for spelling, accuracy and completness. If files are not set up accurately in the first place the process of correction interferes with normal system operation and may in the meantime have caused problems with customers or suppliers.

Files should be audited periodically for active and inactive records. Standard checks can be made to delete files if, for example, they have not been active over a full financial year.

Final operator training

By this time most of the people who are likely to use the system will have a reasonable idea of the basic features of the various computer devices to be installed. Ideally the final stage of operator training will take place on the supplier's premises, for two reasons. Firstly, he is likely to have classroom facilities with adequate resources and visual aids to ensure that training takes place in the correct manner to a predefined programme, away from the normal working environment. Secondly, the ideal is that systems testing of all programs, both packages and custom built, take place immediately following the training session so that all of the customer's staff have an opportunity to involve themselves with the system before it is actually installed in their own premises.

Systems test on supplier's premises

This stage is the one opportunity to test the programs to destruction. Every conceivable sort of transaction and odd query should have been collected by the customer's project manager over the preceding weeks. In concert with the operators and the supplier's technical staff he should process a full period of normal transactions, or a representative selection depending upon available time, in addition to every separate condition he has been able to dream up over the life of the project thus far.

Systems testing at the supplier's may take a couple of hours or a week: it represents the last real opportunity to ensure that the system complies with the requirements specification.

At the end of this period of testing the supplier is likely to request a formal sign-off of acceptance of the system.

Install equipment

By now the site at the customer's premises should be prepared. Usually the microcomputer system will only require a single phase supply so that assuming there is enough space and the site has been approved by the installation planning representative, installation is merely a matter of delivering and uncrating the system. This exercise is likely to take only an hour or so. Nevertheless it will probably be more convenient to arrange the delivery to take place over a weekend or after office hours.

In-house systems test

This phase should be more or less a repeat of the tests at the supplier's premises. The object of this second series of tests is more for staff reassurance than for technical purposes. The tests can also formally signal the beginning of the parallel run phase although it is rather unlikely that the exact timing of the delivery of a machine and the beginning of a financial period will coincide, so that there may be a short hiatus before formal commencement.

During this period it should be possible to complete the education of non-computer staff and to rehearse standard routines such as loading and unloading files, loading stationery and start up routines. Back up routines should not be rehearsed until all operators have a firm grasp of normal operating procedures.

Documentation

Before final acceptance of the system, which may include final payment, care should be taken to ensure that the supplier has supplied all the manuals necessary to ensure satisfactory routine operation of the system. These manuals should include an operator's manual for the machine and for each different device where they originate from several sources; this is more the rule than the exception with microcomputers. A user manual should be provided, detailing all the normal facilities, input and output types, error messages and procedures.

The supplier should also provide a full set of programming specifications where the program has been specially developed for the customer. This will ensure that another supplier can take over maintenance of the programs if it proves impossible for the original supplier to support the installation at a later stage.

It is important to ensure that all manuals are complete and up to date and represent the exact model and release of all hardware and software being used.

Educating other staff

This may or may not be necessary depending upon the size of the organisation or perhaps the insularity of a particular department. Where it is deemed to be necessary a short talk and demonstration is all that is required, under normal circumstances. The objective is to gain acceptance of the new procedures, to enhance awareness and to remove any doubts or fears. This is best achieved by the demonstrator taking time to explain the impact of the system on the daily routine of staff not directly concerned with the computer.

It is particularly important that this process goes on in

several directions. Management must be informed as well as the staff already mentioned. Their comments and suggestions also need to be absorbed into the routine running of the system, if not for further system enhancements. For example, many of the newer microcomputer systems are now capable of running word processing packages. At the moment the word processing package is likely to require the use of the whole machine, therefore it cannot share the use of the machine with other programs. It will also require a different sort of printer, more often than not. Nevertheless, management and other staff need to be aware of this and other supplier-planned facilities to enable planning to take place on an informed basis.

Customers and suppliers

There can hardly be an adult alive who has not suffered from or been amused by the results of some computer system or other. It is a sensible precaution to inform the more important customers and suppliers that the change is taking place, possibly to be followed up by personal telephone calls or further letters where there is likely to be a change in procedure for certain people.

Normally the idea of an improvement in service levels is enough to attract customers but suppliers may not be equally enamoured of this potential improvement in efficiency, so it may need careful handling in some cases.

Parallel running

This procedure represents the final bedding down and phasing over from one system to another. In practice it means that both the old system and the new system are run in concert. The object is to ensure that the results match each other as far as is possible.

The difficulty during this period is that many pieces of paper go through an extra handling process and temporary staff may need to be recruited to run down the existing system.

As a result the new system may not appear to perform as well as expected, especially if technical teething troubles are encountered, which must be anticipated.

Parallel running can be a very trying period. Nevertheless it is vital if the system is to gain full acceptance by everyone. With adequate planning this period may be reduced to no more than two months for financial systems, possibly a lot less for more straightforward analysis systems.

Go live

On the planned date parallel running is stopped and the computer systems then operate without the back up of the older systems. With the right sort of project planning and control any problems encountered will be relatively minor. Nevertheless procedures for fixing faults and minor program changes must be agreed with the supplier. No computer program ever written is perfect for all users, and changes are certain to be required from time to time. If these changes do not seriously effect the business it is usually better to wait for a few months and gather all the small changes together in the form of a request for program modification and then to ask for the changes to be made, subject to price and implementation time. This method generally causes relatively minor inconvenience whereas constant small changes can quite easily disrupt a system.

At various stages during the normal running of the system the project manager should ensure that staff do a fire drill. Ideally without warning, he should rehearse a 'crisis'. For example a disk might malfunction, the printer may need repair, there might be a full power loss. Every conceivable external factor that may cause problems should be anticipated and then presented to the operators as a real life problem. In this way, when the problems do occur, finding the solution is likely to have less impact.

Systems audit

After a period of routine running it is useful for the project manager, or a member of management, to review procedures to ensure that changes have not crept in over the months of familiarity, unless they are improvements. He should also review results achieved against the original anticipated benefits, as much for monitoring management's performance as for drawing up a case for enhancements to the system.

The results of such an audit are usually most revealing. The benefits that transpire as being of most value were often not anticipated at all during the requirements specification phase; the reverse is true on occasion.

Summing up the administration project

Obviously the project discussed has of necessity been fairly vague but this has been a deliberate choice. Anyone installing a small business computer knows his own problems and business. Nothing said here could change that, but the impact of a computer on the business does have certain consequences and it has been the aim of this section to highlight the most important of these.

Naturally the narrative has tended to be somewhat hypothetical; for example the sequence of many of the activities could be interchanged, a few eliminated completely. The important thing is to think through all the steps involved before making the initial move. Once a supplier has been chosen and once a system has been installed it will be part of the business in one form or another for as long as the business exists.

For a small business it can be the single most expensive item of capital investment ever made and should be treated in that manner from the beginning of the project.

GLOSSARY

The glossary is made up from abbreviations, jargon, acronyms and terms used by professionals in connection with computers and microelectronics. It is not meant to be a full and definitive glossary of data processing terms.

All manufacturers subscribe to generally accepted jargon but also seek to propagate their own unique terminology as a marketing device. Where a particular manufacturer's jargon has become so broadly accepted that it is now part of the industry's language it is included here.

It will be apparent that many aspirants to that status have not been included in this glossary, either because they are specific to a single supplier or because they are so esoteric that, for the present at least, little purpose can be served by spreading the awareness of the term.

Using the Glossary

If the abbreviated form, or acronym, is more commonly used than the full version of the term, then the definition will be found at the entry for the abbreviated version. The entry for the full version will direct the reader to the abbreviation.

If the term is known only by its shortened form, it will only appear once.

For quick reference, there is a list of abbreviations and acronyms on page 252.

Cross-references are written in SMALL CAPITALS, but not every headword is cross-referred every time it appears. Cross references are only used when the understanding of the reference will expand the comprehension of the entry in question.

Other entries in a related area are indicated by the use of an arrow.

A

A ◊AMPS.

A to D ◊ANALOG TO DIGITAL CONVERTER.

Abbreviated addressing a technique for shortening the direct address by using only part of the full memory address. This results in a quicker way of processing data since the truncated address is decoded by the computer's central processing unit in less time than the full address would require.

Abort to spontaneously halt the execution of a computer program. To cancel an operation partway through after evaluating initial results.

Absolute address a specific fixed location of discrete data in storage; an address that the control unit can interpret directly. The label assigned by a programmer to a particular storage area in a computer. Code that identifies a unique storage location or device. (Synonymous with MACHINE ADDRESS.)

Absolute assembler a unique type of ASSEMBLY LANGUAGE program created to produce binary programs containing ABSOLUTE ADDRESSES and address references only.

Absolute code a code using ABSOLUTE ADDRESSES and absolute operation codes. A code that indicates the exact location where the data concerned is to be found or stored.

Absolute loader a program which places programs and data in ABSOLUTE ADDRESS format into memory.

Absolute value the value of a number ignoring any qualifying plus or minus prefix, e.g. the absolute value of -1 is 1.

Absolute zero taken from the fundamental, or absolute scale of temperature. This scale is based on the Second Law of Thermodynamics, as applied to a theoretical 'perfect' gas. In this scale 'absolute zero' corresponds to -273°C.

AC or ac ◊ ALTERNATING CURRENT.

Access the process of gaining entry. For example, to access a record, its device, location and specific address need to be obtained before the computer can gain entry to that precise area of storage containing the data required.

Access time the time taken from when data is requested from a storage unit to its delivery. The time from when that data is presented for storage until the data is stored. A value often used for comparison between different computer systems.

Accounting machine mechanical or electro-mechanical devices which were largely used for basic arithmetic functions. As a result they were widely used for commercial or accounting purposes. They have now largely been replaced by calculators or microcomputers.

Accumulator one or more registers associated with the ARITHMETIC LOGIC UNIT which are used as temporary storage areas for data and for results of the computer's central processing operations.

Accuracy specific to a TRANSDUCER or SENSOR. The ratio of error to total output, expressed as a percentage.

Acoustic coupler a device which converts voice signals to digital signals. Used to transmit data along voice telephone lines using a normal telephone handset as the input device for a computer system.

Acquisition ◊DATA ACQUISITION.

Acronym when applied in the computing sense it refers to the formation of an English language word from a selection of the initial letters of a phrase it is designed to represent. It is used to abbreviate long, clumsy or tongue twisting terms, e.g. COBOL, COmmercial and Business Oriented Language.

Active element an element in its excited or active state or a file, record or routine which is being used by the processing unit. More typically applied to electronic devices, e.g. transistors, or Cathode Ray Tubes.

Actuator a device used to convert electrical energy into mechanical energy; an output TRANSDUCER. When energy is to be directed in a straight line it can be called a 'linear actuator'.

Adapter a connecting device for parts that would not otherwise fit together, usually a standard plug or connector.

Address a coded instruction specifying the location of data or program words in storage. An address may refer to storage in registers or memory or both. An address code itself may be stored so that a memory location may contain an address of data rather than the data itself. This technique is known as 'indirect addressing'.

Address bus parallel connections (hardware circuits) used to carry binary addresses from the CENTRAL PROCESSING UNIT to memory.

Address field that part of a computer word that contains either the address of the data or instruction, or the information necessary to locate an address.

Address register a BYTE (8 bit) or word (generally 16 bit) used for temporary storage of an address transmitted during an input/output cycle. The register is used by the computer itself and is normally not available to the programmer.

Addressing, common data bus on some systems referred to as MEMORY MAPPED I/O ADDRESSING. Instructions and data contained in or required by a program are stored into and loaded from specific memory locations, the ACCUMULATOR, or selected registers. Because some microprocessors' memories (read/write and read-only) and peripherals are on a common DATA BUS, any instruction used to address memory may bc used to address peripheral devices.

Addressing mode the means by which a program can find a specific memory location. There are numerous methods by which memory can be addressed. The more sophisticated the method of addressing memory, the faster and more economic will be the program execution.

One of the main differences between microcomputer systems is in the wide range of addressing methods available. Typical techniques include: sequential forward and backward, indexed, indexed sequential (indirect), 16 bit word-addressing, 8 bit byte addressing and stack addressing.

ADP Automatic Data Processing, synonymous with EDP (Electronic Data Processing) and DP (Data Processing). The generic term for the computing process.

Agent an independent salesman or sales organisation which sells a supplier's products for a commission, or a discount. Does not hold stock of the product. Normally offers very limited support.

ALGOL an abbreviation for ALGOrithmic Language. Like FORTRAN a high level computer language specially suited to mathematic and scientific problems.

Algorithm a clearly-specified set of rules defining a finite number of operations required to solve a particular problem.

Alignment pin the pin or device that ensures correct connection of two components to be connected.

Allocate to assign main software routines and subroutines to storage. Carried out in the coding or software definition phase of programming and then looked after by the computer's operating system.

Alphanumeric information containing a combination of alphabetic characters and numbers.

Alternating Current (AC or ac) an electric current which flows in positive and negative cycles. The measure of the current is its algebraic average. The cycles per second are referred to as Hertz (Hz).

ALU ◊ARITHMETIC LOGIC UNIT.

Ambient, ambient conditions the conditions of the surrounding environment. Refers to temperature, light, noise, atmospheric pressure, etc. A computer system or an electronic device is designed for a particular set of ambient conditions, within a given tolerance. If the ambient conditions fall outside the specified tolerance compensation must be made in the form of insulation, air conditioning, etc.

American National Standards Institute ◊ANSI.

American Standard Code for Information Interchange ◊ ASCII.

Amplifier a device used to intensify or increase an electrical signal. There are numerous types producing either linear or non-linear resultant outputs.

Amplitude normally used to describe the peak value of a sine wave form. In the electronics sense it refers to the peak values (positive and negative) of an alternating current.

Amps (A) an abbreviation for Ampère, it defines the measure of the constant current flowing in a circuit.

Analog(ue) a system in which the output signal bears a continuous relationship to the input signal, as opposed to the discontinuous, or discrete signals, used by DIGITAL circuits. The term is usually spelled 'analog'. A typically 'analogy' of the differences between analog and digital techniques is illustrated by the immediate differences between an analog watch and a digital watch. A slide rule is a type of analog computer.

Analog computer a computer that operates on voltage levels rather than digital values.

Analog to Digital converter (A to D) a device which samples an analog signal and converts the observed value to a BINARY number for use by a digital circuit.

Analyst/Systems Analyst the computer professional whose job is to convert a problem into a format so that it can be converted into computer programs by a programmer.

Analytical engine Charles Babbage's design for a mechanical computing machine which embodied all of the main principles implemented in modern computers, with the exception of the stored program.

AND gate a discrete component used in logic circuits which requires two input signals to generate one output signal. A Boolean logic operator. See appendix for LOGIC CIRCUITS.

ANSI American National Standards Institute: formerly American Standards Association (ASA), and, prior to that, United States of America Standards Institute (USASI). This organisation convenes committees from suppliers, users and other interested bodies to provide standards for the computer industry, e.g. ANSI COBOL.

APL an acronym for A Programming Language. A high level and efficient language developed by Dr Kenneth Iverson of IBM. It has been used almost exclusively by timesharing systems so far, but there are indications that it may find a use in microcomputer systems.

Application the specific task to which a computer or program is dedicated, e.g. payroll, sales ledger, etc.

Applications program a program that does actual problem solving. More usually this is a suite of programs, applied for users' problem solving, e.g. payroll, ledgers, stock control, etc.

Architecture a general term used to describe the philosophy of the construction of specific computer systems or software products.

Archive historical data, usually contained on tapes or disks but may be in other media.

Arithmetic Logic Unit (ALU) the arithmetic logic unit is one of the three essential components of a microprocessor (the other two being the REGISTERS and CONTROL BLOCK). The ALU is contained in the computer's central processing unit and carries out arithmetic and BOOLEAN logic operations on data presented in a BINARY form.

Arithmetic registers those on which arithmetic and logic functions can be performed; the register can be a source or destination of OPERANDS for the operation.

Array a matrix or two dimensional grid used to indicate a collection of memory locations, or a description of inputs and outputs on, for example a PRINTED CIRCUIT BOARD.

Artificial intelligence a type of program that allows a computer to operate certain functions on its own. For example, learning adaptation, simple reasoning, improvement and optimising. (Synonymous with CYBERNETICS.)

Artwork the preparatory design work for a PRINTED CIRCUIT BOARD. It refers specifically to the film-based design which is then used in subsequent etching processes before the printed circuit board is produced.

ASA American Standards Association. ◊ ANSI.

ASCII American Standard Code for Information Interchange: standard binary notation for numbers, letters and control characters. See appendix for CODES.

Assembler software programs which translate instructions written in assembly codes (e.g. mnemonics, or SOURCE CODE) into MACHINE LANGUAGE instructions (OBJECT CODES) which can be directly loaded into a computer and recognised by the machine's central processing unit.

Assembly language a machine-oriented language, used for writing the SOURCE CODE programs. The program is written as a series of source statements using mnemonic (or symbolic) codes that suggest the definition of the instruction. The symbolic codes must be translated by the assembler program into object (or machine) code before it can be used by the computer.

Assembly listing a printed list produced by the ASSEMBLER to document an assembly operation. It shows, line for line, how the assembler translated the assembly language program.

Associative storage a computer memory in which storage locations are identified by their contents, not by names or positions.

Asynchronous a mode of operation in which events are started by the completion of another event, not by a clock.

Attenuation the reduction or loss of signal in passing along a circuit, due to resistance, leakages, etc.

Automatic Data Processing ⇨ ADP.

Automatic loader a loader program contained in a special ROM that allows loading of BINARY paper tapes into the first record or sector of a mass storage device.

Auxiliary storage a peripheral storage device additional to the main memory of a computer, e.g. paper tape, magnetic tapes, disk or magnetic drum. Auxiliary storage holds much larger amounts of information than main memory, and takes a longer time to access. This type of storage can be known as on-line storage or backing storage.

B

Back up a term used to denote skilled resources when applied to a computer system supplier. When applied to the process of computing it refers to the taking of a copy or copies of programs or data, for archival purposes or for security. Back up can also be applied to a second or further computer systems on which programs and data may be processed in an emergency.

Background a term used in connection with computer operating systems. It implies that there are programs with varying levels of priority. The lower priority levels are run in background, i.e. in the computer's spare time or unused memory locations. The more important, higher priority jobs are run in foreground. An operating system with this level of sophistication is more typically to be found in mainframe and minicomputers, since it normally occupies a large amount of memory.

Background processing the automatic execution of lower priority computer programs when higher priority programs are not monopolising the computer system.

Background program the program with lower priority. Background programs normally execute from batched input. The real time tasks take the higher priorities.

Backing storage ◊ AUXILIARY STORAGE.

Backplane a term describing the connections and wiring units which enable the various modules of a microcomputer system to interconnect and communicate.

Backslash/slash the American term for the English oblique symbol, the solidus. (/,\), used for many different purposes in the grammar of programming languages.

BAL ◊ BASIC ASSEMBLER LANGUAGE.

Balance the arithmetic task of adding groups of numbers so that they may be correlated. Balancing is a common process used in editing data in computer systems, to ensure that all important data is present and that only valid data is processed by the computer system.

Bank switching the concept of switching from one section of directly addressable memory to another. Bank switching takes place under program control.

Bar chart a display used to illustrate the progress of activities in project management, for example. The chart employs a bar or lines to denote the point in time a particular activity may have reached.

Bar code a method of identification for data recognition purposes. Used widely in computer systems in retailing. The code, which varies with a number of conventions, comprises a number of lines of varying thickness. The lines are used to describe a product, within the definitions of a particular convention. The codes are read by a scanning device which a computer system then accepts as input.

Barrier effect an active component such as a TRANSISTOR can exist in more than one state. The transistor can perform as a resistor or an amplifier. A phenomenon which facilitates this transformation is a resistive barrier, or a high resistance zone in the transistor, which can be created or removed by applying very precise levels of voltage to the transistor.

Base the immediate region in a bipolar transistor, between the emitter and collector regions, to which electrodes are attached. ⇨'BIPOLAR'.

Base number the number which forms the basis for the particular mathematical system a computer or circuit may be using. Base number systems in common use in computer systems are

Binary	base 2
Octal	base 8
Decimal	base 10
Hexadecimal	base 16

BASIC Beginners All-purpose Symbolic Instruction Code: (N.B. in common with many other computer related acronyms, more than one definition can be encountered, for example 'Beginners Algebraic, etc.)

A high level programming language. One of the easiest to learn languages. It is used in most small computers. BASIC runs efficiently in most computers and requires less memory than many other languages. BASIC is also used as a conversational language, where the grammar of the language prompts the programmer to respond in a specific manner.

Basic Assembler Language (BAL) a low level computer programming language, used by expert computer programmers for efficient use of the computer's memory. An ASSEMBLER program converts the BAL program into machine-readable BINARY code.

Batch processing the term describing a computer task where each step is taken sequentially for a group of transactions. For example, in a payroll system all the time cards and personnel and rate changes would be punched up as a batch before being entered into the computer for processing. Thereafter there could be several other batch tasks such as file update, error listings, batch totalling, payroll calculation, payslip printing, credit transfer or cheque printing. By contrast, in an on-line system each transaction is handled separately and completely.

Battery back up a technique to protect the contents of RAM (Random Access Memory) even when power has been lost for a while, in which the battery assumes the task of supplying power to the circuit for a limited period. Usually measured in minutes or hours rather than days.

Baud a unit of rate of serial data transmission roughly equivalent to bits per second.

Baud rate the signal transmission rate measured in bits per second. It is used as a measure of serial data flow between computers, communication equipment and peripheral devices.

Baudot the baudot code is similar in concept to ASCII. It assigns codes to letters of the alphabet, numbers and punctuation marks. Baudot code uses only 5 bits for 32 possible combinations and does not have a unique code assignment for each character. Two codes are used for case shifting (letters and figures) which allow a total of 60 different characters to be represented. ASCII and EBCDIC are much more widely used codes because they are more extensive and easier to use. See appendix for CODES.

BCD Binary Coded Decimal. A system of representing numerical values where each decimal digit is replaced by its binary equivalent.

It uses the base 2 and codes each decimal digit into a 4 bit word. For example:

Decimal Number	*Binary Number*
0	0000
1	0001
2	0010
3	0011
4	0100
5	0101
6	0110
7	0111
8	1000
9	1001
10	1010
11	1011
12	1100
13	1101
14	1110
15	1111

See appendix for CODES

Benchmark a standard or point of reference used to measure performance or value. Datum is the engineering equivalent.

Benchmark tests tests used in measurement of system performance under typical conditions. A group of programs can run on several computers for the purposes of comparing speed, throughput, ease of conversion and overall performance. There are several different conventions for evaluating the results of benchmark tests but they are generally only applied to the very large installations since the costs involved can be prohibitive.

Best straight line when calibrating an instrument, a TRANSDUCER or a SENSOR, the range of output values plotted against input appears as two curves, one for the upper limit of tolerance, and one for the lower. The best straight line plotted between these two curves is defined as the nominal performance for the instrument being calibrated.

Bidirectional a BUS structure in which a single conductor is used to transmit data or signals in either direction, usually used for data transmission between a peripheral unit and a central processing unit or memory.

Binary a system of numbers using 2 as a base whereas the decimal system uses 10 as a base. The binary system requires only two symbols: 0 and 1. ◊ BCD: BINARY CODED DECIMAL.

Binary Coded Decimal ◊BCD

Binary digit ◊BIT.

Bipolar having two poles, positive and negative. When applied to TRANSISTORS it refers to the type of transistor construction which has two positive regions (p-regions, the emitter and collector), one on either side of a negative region (n-region, the base). The opposite construction is also employed where two negative regions sandwich a positive region. These are known as pnp and npn transistors, respectively.

Depending upon the voltage applied the central region will become resistive, thus preventing the flow of current, or become conductive, thus permitting the flow of current. In this way a bipolar transistor can be used as an amplifier or a switch. The bipolar transistor principle is widely used for memory technologies.

Bistable a TRANSISTOR circuit designed to divide a value by two. It exists in a BINARY state, either as a zero value or a one. A FLIP-FLOP circuit is bistable.

Bit binary digit. A single binary digit may be a logic 1 or 0. In microprocessing terms the logic states are represented by voltage levels; the voltage being considered either on or off when it falls outside preset values. These values vary with the technology, e.g. TTL, CMOS, etc.

Bit parallel a method of simultaneously moving all bits in a group over separate wires.

Bit serial a method of sequentially moving a grouping of bits one at a time over a single wire.

Bit test instructions special low level programming instructions to examine the status of any main memory bit. The instruction can test, set or reset a memory bit. These instructions are for setting flags, or signposts for data, and for monitoring and controlling on-off functions such as switches, relays, valves and indicator lamps. Not present in all systems. More commonly found in industrial microcomputer systems.

Bits per second ◊BPS.

Black box any piece of equipment, usually electronic, which is considered only as a functional item, thus only the input and output are evaluated. In practice this approach is generally followed with regard to electronic products. Most people are not interested in the workings of a TV set or washing machine provided it functions. A flight recorder is the archetypal black box.

Black-out the loss of performance in a device immediately following a SPIKE or abnormal transient signal.

Block diagram a functional representation or diagram of a system, instrument or computer. Intended to diagramatically illustrate rather than specify function.

Board a commonly used term to describe a printed circuit board. ◊PCB.

Bonded metallic components connected in a circuit to provide the impression, electrically, that they are physically bonded, and thus at a common voltage.

Boolean algebra a notation which uses an algebraic method for describing logic states. Named after thc 19th Century English mathematician, George Boole who originally developed his system to describe true or false mathematical statements in such a manner that they could not contain any ambiguity nor be misinterpreted.

Boolean algebra has been adopted by logic circuit designers and is now used to describe the logic states which make up the logic gates used in a computer's Arithmetic and Logic Unit. See appendix for LOGIC CIRCUITS.

Bootstrap a technique or device designed to initiate itself, e.g. a program whose first few instructions are sufficient to bring the rest of itself into the computer from an input device. Can be used either as a noun or a verb to describe the device or the process.

Bootstrap loader this device is used where there is no loader in main memory. It will load into memory any sequential series of BYTES, usually unchecked. It may be keyed into the computer but is more normally stored in Read Only Memory (ROM). The bootstrap loader must be as small as possible in case it has to be input manually.

Box an enclosure or case for an industrial or inherently safe system.

bps bits per second. In serial transmission, the speed with which a device or channel transmits a character in bits. ◊BIT

Branch a logical decision point in a system, or a program instruction. Refers to the capability of a computer to modify the function of a program sequence and depends on the content of the data at a particular instant. A means of departing from the main program out to a subroutine, based on a decision presented by the software. (Synonymous with JUMP.)

Breadboard the initial design model, usually of a circuit. This is normally the very first phase of design for an electronic circuit or system, aimed at proving principles and function, not appearance. The term is not used with reference to software except where software is an integral part of the hardware.

Breakpoint a point in a program where the program expects some external event to happen. For example, it might expect an operator to key in his personal code or an authority before it will proceed to the next step. ◊CHECKPOINT.

British Standards Institute ◊BSI

BSI British Standards Institute, the body responsible for defining standards throughout British industry.

Bubble Memory one of the newer technologies offering a much higher density than conventional memories. There are several different types of bubble memory but the general principle involves the recognition of magnetic bubbles in a non-volatile storage medium. As the presence or absence of bubbles can be recognised as a binary value and as external fields can manipulate this data, bubble memories can replace the more conventional technologies. The specific principle behind bubble memories is based on the phenomenon that if a thin slice is cut from a crystal of certain ferromagnetic materials the observable magnetic patterns, or domains, on the surface of that strip form wavy lines, having alternating directions of magnetisation. The sum of the volume of domains magnetised in one direction equals the sum of the volume of domains magnetised in the opposite direction.

If this crystal slice is then subjected to a magnetic field of increasing strength the domains begin to change in shape until, at a precise point, they reform into perfect cylinders, or bubbles. If the magnetic field continues to increase in strength, at a certain point the bubbles will dissipate.

Thus within certain predefined limits magnetic bubbles exist, to a known magnetic strength. Outside these limits they do not exist;

hence they can be interpreted as binary digits.

Buffer a circuit connected between other circuit elements to prevent interactions and provide additional drive capability. Also a storage device to compensate for differences in speeds of peripheral devices or events being monitored by the computer.

Bug a jargon term used to describe an error or fault in either the hardware or software of a system. 'Gremlin' was its predecessor in World War II engineering jargon.

Bureau a company which offers a service whereby customers may pay for the use of time on a computer. The bureau may also offer programs and operating personnel as part of the service. The service is generally thought of as 'buying computer time'.

Burn-in testing and running of a product, system or component through the range of its operating environment to ensure that an early failure does not occur. In effect the manufacturer is simulating the use of the product by subjecting it to a series of tests.

Bus a collection of wires carrying parallel binary data. Several bus users (modules, e.g. memory) can send or receive data along the bus. In general only one 'sender' and one 'receiver' are active at any one instant. Buses facilitate the transfer of data between memory, input/output services and the central processing unit of the computer.

Bus driver an integrated circuit which is added to the data bus system to give the correct 'drive power' to the computer's central processing unit when several memories are connected to the data bus.

Bus multiplexing the concept of transferring data and/or instructions on the same line or wire at different times, under system control.

Bus system a network of paths inside a computer which facilitates data flow.

Bypass a path around one or more elements of a circuit.

Byte a usable unit of data: 8 consecutive BITS treated as an entity. Byte and character are often used synonymously. This is not necessarily accurate since alphabetic characters generally occupy more storage space than numeric characters.

C

CAD Computer Aided Design the use of a computer for automated industrial design. It employs graphic screens, digitisers, plotters and automated drafting equipment in addition to more conventional computing hardware.

Cabinet a container or enclosure for a rack containing printed circuit boards.

Cable flexible conductors (wires), insulated from each other and contained within an insulated outer covering. Cables in use in computer and electronics systems range from two insulated wires, known as a 'twisted pair' up to multi-core cables of complex configurations. It is possible to contain hundreds of conductors in a single cable.

Calculator a device or integrated circuit capable of performing mathematical operations.

Calibration the process of establishing the actual value of an instrument or device by measurement. This compares to the design, nominal or rated value which may not be strictly attainable due to errors, losses, leakage, etc.

Call a software technique. Program subroutines are 'called', which has the effect of transferring control to the subroutine. The call instruction automatically saves the return address for the main program at the top of the stack so that control is returned to the main program when the subroutine has completed its task.

CAM Computer Aided Manufacture the widespread use of computers to aid and improve the manufacturing process. Includes such processes as numerically controlled machine tools, computer aided production control and materials planning.

Capacitance the ability to store an electrical charge, measured in Farads (F), more practically in microfarads (μF) or picofarads (pF). A capacitor has the ability to store charge and discharge, hence its capacitance defines the value of the capacitor.

Capacitor an electronic component consisting of two metal plates separated by an insulator. Sometimes called a condenser. Each metal plate is a conductor, or electrode. The insulator, or dielectric, is designed so that the two conductors have equal electrical charges but opposite polarity.

Capacity the size of computer memory, used as a comparison between models of computer. Measured in BYTES or WORDS (sometimes characters).

Card a punch card is literally a specially designed piece of card which is punched with holes representing codes which can then be read by a computer. There are several standards in use, in terms of size and coding.
Card is also loosely used as a jargon term for a printed circuit board (PCB).

Card column a line of punch positions running from the top to the bottom of a punch card. The most commonly used punch card convention has 80 rows running horizontally and 12 columns running vertically.

Card punch an electro mechanical device for punching holes in cards in specific codes for the purpose of storing information in a punch card.

Card sensing the converting of information contained in punched cards into electrical impulses by a unit in a card reader; an input device for a computer system.

Carriage return as used in typewriter operation. A key on a keyboard, or a program instruction, causing the print head or cursor on the display to return to the beginning of the next available new line.

Carry (bit) used in the normal arithmetic sense. Actually an extension bit called the carry bit is added into the accumulator. See appendix for LOGIC CIRCUITS.

Cascade connecting programs, routines or circuits together so that the output from one becomes the input of the next. Compare to 'DAISY-CHAINING'.

Cassette a magnetic medium for the storage of data. Magnetic tape in an enclosure.

Cathode Ray Tube ⇨ CRT.

CDD ⇨ CHARGE COUPLED DEVICE.

CCITT Consultative Committee International Telegraph and Telephone. A committee within the International Telecommunications Union. It concerns itself with the conventions which enable transfer of data over compatible links, either internationally or between devices from different manufactures. Conventions exist which define plugs, cables and software routines for handling data, to facilitate interchangeability of programs and devices between different manufacturers' products and across geographical boundaries.

Central Processing Unit (CPU) the heart of any computing system comprising groups of REGISTERS and LOGIC. Basically the CPU is made up of storage elements called registers, computational circuits in the arithmetic and logic unit, and the CONTROL BLOCK and input/output circuitry. Also called the processor or the central processor.

Central processor ⇨ CENTRAL PROCESSING UNIT.

cgs system an earlier system of measurement, based on centimetre, gram, second. Now susperseded by SI Units. ⇨ SI MKS.

Chain a set of operations to be performed sequentially under program control.

Chain printer a type of high speed impact printer where the characters are all contained on a continuous metal chain. The commonly used characters are repeated two or three times to reduce access time. The chain moves across the paper continuously. Under program control a 'hammer' selects a character and strikes it from behind thus causing printing to take place on impact with the paper. The print head is a slug, or etched positive impression, of the letter to be formed. Drum printers also use a similar technique.

Channel a hardware path, wires, along which signals may be sent, e.g. a data channel, output channel, etc.

Characters the letters A–Z, numerous special symbols and the numbers 0–9, coded for use by a computer.

Charge the quantity of unbalanced electricity in a body. An excess or deficiency of electrons, giving the body negative or positive charge.

Charge Coupled Device (CCD) a memory technology in which packets of electrical charge are separated by an insulating barrier in the semiconductor circuit. These packets, or minute charges, can be moved step by step, in a DAISY-CHAIN fashion backwards and forwards along the chain.

Each packet, or charge, represents a BINARY digit. Each movement of the charge moves the binary digit into a new memory position.

CCD are used for some computer memory applications but their inherent speed makes them eminently suitable for scanning and TV camera purposes.

Chassis the metal frame which houses the printed circuit boards (PCB), power supplies, etc. which comprise the central processing unit of a computing system.

Chatter rapid closing and opening of contacts on a relay or switch.

Checkpoint a convenient point in a program for stopping and restarting or for the use of external events. ◊ BREAKPOINT.

Chemical etching part of the process of photolithography in which the required circuit is protected by an etch-resistant material whilst the unwanted portions of the material are chemically eroded so as to leave only the exact circuit, or conductive path, remaining on the insulating base material.

Chip the SEMICONDUCTOR material on which integrated circuits are printed. A rectangular or square silicon chip is cut from a circular silicon wafer in mass production. The chip is normally to be seen mounted in a rectangular plastic package, ◊ DIP/DIL, SIP/SIL. This rectangular package contains the packaging material, external connections and the chip itself which cannot normally be seen. There are literally thousands of different types of chip, only a few of which are microprocessors.

Circuit a combination of conducting electrical paths and devices constructed for a specific purpose.

Circuit breaker a device that opens electric circuits under anticipated but unusual conditions, e.g. overload of current, heat, etc.

Circuit diagram a diagrammatic representation of a circuit employing a variety of conventions and symbols, enabling competent technicians to 'read' a circuit easily.

Clear an activity to zeroise (or blank) one or more memory positions. A program normally clears REGISTERS before beginning an arithmetic task, so that the programmer can be confident there are no errors due to residual contents of registers.

Clock a timer used in a system to originate accurately timed pulses and intervals for the timing of switching circuits. The most accurate clocks are based upon quartz crystal. When an alternating current is passed through a specific type of quartz crystal, mechanical vibrations, or oscillations, occur. The frequency of those oscillations is highly stable and predictable to a very high timing accuracy, thus the principle is widely used for timing purposes.

Clock rate a predefined time rate at which pulses are emitted from the clock within a computer system.

Closed loop a circuit or logic process in which the output signal or value always returns to start for comparison. Used in servo systems and analog control systems.

CMOS Complementary Metal Oxide Semiconductor. A SEMICONDUCTOR technology, using both positive and negative devices on the same silicon substrate. Its construction employs positive and negative channels in series, only one being switched on at one time. This gives the advantage of low power dissipation. CMOS also offers good immunity to electrical noise, or interference.

Coaxial cable a special purpose group of cables in which the conductors are arranged in cylindrical layers around a central core. Each cylindrical layer is insulated from the conductors on either side. Conductors may be made up from flexible wires, tubing or braid, for example. Insulation may be any of the normal insulating rubber or synthetic materials but the outer skin is normally quite thick, or armoured, to protect the contents.

COBOL an acronym of COmmercial and Business Oriented Language. The most widely used high level computer programming language for business data processing.

Code a communication for conveniently representing characters in a form the computer can understand, e.g. binary code. To code also describes the act of writing down the mnemonic instructions that form a program. The term 'program writing' is interchangeable with 'coding'.

Cold Start a system start up following a lengthy period of inoperation. An initial start up.

Coil a circular wound conductor, or group of conductors.

Collate the combination of data, or documents, into a predefined sequence.

Collector an n or p region in a semiconductor. ◊ BIPOLAR.

COM ◊ COMPUTER OUTPUT TO MICROFILM.

Command a pulse, signal or group of signals to start or stop an operation. A computer instruction which starts or stops an operation, or confirms an instruction to continue.

Comment a programmer's notes enabling a program to be understood by other people. Comments are written in areas that enable the program to ignore them except for storage, printing and display. They are external to program logic.

Compatibility the extent to which computers, peripherals, programs and circuits can operate in concert, without use of special interfaces, buffers, etc.

Upwards compatibility refers to the ability to take programs from one machine and run them on another, larger and more powerful machine from the same supplier.

Compensate the provision of program logic, a circuit or a special device to counteract known sources of error.

Compiler a program which translates (assembles) higher level languages into machine code instructions which can be recognised by the computer's central processing unit.

Complementary Metal Oxide Semiconductor ◊ CMOS.

Complements unless a microprocessor has a specific calculator chip all simple arithmetic has to be performed by software. Since the assembler language used on a microprocessor operates at the binary level a technique to perform arithmetic within the binary notation has to be employed. Many microprocessors do not include a calculator facility. Not all microcomputers utilise a calculator chip, which poses an extra problem since the processor can only add, it cannot subtract.

The technique employed to overcome this limitation is known as complements, or 'twos-complement' for a binary system.

For example in a simple decimal subtraction of 2 from 9 the sum appears: $9-2=7$.

The binary equivalent of this calculation, using binary addition to achieve the same result as the decimal subtraction of $9-2$ is as follows.

(a) Find the twos-complement for binary equivalent of decimal 2.

(b) Add the twos-complement of decimal 2 to to the binary value of decimal 9.

(c) Ignore any carry bit in the result.

Thus, to find the twos complement of decimal 2.

(a) (i) Decimal 2 = binary 0010.

(ii) Replace all 1 bits with 0 bits.
Replace all 0 bits with 1 bits.
thus 0010 becomes 1101.

(iii) Add a 1 bit to the result
thus 1101 becomes 1110.

Therefore the two-complement of decimal 2 = 1110.

(b) Add binary value of decimal 9 to twos complement of 2.

	1001
	1110
carry 1	0111

(c) Ignoring carry bit the result is 0111, equals *decimal* 7.

See section on LOGIC CIRCUITS in appendix.

Component Value the rated value in terms of voltage, current, capacitance, etc. of a given electronic or semiconductor device.

Computer an assembly of central processing units and peripheral devices, having the ability to:

store programs and data
manipulate data
perform arithmetic and calculations on data
compare data and make yes/no decisions
perform input and output operations on data and programs.

Computer Aided Design ⇨ CAD.

Computer Aided Manufacture ⇨ CAM.

Computer bureau ⇨ BUREAU.

Computer Output to Microfilm (COM) a computer output device; it may be a printer or a typesetter that has an option to output microfilm as well as normal printing. It may be a special purpose COM device, perhaps using laser techniques.

Concatenate a programming term meaning to link together, referring to either data routines or whole programs.

Concentrator a device which enables several computers to share a single telephone line when operating teleprocessing links. The term is sometimes used as a synonym for 'multiplexer' but this is not a strictly accurate use of the term concentrator.

Conditional refers to the action to be taken at a decision point in a program. The action may be to BRANCH, JUMP or ABORT.

Conductance the ability to conduct electricity.

Conductor material or devices that carry, or conduct, electrical current.

Configuration a specific arrangement of peripherals and processor which clearly defines a computer's capacity. The term may also be applied to an arrangement of chips or components.

Connect time the time that passes between logging-on and logging-off a time-sharing computer system. Used as the basis for billing a system user.

Connector a device enabling components to be connected into a circuit. A plug or adaptor which enables current to pass from one device or circuit to another.

Console the control panel or control devices for a computer. The central device containing start/stop keys, power keys, status display lights and keyboard for input of variable key data, e.g. password, date, program name, etc. Often contains basic printer or display for operator messages.

Constant a value which is fixed, for use by a program. For example, on any given day, the date is a constant.

Contact a current-carrying component of a relay, switch or connector designed to open or close electrical circuits.

Continuous signals ⇨ ANALOG.

Control block this is the section within the central processing unit which performs the control functions. It is responsible for decoding microprogrammed instructions and then generating the internal control signals that perform the operations required.

Control bus a group of connecting paths which conveys control signals to regulate system operation.

Control character a character whose recognition by a program or system starts, stops or changes a control function.

Control program a sequence of instructions that will inform and guide the CENTRAL PROCESSING UNIT through the various operations it must perform.

Convention a standard, accepted procedure. In computer terms this relates to symbols, acronyms and so on.

Conversational language a language that looks like a version of standard English enabling rapid assimilation of the features of a system. Generally used in time sharing and enquiry type applications, e.g. APL and BASIC.

Converter a method or device for changing alternating current to direct current or vice versa. See SIGNAL INVERTER.

Core an assembly of very small ferrite rings or cores which when magnetised in one direction represent 0 and in the other 1. Core memory was the earliest form of non-volatile Random Access Memory (RAM) and was the basic memory technology for many years. Core is now being superseded by solid state memory for reasons of economy, space and performance.

Corruption damage or loss of data due to computer or software malfunction.

Counter a circuit designed to count pulses or a memory location which can be set to an initial number and incremented or decremented by signals received.

Couple circuits two circuits (or more) connected so that they interact electrically.

cps cycles per second. ◊ CYCLE, FREQUENCY, and HERTZ.

CPU ◊ CENTRAL PROCESSING UNIT.

Crash usually refers to physical contact between a disk and a reading head, causing damage to both. Can also refer to a dramatic failure of a computer program. In either case a failure of significant proportions.

Critical Path a term to denote the shortest route, path or time to reach a given objective. Used in connection with critical path network techniques. ◊ PERT.

CROM Control Read Only Memory ROM that is designed to decode control logic, in the processor.

Cross assembler a process by which a program is assembled by one computer to enable it to run on another computer. Used frequently in microprocessor systems since there are so many different versions of programming languages that the only practical way of using one computer to generate programs for other types is by using cross assemblers.

Cross talk a phenomenon which occurs when signals from one circuit interfere with another. The source of the signals is the 'disturbing' circuit, the other is the 'disturbed' circuit.

CRT Cathode Ray Tube. A display unit output device resembling a television tube or monitor. It is the display device used in a VDU (video display unit).

Cryoelectronics the field of study which concentrates on the behaviour of conductors at very low temperatures. The JOSEPHSON JUNCTION and the superconductor devices originally required cryogenic conditions.

Crystal ⇨ GRAIN.

Crystal oscillator an energized crystal whose vibrations produce a constant frequency electronic oscillation. Dividing components or circuits are provided to create the exact frequencies required.

Current the rate of flow of electricity through a conductor, measured in ampères, or amps. Stated to be a direct or continuous flow (dc or DC), or flowing in pulses (ac or AC).

Current carrier an electrical conductor, which permits the free flow of current within the limits of its electrical resistance.

Current loop a communication line on which the presence or absence of current is used to represent data transmitted over that line.

Cursor a position indicator to enable the use of a VDU to see exactly where the next input character may be placed, or to keep tracking position. A visual indicator, it is analogous to the typing position on a typewriter.

Customer Engineer ⇨ FIELD MAINTENANCE.

Cybernetics the study of man/machine interaction. It is generally taken to mean FEEDBACK control systems but can be much more broadly defined to include complex modelling, artificial intelligence, robotics and other advanced application areas.

Cycle the wave pattern of, for example, a sine wave. The wave alternates from positive to negative through 360°. When applied to alternating current, cycles are measured in cycles per second. In SI units this is measured in HERTZ, (Hz).

Cycle, instruction time the time taken to fetch an instruction from memory and then to execute it.

Cycles per second ⇨ CPS.

Cycle stealing when an input/output device uses DIRECT MEMORY ACCESSING (DMA) techniques, it avoids the need to use the central processor, so that the input device talks directly to memory. It can hold up the use of the input/output bus for an indefinite number of cycles while it accesses system memory. This technique is used to speed up certain priority tasks.

D

DAC ◊ DIGITAL TO ANALOG CONVERTER

Daisy chain a specific method of directing signals along a BUS. The devices not needing a signal pass it on to the next device which requires a signal. This technique facilitates the allocation of priorities between devices along the bus.

Damped a system to control oscillations down to required amplitude and frequency. Damped oscillation is sometimes termed 'ringing'.

Data information or signals to be processed, usually considered as binary WORDS.

Data acquisition the generic term for a system or device that captures data from various sources and converts it to BINARY code for subsequent use by the computer.

Data bank the combined contents of a number of separate data bases.

Data base the entire file or collection of data relevant to a company or organisation or an individual computer system or program.

Data bus a group of connecting paths which conveys data to and from the CPU, memory storage and peripheral devices.

Data communications the process of interconnecting computers over telephone line links.

Data link the device which undertakes the transmission of data in a data communications or teleprocessing network. The data link may be a computer in its own right or may have a limited capacity which merely enables it to transmit and receive data. Once data has been read by the input device on the data link, (for example a tape reader), the data is converted into a form where it can travel along a telephone line like voice signals. This is accomplished by means of a modem, or MOdulator/DEModulator, which converts digital input to digital signals analogous to voice signals. Modems and data links also perform 'receive' as well as 'send' functions.

Data logger a computer or electronics device which captures and records data, often via sensors, for later analysis or computer processing.

Data pointer a register holding the address of data to be operated on by an instruction. The register points to the data's memory location.

Data processing (DP) relating to the computer activities of receiving data, performing the desired operation under stored program control and producing the desired results.

Data recording the process of converting data into a medium which can be used for input to a computer system, e.g. punch cards.

Data reduction the process of eliminating unnecessary detail from data and reducing it down to a manageable and simplified format or volume.

Data store memory that contains data.

Data word size the specific length of data word a particular processor is designed to handle. Thus the term 2, 4, 8 or 16 bit microprocessor refers to data word size.

The length of the data word affects data throughput, efficiency of storage and programming, programming language facilities, precision and many other factors. In general greater word length offers greater facilities but higher cost. Programs are not directly transferable from one word length machine to a different one.

DC ⇨ DIRECT CURRENT.

Dealer a sales agent. Generally not a stockist. Acts as a sales outlet for the manufacturer.

Debug a term used in connection with software or hardware. Debugging involves searching for and eliminating sources of error in the operation of a computer or its software.

Debug monitor a memory-resident debug program that provides real time BREAKPOINT potential, in order to examine and alter system memory locations and system variables. It enables user programs to call down operating system routines.

Decade a ten position device; the term is commonly applied to switching devices.

Decay the time taken for a signal to fall to a level below which it ceases to operate a circuit or system. Applied particularly to Cathode Ray Tube image creation and change.

Decimal a number system using the base 10.

Decimal arithmetic capability the ability to perform decimal arithmetic in one or two instructions; may be a hardware decimal adder or an instruction that 'corrects' a binary result.

Decision gates ◊GATES. See appendix for LOGIC CIRCUITS.

Decision tables an array of data held in main memory which informs the main program of action to be taken when a branch or jump instruction is executed.

Decode to translate data or symbolic representation in order to decide how and where resultant signals are to be sent.

Decoder an electrical circuit for decoding ADDRESS signals.

Decrement the process of reducing the value held in a counter or register.

Dedicated a dedicated computer is one that has been specifically programmed for a single application.

Default a value assigned to a variable by a program if it does not have any associated value when read by the program.

DeMorgans theorem facilitates the expression of Boolean algebra in terms of AND and NOT. See appendix for LOGIC CIRCUITS.

Demultiplex the device that reconstructs multiplexed signals into a coherent stream. ◊ MULTIPLEXING

Density the measure of the number of GATES and INTEGRATED CIRCUITS present on a given surface area of a silicon chip. ◊ SSI, MSI, LSI, VLSI.

Depletion the region in a SEMICONDUCTOR that changes state under the application of externally applied voltage to facilitate the change from resistor to amplifier, or amplifier to resistor, is known as the depletion region. This phenomenon occurs at the junctions of the positive and negative regions of a BIPOLAR transistor.

Desk check the act of physically reading through a coded program or source listing prior to submitting it to the computer for compilation. The object is to shorten and simplify debugging by locating any logic and syntax errors.

Detect the process of recognising the presence or absence of a signal or specific item of data.

Development system a collection of printed circuit boards (PCB) and MODULES comprising central processor, memory, and peripherals to enable programs and hardware systems to be developed and tested. A development system also requires ASSEMBLER level programming tools and a software EDITOR. Often has a facility to program ROM and in circuit emulation facilities. ◊ IN CIRCUIT EMULATION.

Device independent a method of writing programs which ignores any special characteristics of specific computers. In this way the computer is 'transparent' to the program, thus the program may be interchangeable between machines.

Diagnostic routine routines for helping a programmer or engineer locate faults in programs or hardware. Hardware in particular is now being developed to the point where it can run self-diagnostic routines which tell the engineer the potential sources for future malfunction.

Dice the plural noun for the completed chips cut from a silicon wafer.

Dicing the process of cutting a die from the silicon wafer.

Die the singular noun for the completed chip cut from a silicon wafer.

Difference machine Charles Babbage's first attempt at constructing a calculating machine based on the principle of mathematical first and second order differences.

Differential amplifier a device or circuit deriving an output signal based on the differential of two input signals.

Diffusion a process by which selected chemicals, called dopants, are enabled to enter the crystalline structure of semiconductor materials in order to change their electrical characteristics. ◊ DOPANT.

Digital a system that handles information as numbers.

Digital computer a system that requires information to be transmitted in the form of separate signals, as distinct from an analog computer which receives a continuous signal. Each separate signal is regarded as a BINARY digit in a digital computer.

Digital to Analog converter (DAC) a device for converting discrete digital signals to a single continuous signal.

Digitise the conversion of analog input signals into digital output signals. Scanning an irregular shape to produce XY co-ordinates on a plotter is a typical use of the technique.

Diode a two terminal device which conducts electricity easily in one direction and with difficulty in the other. It can be used to inhibit current flow in one direction.

Diode-Transistor Logic (DTL) a convention for the construction of logic circuits before the advent of the cheap transistor. Diodes were used as resistors and conductors, transistors as amplifiers and switches in this convention. Was superseded by TTL, Transistor-Transistor Logic.

Direct addressing an addressing mode characterised by the ability to reach directly any point in memory storage.

Direct Current (dc or DC) a stream of current flowing at a constant rate, in one direction.

Direct Memory Access (DMA) a method of gaining direct access to main storage or other high speed storage devices, without involving the processor. ⇨ CYCLE STEALING.

Directory a library of files or programs, generally held on a magnetic storage medium.

DIP/DIL Dual In line Package. A device on which a chip can be mounted to connect it directly to a printed circuit board (PCB). It includes packaging and parallel connection pins. ⇨ SIP/SIL.

Disassembler a program that reverses the assembly process, i.e. it converts machine language to the original higher level language. It is normally only an approximate conversion.

Disc ⇨ DISK.

Discrete device a single-function packaged component; for example, a diode or transistor.

Disk (disc) a magnetic storage device which rotates on a spindle and can be accessed by a RECORDING (read/write) head. Models range from the mass storage variety capable of storing over 1 billion characters down to the single sided floppy disk, storing 250,000 characters. The disks are known as packs, cartridges, drums and by various other supplied-originated names.

Disk drive the peripheral device containing motor, enclosure, etc., to permit use of the magnetic disk and its read/write functions.

Display the face of a cathode ray tube or monitor, on which output may be viewed.

Dissipation loss of power due to resistances, leakages, etc. ◊ATTENUATION.

Distributed intelligence a system where the devices capable of being programmed are spread around the system user's premises. Formerly only the central computer was capable of being programmed. With the advent of the microcomputer many terminals, printers and other devices are capable of being programmed independently of the central computer.

Distributor a sales agent for a system manufacturer who also holds stock of finished products and spares. Typically also employs support staff to ensure successful installations. A distributor is normally appointed only if the system supplier does not manufacture the product in the country where the distributor is based.

There is a different pattern for semiconductors where it is the normal practice to buy from distributors in all countries unless the customer has very significant purchasing power.

DMA ◊ DIRECT MEMORY ACCESS.

Documentation the generic term for any set of drawings, parts lists, flow diagrams, operating instructions and so on concerning a system or part of a system.

Domain the term given to the area of magnetisation on the face of the material from which bubble memories are fabricated.

Dopant an impurity which is deliberately introduced into a SEMICONDUCTOR, to achieve a known level of conductivity. ◊DIFFUSION.

DOS (Disk Operating System) an operating system for disk based machines.

Dot matrix a type of printer that uses a similar process to the way characters are represented on CRT screens, by building them up with dots. Any character to be printed occupies an area defined by the supplier as a matrix, e.g. $16 \times 11, 9 \times 7, 7 \times 5$. This means in the case of a 7×5 matrix, 7 vertical dots and 5 horizontal dots. Any commonly used character can be fabricated from this array.

The action of selecting the dots to form a character, from data held in ROM in the printer, causes selected print heads, or elements, to impact the character outline onto paper.

Double precision (extended precision) the use of two words for arithmetic functions, thus doubling the accuracy of the results.

DP ⇨ DATA PROCESSING.

Drain a semiconductor's electrode. ⇨ ELECTRODE.

Driver a circuit controller or one that provides the input for a device or another circuit.

Drop in foreign objects on a disk causing the read head to sense information that was not recorded.

Drop out when the voltage level falls below minimum design requirements. The result can be to stall a system. Drop-out also refers to a disk's reading head failing to read data. ⇨ SPIKE.

Drum printer a computer output printer similar in operation to an impact or line printer except that the characters are presented to the printer hammer at the printing position, rotating vertically on a horizontally mounted drum of printer characters. Compare this to the horizontal chain on a CHAIN or LINE printer.

Dry joint a faulty electrical connection caused by inadequate soldering. A chemical condition.

DTL ⇨ DIODE-TRANSISTOR LOGIC.

Dump a deposit of all preselected data, or programs, onto a printed output. Dumping of data can take place via other media but the principle remains the same.

Dynamic Memory Dynamic RAM (Random Access Memory) can only hold data for a few milliseconds, therefore it has to be constantly refreshed by having its contents rewritten. Dynamic RAM is the cheapest type of random access memory available at the moment so the refreshing process can be an economic saving but a technical drawback.

E

EAROM Electrically Alterable Read Only Memory. These are non-volatile memories, used to store static data and programs. It has a slow write time (2 microseconds) thus does not require special equipment for programming as distinct from EPROM (Erasable Programmable Read Only Memory) which is programmable using short wavelength ultra violet light and requires special programming equipment. EAROM can be programmed in circuit, e.g. in position. The whole of an EAROM, or just one part of its memory, may be reprogrammed. ◊EPROM, PROM and ROM.

Earth the point taken to be an arbitrary zero in the scale of electrical potential. To physically connect an electric circuit to earth, or a device synonymous with earth, e.g. a cold water pipe. Synonymous with GROUND.

EBCDIC Extended Binary Coded Decimal Interchange Code. A standard code. See appendix for CODES.

Edge connector the plated or pure metal conductive connection points specially provided at a convenient edge of a printed circuit board (PCB). Soldered or plug connections to printed circuit boards are generally made from edge connectors.

Edit the process of reading and modifying data or programs.

Editor software designed to enable a user to enter and modify program coding and data for ASSEMBLY LANGUAGE source programs. Used in conjunction with a development system for microprocessor programming.

EDP Electronic Data Processing. The generic term for computing. Synonymous with ADP and DP.

EEROM Electrically Erasable Read Only Memory. Synonymous with EROM and PROM. See also EAROM.

EIA an abbreviation for the trade group Electronic Industries Association (of Great Britain).

Electrically Alterable Read Only Memory ◊ EAROM.

Electrically Erasable Read Only Memory ◊ EEROM.

Electricity the study, disciplines and activities associated with electric charges, such as electrons.

Electrode a device that attracts or emits electrical charge carriers. In a SEMICONDUCTOR the conduit for electrical current is an electrode and can be known as a collector, a drain or an emitter.

Electromagnetic field the environment, or magnetic field, set up when a device which can only be magnetised when an electric current is passed through it is energised. The magnetic field created in this way is volatile and will not exist when current is removed from the device.

Electron the natural unit of electric charge. Electrons exist independently and are constituents of an atom. Electrons moving in one direction within an electric field constitute an electric current.

Electron beam a highly concentrated emission of electrons from a single source. The particular use of the electron beam in SEMICONDUCTOR technology is in describing the microminiature circuits on silicon chips. It is also used for similar purposes in microscopes.

Electronic Data Processing ◊ EDP.

Electronic Industries Association ◊ EIA.

Electronics technology based on the properties, behaviour and control of electrons. A branch of electrical technology.

Electrostatic a printing technology that is based on electrostatic adhesion due to the attraction of two oppositely charged substances. Xerographic based photocopiers employ similar principles.

Embedding the process of introducing DOPANTS into a pure silicon crystal. ◊ DIFFUSION.

Emitter an n or p region in a SEMICONDUCTOR. ◊ BIPOLAR.

Emulate to imitate one system with another such that the imitating system accepts the same data, executes the same programs and achieves the same results as the imitated system. In practice this is very difficult to achieve and compromises have to be accepted.

Enable to program or forewarn the processor to accept an interrupt signal, or priority processing task.

Encapsulate to enclose or submerge an electrical device in an insulating material. The process takes place in a vacuum so that no air or gas remains within the encapsulated assembly. The process gives a much higher electrical and heat insulation to the device, to precise specifications.

Enclosure a suitable box, casing or cover for an electronic product.

End user the computer supplier's customer. The organisation which actually uses the computer to solve its problems, as distinct from all the organisations in the supply chain.

Energise to apply an electrical charge to an electrical device. ⇨ EXCITE.

Enhance to add to or to improve. When applied to computers it generally means to add extra function or facilities to software or to improve the performance or capacity of the hardware.

Environment describes the ambient or required conditions for a computer system. Refers to temperature, humidity, air cleanliness and air pressure.

Epoxy resin an insulating plastic material, commonly used as an encapsulating material. ⇨ ENCAPSULATE.

EPROM Erasable Programmable Read Only Memory. A non-volatile memory, or one whose contents are not lost when electrical power is removed. The contents of EPROM are programmed using an electro-optical programming device; part of a development system.

The programming technique employs a short wavelength ultra violet light with a very fast write cycle of 500 nano seconds.

The whole of an EPROM must be reprogrammed when making a change. Contrast to EAROM.

Erasable Programmable Read Only Memory ⇨ EPROM.

Erasable Read Only Memory ⇨ EROM.

EROM Erasable Read Only Memory. Synonymous with EAROM, EEROM, EPROM.

Error-Message identification of program errors in a listing following an attempt at assembly. The better compilers give comprehensive descriptions of the error thus helping the programmer to correct it quickly.

Excite to apply a voltage to an electrical device. ⇨ ENERGISE.

Exclusive OR gate similar to the OR gate but producing an inverted signal. See appendix for LOGIC CIRCUITS.

Execute a function following on from a statement in the program where a command is performed on the ADDRESS indicated by the register, under program control. An imperative statement.

Execution Time the time necessary to carry out an instruction.

Executive a program designed to organise and run other programs.

Exercisers a basic development system. Usually a HEXADECIMAL keyboard and display, designed to handle one specific microprocessor.

Exorciser a widely used development system manufactured by one of the leading semiconductor manufacturers for use on his own proprietary products.

Expression an ALGORITHM or representation of mathematical terms.

Extended Binary Coded Decimal ⇨ EBCDIC.

Extended precision the ability to add or subtract using a double WORD length and the CARRY instruction or facility. Thus when the results of a mathematical operation become larger than a single word length they can overflow into the adjacent memory word. See COMPLEMENTS for an illustration.

Extrapolate to forcast (or estimate) results based on previous data; the reverse of INTERPOLATE.

F

F ◊ FARADS.

Fabricate when applied to SEMICONDUCTORS the term refers to the process of creating an INTEGRATED CIRCUIT from a wafer of silicon.

Facilities Management a totally subcontracted computer operation in which the client supplies the computer and the premises and a subcontractor provides all the staff necessary to provide an in-house service. This approach is mainly used by some of the larger computer users with a very high data processing expense budget.

Farads (F) a measure of the capacitance present in a circuit or produced by individual components. ◊ CAPACITANCE.

Feasibility Study a formal survey to establish the economics, practicality or technical implications (or all three) of following a certain course of action. For example, installing, replacing or upgrading a computer. Another typical example covers the studies aimed at replacing conventional technology in a product or process with the newer, current technologies.

Feedback in a circuit which contains an energising device and other devices which consume a portion of that energy, the status of the devices may be monitored by feedback signals. The feedback, or data concerning the status of various devices in the circuit, enable the energising device to adjust its output to conform with the demands of the system.

Feedback systems can therefore be self-regulating. Servo systems are a name for a particularly sort of feedback system, where the output signal is determined by the input signal according to a formula in memory or preset mechanism.

Ferrite Core ◊ CORE.

FET Field Effect Transistor (see p. 54). A transistor controlled by voltage rather than current. The flow of current through a channel is controlled by the effect of an electric field resulting from the voltage applied to an area called the gate. Note that the use of gate in FET applies to an area of the semiconductor used to prohibit or enable the free flow of electrons, and is not to be confused with a logic gate.

Fetch getting the next instruction from memory.

Fibre optics the process of transmitting light images along fine filament fibres. The fibres, made from glass or perspex, have highly polished surfaces with a refractive index which allows very little of the transmitted light to escape, or attenuate.

Field in programming terms a logical block of storage, of any length recognisable by the computer, in which a particular part of data or program is held and decoded.

In an electrical or magnetic definition a field is that region where the interaction of bodies of particles exert their influence, giving rise to a electrical field or a magnetic field.

Field maintenance the industry dedicated to the servicing and repair of products once they are installed on a customer's premises. In the computer industry this service is normally carried out by the supplier's own maintenance staff called 'customer engineers', in fulfilment of a maintenance contract. However, independent field service operations are beginning to replace the suppliers' own services.

Field test the process of testing a product in a real life environment, as opposed to laboratory tests.

FIFO First In First Out. A method of storing data in a stack or table and retrieving first the first item stored. ◊ LIFO.

File data categorised as being of a certain type or having a specific relationship may be treated as a specific entity, or a file. The literal term refers to the computer-readable medium on which the data is to be stored, which can include card, tape, magnetic tape or disk or computer memory.

File maintenance the procedures involved in keeping files up to date with addition, deletions and amendments to data.

File name a unique acronym or grouping of characters which identifies a specific file to the system.

Filter an electrical device or circuit designed to transmit and accept signals only within predefined limits. Any signal falling outside these limits will be suppressed. Used as protection against SPIKES etc.

Firmware software instructions which have been permanently stored in ROM (Read Only Memory). The memory converts these instructions into machine language on demand by a program.

Fixed head disk a type of disk drive where the read/write head does not move across tracks. Instead there is a separate read/write head for each track.

Fixed point notation (arithmetic) operations involving a fixed position for the decimal point, which means that the program, rather than the hardware, has to keep track of the decimal point position.

Flag an information BIT (or bits) which informs of a specific condition within the central processing unit.

Flame proof an industrial enclosure or device which has to conform to very rigorous standards in order to operate in a dangerous or hostile environment, for example in mine shafts, is said to be flame-proofed. The standards are aimed to ensure that the device itself cannot trigger an explosion or fire, hence it has considerable safety packaging and insulation.

Flat pack a printed circuit board (PCB) assembly having the leads, wires or pins extending from the board in the same plane. Such a low profile package has its application where space is at a premium.

Flip-flop a circuit capable of assuming one of two stable states depending upon signals input to the circuit.

The term can also be applied to a bistable device which is capable of acting as a binary counter, or as a type of toggle to control logic gates. See appendix for LOGIC CIRCUITS.

Float when tri-states are used an output need not be held at either the '1' or '0' level; it can be in the third state, when the output is allowed to 'float'.

Floating point arithmetic the reverse of fixed point arithmetic. A hardware operation in which the computer calculates the decimal point position after completing calculations. It extends the limits of fixed WORD length operations and also reduces the programming tasks for calculation.

Floppy disk a combination of magnetic tape and disk technologies. It is a flexible oxide coated disk (in appearance similar to a 45 rpm record) used for memory storage. Capacities vary from around 250,000 characters, up to 1,000,000, i.e. double-density, double-sided: the 'flippy floppy'.

Flow chart a sequence of operations depicted by symbols and diagrams to indicate an executive program. Flow charts give a visual indication of the procedure necessary for each section of the program. Synonymous with 'flow diagrams'.

Flow diagram ◊ FLOW CHART.

Foreground the partition of computer memory in which the highest priority tasks are executed, e.g. 'real-time' operations. ◊ BACKGROUND.

Format the physical layout and appearance of a computer record, file, input field, report, etc.

FORTRAN an acronym for FORmula TRANslator, a widely used language for mathematic and technical programming. Does not have the flexibility of COBOL for commercial work, especially in report writing, i.e. producing print outs to the desired format.

Frequency the measure of the number of repeats of a pulse per unit of time. For example, the cycles per second of sine wave pulses (AC) is now expressed in Hertz. Hertz, like many other multiple measurements, can be expressed in kilo, mega, etc. values. Thus 1 KHz is 1000 cycles per second (cps).

Full duplex simultaneous transmission over a communications channel or series of wires, in both directions.

Function a predefined and specific task, for example, some keys on keyboards have one specific function. They are usually called function keys. A function key could access a ROM (Read Only Memory) which contained a standard item of information which formerly needed to be repetitively keyed in, such as part number or account number. In word processing applications a format description could be held in a ROM associated with a function key.

Fuse a failsafe device inserted into a circuit to fail when the current flowing in the circuit exceeds the desired rate.

Fusible link in one type of Programmable Read Only Memory (PROM) the BIT patterns are destructively formed by fusing links together. This technique uses a heavy current PROM 'blower'. Once blown this PROM is permanently programmed and cannot be erased or altered.
◊ PROM.

G

G^3 Gallium. An abbreviation for gadolinium gallium garnet. This is a form of garnet which can be grown as a crystal and used in the production of bubble memories. Specifically it is used as the non-magnetic substrate. ◊ BUBBLE MEMORY.

Gain the measure of a circuit to increase the magnitude of an input signal. For example in a description of power amplifiers gain is used to denote the ratio of output signal to input signal.

Gantt chart a type of bar chart, used to illustrate the progress of a project or relative values: ◊ BAR CHART.

Gate In a Junction Field Effect Transistor (JFET), the gate, or control gate is the mechanism used to control the width of the transistor's conducting channel. If the gate is closed the transistor acts as a switch in the off position, if the gate is opened, it acts as a switch in the on position.

Contrast this definition to the gate in a logic circuit, see below.

Gates these are effectively a discrete component version of the relay. They are circuits having two or more inputs and one output. They allow a signal to pass (or not) when certain predefined criteria are met. Varieties of gates are based upon the premise that in Boolean algebra (mathematical logic), a proposition is a statement that is either true or untrue, without ambiguity.

See appendix for LOGIC CIRCUITS.

General purpose a computing system that is not designed for a specific type of work but can be applied to a whole range of tasks is termed a general purpose data processing system.

Generator any mechanism that converts mechanical movement or energy into electrical energy.

Germanium (Ge) a material which, like Gallium and Silicon, is used as a substrate, in its crystal form, for semiconductor fabrication.

Giga a term implying a 'gigantic' value. In the United States and France this prefix denotes one thousand million, i.e. 1,000,000,000 or 10^9. In Great Britain this prefix means one million million i.e. 1,000,000,000,000 or 10^{12}.

GIGO Garbage In Garbage Out. A computer slang term abbreviating the practical reminder that if a system receives bad, inaccurate or incomplete information the output will have similar deficiencies.

Glassy metal a term now being used to describe the wire being produced by rapid refrigeration of exotic alloys. It is anticipated that 'glassy metals' will be used as superconductors since the singular method used for manufacturing the material virtually eliminates its electrical resistance.

Glitch an expressive American term for bug or gremlin.

GO-TO a software term or programming instruction. To 'go-to' an address causes the next instruction to be fetched from that address.

Grain the crystals which constitute a metal or alloy tend to align themselves along their axis. The term grain is used synonymously with crystal. Grain size and alignment depends upon the method of finishing or heat treatment used to purify the metal or to reach the desired metallurgical and surface hardness specification. Grains can become enlarged by absorbing other grains under certain temperature conditions. ⇨ GLASSY METAL, SILICON.

Graphics display a special video display unit used to display two or three dimensional images in outline form. Coloured graphics displays are now quite common. Typically used in the area of industrial design, Computer Aided Design (CAD), and Computer Aided Manufacturing (CAM).

Graticule one of the optical measuring scales used in connection with design and layout of integrated circuits.

Ground a term used in the United States as a synonym for the term used in Great Britain for electrical earth. ⇨ EARTH.

H

H ◊ HENRYS.

Half-adder a circuit using binary signals, having two inputs and two outputs.

Half byte 4 bits or binary digits. Some programming languages make it possible to address a half byte of memory. In this case it means that the memory may be more efficiently utilised than those machines where a full byte (8 bits) is the smallest module of memory which a programming language can address.

Half-duplex alternate transmission over a communications channel, in both directions. ◊ FULL DUPLEX.

Hall effect a phenomenon which takes place when a conductor is placed in a magnetic field where that conductor is perpendicular to the magnetic field and current. This effect is exploited by, for example, proximity switches. In operation the proximity switch creates its own magnetic field which is affected by bodies passing through it. The alteration to the magnetic field can be observed and measured.

HALT a condition that interrupts the normal RUN mode of a processor, enabling only certain very specific commands to be entered via the system console.

Handshake receive and transmit signals. A synchronous process can more easily pass data if two or more handshake signals are provided. Typically the transmitter requests attention, and the receiver acknowledges completion. It is used to synchronise data transmission systems. In practice it enables a receiving device to tell a transmitting device that it has received data.

Hard copy printed or graphical output produced on paper by a computer system.

Hard disk a hard disk has much greater storage capacity than a floppy disk, the actual capacity depending upon the manufacturer and the specific design of disk drive and read/write head. The disk itself is made from a rigid alloy plate and coated with mylar, a magnetisable compound. ◊ DISK, FLOPPY DISK.

Hardware the individual components, i.e. mechanical, electro-mechanical, magnetic and electronic devices that comprise any computer system. ◊ FIRMWARE and SOFTWARE.

Hardwired logic systems built up with transistors and integrated circuits requiring wired connections, where the interconnecting pattern determines the operation. Compare to systems implemented in Random Access Memory (RAM) or Read Only Memory (ROM), which can be relatively easily altered, by program changes.

Hash a technique used by programmers to check that accumulated totals are accurate. Hash totals are often a system-generated approximate sub total to give an order of magnitude that will easily validate values in a register or accumulator.

Hazardous environment an environment where physical danger exists. An environment where failure to meet laid down safety criteria could result in damage or even danger to human life. Met in conditions of radioactivity, high/low temperatures, explosion risk, etc.

Header data information printed at the start of a run to identify the program and data being used, file generation, date and so on.

Heat Sinks the generic term for any device, method or material which can be used to dissipate unwanted heat from an electric circuit, or any other source of heat.

Henrys (H) a measure of the inductance present in a circuit or produced by individual components such as coils. The SI unit of inductance. ◊ INDUCTANCE.

Hertz (Hz) The SI Unit of frequency; the count of cyclical phenomena occurring each second. It replaces the old cps or cycles per second unit of measure. ◊ CPS, CYCLE, FREQUENCY.

Heuristic a programming technique to enable a system to gradually create an optimum value for a specific variable by means of learning from previous operations. A technique used in programming cybernetic or artificial intelligence systems. ◊ STOCHASTIC.

Hexadecimal a system of numbers and letters using 16 as a base. It uses the characters 0 to 9 and A to F and is interchangeable with binary. The system is easier to use and remember than binary. It can offer more efficient use of memory.

Decimal	Binary	Hexadecimal
0	0	0
1	0001	1
2	0010	2
3	0011	3
4	0100	4
5	0101	5
6	0110	6
7	0111	7
8	1000	8
9	1001	9
10	1010	A
11	1011	B
12	1100	C
13	1101	D
14	1110	E
15	1111	F

See appendix for CODES

Hi (High) where there are two or more BITS, or BYTES, used for software addressing purposes, the address numbers go from Lo (Low) to Hi (High). They may be directly addressed as Lo or Hi.

High level language a computer language which is easy to understand and use, but which requires extensive translation (compiling) into machine code before it can be used by a computer system. The general aim of high level languages is to offer English-like instructions. Thus programmers who do not have ASSEMBLY LANGUAGE experience can still be productive fairly quickly since high level languages are easy to learn. However, they are inefficient in use of memory compared to assembly or machine level languages. In microcomputers therefore, many high level languages are in fact a sub-set of the original. Examples of high level languages are: COBOL, FORTRAN, BASIC and PL/1.

High threshold METAL OXIDE SEMICONDUCTOR (MOS) logic which switches at 4V to 5V; not directly TTL compatible.

Hobbyist someone who uses a home computer for pleasure and not for a profession.

Hollerith code named after Dr. Herman Hollerith who invented a punch card code in 1891 in order to reduce the data analysis task of the American census. The census took place every 10 years; in 1891 he calculated that it would take 20 years effort to analyse the results of one 10 year census. He therefore devised a punch card code, based on Jacquard's much earlier principles used in conjunction with weaving looms. Hollerith also designed machines to punch and interpret the code, to sort, collate and calculate. This generation of machines, sometimes called unit record, i.e. one record per card, was later taken up by commercial companies including IBM, NCR, Remington, Power Samas and many others.

The code comprises up to twelve vertical positions, from top to bottom representing 0 to 12. Depending upon manufacturer the card then had from 40 to 80 horizontal rows.

A combination of zero punched holes to three punched holes in any column could then represent anything from absence of data (blank) to full numeric and alphabetic codes together with a range of special characters.

Home brew the type of computer used by a hobbyist. Synonymous with Home computer.

Home computer also known as hobbyist or 'home brew' computers. Cheap, limited facility, programmable microcomputers. Designed for use in the smaller business or the home. Designed to a price level, they are useful tools for an introduction to the microcomputer as an office or laboratory based problem solving aid.

Hostile environment synonymous with 'hazardous environment'. In practice there are some differences in performance standards and requirements. The usage of the term 'hostile' emphasises physical discomfort.

Hot start a system restart following a very brief period of inactivity. Virtually an immediate restart.

House keeping part of file and program maintenance where fields are reset to zero in programs and copies of files are created. The tasks that are important to the smooth running of an installation but are not directly productive.

Housing a case, box, cabinet, etc. which contains an electronic product or chassis.

Hybrid a small electronic module in which passive elements and circuits are fabricated onto a substrate to which the active devices (for example, transistors) may be added, usually in chip form. A mixture of TTL and SOLID STATE technologies.

Hybrid computer a mixture of analog and digital technologies and principles.

Hz ⇨ HERTZ.

I

IBM International Business Machines Corporation. One of the major forces in the computing industry ever since its inception. During the 1970s the term IBM become synonymous with computing systems through the medium of novels and films.

ic ◊ INTEGRATED CIRCUIT.

IEE abbreviation for the Institution of Electrical Engineers. IEE are the British professional body responsible for educational and industrial standards.

IEEE abbreviation for the Institution of Electrical and Electronics Engineers Inc; an American body widely concerned with the definition of standards.

I^{2}L ◊ INTEGRATED INJECTION LOGIC.

Illegal (address, character) a dramatic term used by programmers to describe data or parameters that are unacceptable to the program being run.

Immediate, immediate data constants which are included as an extension to the 'immediate' class of instruction. This avoids additional memory accesses since data defined in this way is immediately available to the program.

Impedance (Z) a measure of the total effective resistance or individual resistance in a circuit when the current flow is alternating (AC).

Impurities foreign bodies deliberately introduced into semiconductors to produce a desired performance. Such impurities deliberately introduced are called dopants. ◊ DOPANTS, DIFFUSION.

In circuit emulation a phrase attributed to Intel, a leading semiconductor fabricator; equivalents are available from other manufacturers. It refers to the ability to plug a prototype into a development system in order to simulate the real life environment. Thereafter the development system tests the prototype thus enabling laboratory simulation of the working environment to take place.

In-house describing facilities and expertise within an organisation.

Incident light natural light. ◊ PHOTORECEIVERS.

Increment generally the software descriptions of the operation of the STACK POINTER in a central processing unit. When a BYTE of information is removed from the stack the stack pointer is incremented (moved up) one place and when a byte of information is put into the stack the stack pointer is decremented (moved down) one place. More generally means adding to in very small values. ◊ DECREMENT.

Indexed addressing this addressing method enables the programmer to address any location in memory through the use of the pointer register and displacement (system or programming language facilities which keep track of data). The contents of the index register are not modified by indexed addressing. This method of addressing enables the computer to allocate storage in a random fashion thus making good use of all available space.

Indicator a device to draw attention to a specific condition. Could be an LED, flashing light, or asterisks on a report or on a video display unit.

Indirect in the indirect mode, an address is used to point to data which is in turn the address of the required data. This refers to any level of addressing other than the immediate direct method. Indexed addressing is a form of indirect addressing.

Indirect Addressing ◊ ADDRESS.

Inductance the measure of energy stored in a magnetic field, which is set up by an electric current. The unit of measure of inductance is the Henry (H).

Inductor a device which creates inductance, typically a coil of wire wound around an iron core. ◊ INDUCTANCE.

Industry marketing the practice of developing a product for a single, specific industry or industrial or commercial sector, and then marketing that product exclusively to the sector for which it has been developed. For example, a company might develop a computer system especially for newspaper production; this would be regarded as Industry marketing. The term vertical integration is synonymous with Industry marketing.

Inferiors used in mathematics and the physical sciences to denote an iota or qualifying letter or numeral. The character is written slightly below the main script. Synonymous with subscript.

Inherently safe any product which complies with the requirements which surround hazardous or hostile environments and can be expected not to cause fire or explosions, even under extreme circumstances, is termed inherently safe.

Inhibit to prevent a system from reacting in a certain manner to certain conditions. For example, it is possible to inhibit certain programs from accessing nominated files or memory arrays. It is also possible to inhibit anyone but an authorised person accessing privileged data.

Initialise the process of setting all memory and counters, timers, etc., to zero or start values. This is the normal commencement routine for a program and minimally involves clearing registers.

Ink jet a technology used in computer printers, where small jets impel ink onto the paper. The character which is created is made up of dots of ink. The dots themselves are contained in an array, or matrix, and can be individually switched on and off under program control to form a complete character.

Input the signals that are given to a computer for processing. Input devices are the means and media to transmit those signals to the computer, more specifically to the central processing unit.

Input/output/(I/O) Ports connections to the internal BUS system of the central processing unit to interface the computer to other modules and peripherals.

Instruction a binary word which is interpreted by the central processing unit instruction decoder as a command to carry out specific tasks. A program is made up of instructions.

Instruction decoder an array of logic gates or circuits or a small Read Only Memory internal to the central processing unit. Used to interpret instructions fetched from memory.

Instruction register a register within the central processing unit which is used to hold instructions fetched from memory.

Instruction set the total set of unique instructions which can be executed by a given computer system, to provide basic information necessary to assemble a program. Every programming language has its own instruction set. Instruction sets from different computers may appear identical but will work in a slightly different fashion to each other.

Instrumentation devices for measuring, recording and controlling physical properties and movements. The application of instrumentation devices. ◊ TRANSDUCER.

Insulation the condition created by surrounding a conductor with insulation (or non-conducting) material so that current is limited to a known path. Insulating material is a non-conductive substance.

Integer a whole number.

Integrated circuit (IC or ic) a semiconductor device containing circuit elements which are fabricated from a single piece of material (e.g. silicon) directly connected to perform a unique given function.

Integrated Injection Logic (I^2L) logic circuitry in which the speed of operation has a linear relationship with the current consumed. A very compact circuit offering high speed operation.

Integration refers to the density of packaging of active elements, for example gates, on a single chip. ◊ SSI, LSI, MSI, VLSI.

Intelligent device a device (for example a terminal) which contains sufficient logic to enable it to be programmed independently of the host computer, to which it may be connected. In practice most computer peripherals now have independent intelligence. Spreading intelligence around in this fashion means that the more complex and elaborate programs which used to be necessary to enable a central computer to run a network of terminals can be broken down into smaller, more manageable programs. Many of these smaller programs can be loaded into intelligent devices to control their specific tasks. ◊ DISTRIBUTED INTELLIGENCE.

Interactive the term given to a device (or system), usually a terminal, which communicates directly with a program in the computer to change values and display the results immediately.

Interchangeable parts the standards set up by international bodies such as IEEE define the measurements and performance criteria of interfaces and devices such that replacement parts may be ordered and fitted with confidence that they will perform as well as the original.

Charles Babbage may have been the first person, through his machine shop foreman (Whitworth), to encounter the need for machine made interchangeable parts when he first built his Difference Engine.

Interface a common boundary between adjacent systems to

enable them to interact. RS232C defines the EIA standard on interfaces. It specifies the preferred plug types, numbers of pins and signals levels which will allow two different manufacturers' products to perform satisfactorily in the same system.

Interlock describing the enabling of one device which automatically inhibits the other, where two devices are operating in concert.

Intermittent a phenomenon which can be observed or experienced with no apparent pattern of occurrence, generally described as random. Intermittent faults on electronic or computer systems are the worst to diagnose since it is not possible to predict when they will reoccur. Often the only way to be sure of curing such a fault is replacement of the whole printed circuit board, or assembly.

International Business Machines ◊ IBM.

International System (SI) an international system of standards that express all units in metre/kilogram/second multiples (MKS).

International Telegraph and Telephone Consultative Committee ◊ CCITT.

Interpolate the reverse of extrapolate. Deducing a result or point on a graph based on readings on either side or immediately before and after the result to be obtained.

Interpreter a program which translates an interpretive-language source program into machine code and executes it immediately, i.e. one line at a time. This contrasts to a COMPILER which produces object code for the whole program before execution.

Interrogate the act of enquiring into the contents of a computer file or program. Involves the use of special enquiry-type languages or programs, e.g. APL.

Interupt the suspension of a normal programming routine of a computer to carry out a specific and immediate task. The computer then transfers control to an interrupt handling program which after execution, returns control to the interrupted program.

Interrupt mask a technique that allows the program to define whether interrupt requests will be accepted. ◊ ENABLE.

Interval timer synonymous with REAL TIME CLOCK.

Inverter a device or signal that converts a signal into the reverse signal. A device that converts Direct Current (DC) into Alternating Current (AC).

I/O ⇨ INPUT/OUTPUT.

Ion an atom, molecule or their groupings that contains an electric charge.

Ion Implantation an alternative to DIFFUSION but having the same objective. In this case the surface of the semiconductor base material is bombarded with ions until the correct performance characteristics are determined to have been achieved. Sometimes used in conjunction with the diffusion process.

ISO International Standards Organisation.

Isolation disconnecting a circuit or device from electrical supply.

Iterate to repeat an instruction or function in software a given number of times or until a desired condition is reached. ⇨ LOOPING.

J

Jack an electrical plug and socket assembly used for easy general purpose connection.

JFET Junction Field Effect Transistor. (see p. 54) Synonymous with FET.

Job all of the necessary programs, data and documentation for a complete run of a program.

Josephson Junction the joint or meeting point of a superconductor and an introduced very thin insulator or slice of insulating material. Due to the superconductive properties of the material a current can actually flow across this junction until an external voltage is applied.

Depending upon the value of the insulating layer and the voltage applied either alternating current (AC) or direct current (DC) can tranverse the insulating barrier. ◊ SUPERCONDUCTIVITY.

Josephson memory an array of memory cells constructed from Josephson Junctions. The memory array is held in a magnetic field at conditions close to absolute zero degrees of temperature. In these conditions the presence of a magnetic field destroys the superconductivity effect; its absence restores the effect. The resulting voltage changes can be sensed at each memory cell as data or absence of data, hence binary information. ◊ JOSEPHSON JUNCTION, ABSOLUTE ZERO.

Joystick a control lever or multiple switch which can be rotated through 360°, with mechanical advantage, to make or break a series of electrical connections. Has practical applications where a particular value or performance characteristic has to be reacted to in an interactive mode or in a closed loop, or servo controlled system. For example, driving a vehicle under varying conditions.

Jump an operation used to control the transfer of operations from one location in a program to another location. ◊ BRANCH.

Jumper a direct connection between two points in a printed circuit, points which were not part of the original circuit. Generally used to improvise a change to the circuit. Known as a 'patch' in programming terms.

Junction the boundary between two dissimilar materials or materials having dissimilar properties. For example the point on which positive and negative charge carrying regions meet in a BIPOLAR transistor.

Justify to align the first or last significant digit of a number by shifting the field left or right in memory. ◊ SHIFT.

K

K Kilo. Commonly taken to mean 1000. In fact this is an approximation. To be strictly accurate K is 2^{10}, or 1024. K is used to describe the memory capacity of a computer, e.g. 32 Kb, or 32,000 BYTES of memory. The exact memory size represented by 32 Kb is 32,768 bytes of memory.

Karnaugh map a particular form of truth table, or an array of values which represent the logic states of inputs and outputs for a given logic gate. The table contains only binary values which represent either the false state (logical 0) or the true state (logical 1) for the particular combination of inputs for a specific logic gate. See LOGIC CIRCUITS in the appendix for a fuller description.

Key a button which can be depressed on any peripheral device, most commonly a keyboard. A key can also be a legend in a program or a very important element in a program.

Keyboard the device that forms a part of an input device, as in the case of a video display unit (VDU), or is itself an input device, as in the case of a Teletype Unit (TTY).

Keypunch a machine that converts the depression of keys on a keyboard to punch holes in a punch card or paper tape to represent the appropriate code.

Kilo ⇨ K.

KISS Keep It Simple, Stupid. An exhortation to programmers in particular. The underlaying advice is very relevant. Several small and simple programs are generally easier to write, test and amend than one large, complex program.

L

Label a name for a software constant, a program or a software routine.

Ladder network a simple software language used in conjunction with PROGRAMMABLE LOGIC CONTROLLERS (PLC), PROGRAMMABLE CONTROLLERS (PC) or sequential controllers. It deals with sequencing, timing of events, and duration.

Language a systematic and formally structured means of communicating instructions and data to a computer. Languages may be user oriented 'English like', i.e. high level languages such as COBOL, BASIC and FORTRAN. They may also be much closer to the way the computer works, i.e. low level languages, such as Basic Assembler (BAL).

Large Scale Integration ⇨ LSI.

Laser an acronym for Light Amplification by Stimulated Emission of Radiation. A laser is the source of a narrow and intense beam of radiation. Many different types of laser and laser materials exist; the principle of the laser is that the atoms comprising the laser material change energy levels in response to an external stimulus or electromagnetic radiation, which causes the laser material to emit radiation. The beam produced can be either continuous, or pulsed, depending upon the laser material. Laser materials include gas, ruby and diodes. The beam is visible in the ultraviolet and infrared regions of the spectrum.

Laser printer a printer which employs a laser beam to describe characters on specially sensitised paper. Normally used where the quality of output printing is more important than cost. Especially useful in the printing and graphic arts industries. ⇨ COM.

Latch a single unit of solid-state memory, which does not form part of an ARRAY, is often called a latch. Historically they were called bistable circuits or FLIP-FLOPS. Used to hold a circuit open in position until the circuit needs to change.

Latency the term for an inherent delay in a system caused by the time taken for memory, disk, etc. to respond to a request. Well organised programs aim to reduce latency by a wide variety of sophisticated addressing and timing techniques.

Layout the result of logical flowcharting and planning of input and output documents for a program or system.

LCD Liquid-Crystal Display. A display utilising liquid-crystal technology. It comprises two clear glass wafers, sandwiching between them a liquid crystal solution. The liquid crystal is an organic liquid whose crystals align themselves under the influence of an electric field. Thus a measured charge can cause liquid crystals to align themselves in the form of pre-arranged alphabetic or numeric characters. Liquid crystal is more sensitive to temperature than most display devices. As such it is limited in application to relatively bland environments.

Leads wires used to make connections between circuits, or a power source and circuit. Usually only for temporary use.

Leakage current finding its own path in a circuit rather than following the fabricated circuit. Usually taken to mean current loss.

LED Light Emitting Diodes. Semiconductor devices that create a low level of light; LEDs have a low power consumption and long life and as such are ideal for use as a display. However, in well lit environments or outdoors they can be difficult to see. Thus for outdoor use in particular the choice of display technology can be difficult. ◊ LCD.

Library a central organisation of complete programs written for a particular computer, normally held on disk.

LIFO Last in First out. A method of storing data in a stack or table and retrieving first the last item stored. ◊ FIFO.

Light Emitting Diodes ◊ LED.

Light Emitting Display a display which utilises light emitting diodes.

Light Pen a pencil shaped device containing a photoelectric cell at its tip. Generally used in conjunction with a video display unit having a sensitised screen surface. Touching the display area of specific data on the face of the screen with the tip of the light pen causes the central processor, or intelligent terminal to decipher the address of the data concerned. If keys on the keyboard are depressed at the same time that the light pen identifies the data a transaction can be processed immediately. In practice this can reduce the number of screen handling programs but often slows down the operation of the system, from the operator's standpoint.

Limit Switches an electro-mechanical device used to cut off power to a circuit when tripped. Used to limit travel, or to engage secondary devices or operations.

Limits and fits systems of tolerances of size employed to ensure interchangeability of parts. Many different systems exist, often directed at a particular type of component, e.g. screw threads.

Line a conductor; a line which transmits energy.

Line printer a computer output device in which characters are printed in a horizontal line before the paper carriage moves the paper up to begin printing the next line. The print chain or transport which contains several sets of the characters moves continuously across the paper. The hammers which hit each character against the paper are selected by software. Speeds of line printers can exceed 1,000 lines of printing per minute. Other technologies such as dot matrix, thermal and ink jet all qualify for the description of line printer.

Line transformer a transformer providing a selection of different voltage and current levels by means of tapping the coil at different positions. ⇨ TRANSFORMER, TAPPING.

Linear referring to two variables that have a direct relationship. More specifically in microelectronics it is applied to outputs varying in a direct relationship to an input.

Linear Actuator ⇨ ACTUATOR.

Link a single-bit register used primarily to hold the 'carry' bit during arithmetic operations. Also used to define the channel or circuit which connects other channels or circuits to each other.

Linker Link edit. The software forming part of the operating system which combines together all subroutines, programs and routines from library, utilities and so on to form a single cohesive program for a specific task. In this way numerous small programs can be linked together to produce a larger and more sophisticated program.

Liquid Crystal Display ⇨ LCD.

Listing a computer print out.

Listing paper standard computer paper, lined for print alignment, sprocket punched for drive.

Literal a value in a computer program whose name describes it literally; e.g. the constant named ONE could also have a value of 1.

Lo Low. ◊ HI: HIGH.

Load to load is to 'copy the contents of'. Synonymous with move. When used in a hardware context, 'load' has its usual electrical meaning. Load and Go means to load a source program and have it immediately translated in machine code and then run, without any intervention.

Load life the time, normally in hours, which a device may operate to pre-defined specifications. These specifications pertain to output characteristics, levels of performance and specific power dissipation.

Lock out generally used in software. A software device for inhibiting a particular operation or preventing access if pre-defined limits have been exceeded.

Log all data pertinent to a minute by minute diary of a system's activities is recorded on a console printer. The print out is referred to as the log. Such information as program name, start and stop times, peripheral identification and halt/fault data is recorded.

Logic the mathematical treatment of formal logic in which a system of symbols is used to represent quantities and relationships (e.g. AND, OR). In applications software it is more generally taken to mean the rules applying to a particular program.

Logic analyser a piece of equipment which can store digital signals from all inputs or from a protoype device it is testing. These signals can be displayed for analysis which enables hardware and software debugging to take place on the same device. ◊ DEVELOPMENT SYSTEM.

Logic card a basic element of a hardware system where the relevant components and circuits are contained on a single printed circuit board, or card. The pcb is mounted in a rack as one of a number of cards which comprise the whole system. Separation of logic in this way facilitates fault finding and correction.

Logic drawings (diagram) a diagrammatic representation of mathematical logic. Used to lay out logic gates on paper before circuit diagrams are drawn. ◊ LOGIC CIRCUITS in appendix for examples.

Logic element a circuit consisting of a gate, or a flip-flop circuit.

Logical circuit a circuit consisting of interconnected gates or circuits. A switching circuit.

Logical one: logical zero in binary notation logical one is taken to mean a logical statement is 'true', logical zero to mean 'false'.

Look ahead a feature of software or of a central processing unit in which a program is scanned for priority tasks. In this way it is possible to override an interrupt request until it is convenient to accept it.

Looping a repetition of instructions until a final condition is determined. Sometimes the word is used interchangeably with iteration.

Low level language a programming language that is very close to the way that the computer actually works. Machine level language and object code (binary codes) are the lowest level languages. The normal usable low level language is Basic Assembler (BAL). The use of such low level language generally ensures a more efficient use of memory than with higher level languages but also requires a more skilled or more highly trained programmer to use the language.

Low threshold TTL compatible MOS logic which switches at 2 V to 3V.

LSI Large-scale integration. This term is generally applied to integrated circuits containing from 100 to 5000 logic gates or 1000 to 16,000 memory bits. Like many definitions of size or quantity in computers and electronics the usage of the term is imprecise. Different fabricators have their own, differing definitions but this is the generally accepted version.

M

Machine address synonymous with ABSOLUTE ADDRESS.

Machine cycle the minimum length of time in which a repetitive operation may be performed. In practice this minimum time is not regularly achieved since the operating conditions vary so much. It is actually the time to perform a predefined operation under laboratory conditions.

Machine language (code) a binary code, the only language that is understood by a computer. All other programming languages must be translated into binary code before processing. Output can be in binary form or can be decoded back into the original language. All computers have their own machine, or machine level, language.

Machine readable media that a computer is capable of interpreting as input. For example, tapes, cards and disks are the well-known machine readable media. OCR (Optical Character Readers) OMR (Optical Mark Readers) and a variety of other media are expanding the range of machine readable media.

Macro a group of program instructions used tor a fixed, repetitive purpose. It has less function than a subroutine but is more powerful than a single instruction.

Magnetic disk circular platters coated with magnetic material to facilitate data recording. Data is written as tracks around logical 'cylinders' on the disk. There are a variety of technologies utilised in magnetic disk recording but the majority employ rotating disks with a read/write head for every surface, moving in and out on a fixed axis. Generally a small number of outer cylinders are used for addressing purposes.

Magnetic flux the measurement of the magnetic field strength through a given area, surrounding a magnet or conductor.

Magnetic tape flexible, standard width, acetate tape coated with magnetic powder. Numerous magnetic codes, all binary based, are used for data recording and error checking. In order to ensure interchangeability of tapes the bps, or bits per inch capacity of the tape drives have to be compatible.

Mainframe computer the generic term given to the earliest computers produced by IBM and other large manufacturers. Initially punch card input machines they all require extensive and sophisticated operating systems to enable economic use, or shared use of the computer. The term has now lost its meaning since the advent of minicomputers.

Mains the plumbed-in power source, distributed nationally. Different countries have different standards. The US distributes 110 V at 60 Hz. The UK 240 V at 50 Hz.

Make to close, or complete, a circuit by means of contacts, switches, circuit breakers, etc.

Mask a photographic plate on which is printed the INTEGRATED CIRCUIT pattern required for a single step of the silicon wafer fabrication process. Mask also refers to a programming technique to enable individual bits to be addressed and manipulated. This technique involves a process of reading a WORD or a BYTE and then ignoring all bits except the particular bit under investigation.

Mass storage the generic term for large scale, bulk, magnetic storage. Drums or the newer disk systems can now store up to 1 billion bytes.

Mathematical operation the performance of a combination of arithmetic tasks by a computer, under program control.

Matrix figures or characters, organised as a tabular array. A DOT MATRIX array is used for printing and CRT display purposes.

Media the name for the basic consumable items on which data is recorded, e.g. card, paper tape, magnetic tape, etc.

Medium-scale Integration (MSI) a term generally applied to integrated circuits containing from 20 to 100 logic gates or less than 1000 memory bits. ◊ LSI, VLSI, SSI.

Mega (M) Meaning times 1,000,000 (10^6), as in megabit or megabyte. To be accurate the term means 1,048,576 or 2^{20} in binary terms.

Memory that part of the computer system into which information can be recorded and held for future use. Storage and memory (and core) are interchangeable expressions. Memory will only accept and hold binary numbers.

Memory address register (MAR) the register in the central processing unit which holds the address of memory being used.

Memory addressing modes the means by which memory is addressed, such as direct, indirect, indexed, relative and sequential.

Memory dump a listing of all or part of the contents of memory or any storage device. Under program control quite detailed selections of memory to be dumped may be achieved.

Memory mapping input/output hardware, addressed as if it were computer memory, is termed 'memory mapped'.

A different use of the same term refers to a map showing addresses and contents of memory, to aid efficient use of memory by programmers. ◊ ADDRESSING, COMMON DATA BASE.

Memory protect a technique which prevents contents of memory from being overwritten by other data or programs.

Merge the insertion of data in the correct sequence into a file of data which already exists. Merging can be performed as a separate operation after sorting the input data prior to updating a file, or can be done in a real time mode, one record at a time, in no particular sequence.

Metal Oxide Semiconductor (MOS/MOSFET) a specific semiconductor technology in which the gate electrode is a metal, silicon oxide an insulating barrier, and carrier doped regions in a silicon substrate become the drain and source electrodes. MOS is a Field Effect Transistor (FET) having a high input resistance. Types of MOS include: p-channel MOS (pMOS or PMOS); n-channel MOS (nMOS or NMOS). ◊ CMOS, VMOS.

Micro (μ) Meaning divided by 1,000,000 (1/1,000,000th or 10^{-6}).

Microcode internal computer code which is not usable by a programmer. Contained in ROM, microcode is very detailed logic which controls the decoding of individual program instructions. Synonymous with Microinstruction. ◊ MICRO-PROGRAM.

Microcomputer a microcomputer is a collection of devices that includes a microprocessor, memory and associated interface circuits to communicate with peripheral devices or other circuits.

Microcomputer analyser a device that is able to record and display on a VDU contents of memory, with location, in HEXADECIMAL CODE.

Microinstruction ◊ MICROCODE.

Microelectronic devices the generic term for electronic components or circuits made to very small dimensions. The density of packaging of certain microelectronics devices, such as memory and logic gates is defined by specific terms. ◊ DENSITY.

Micron (μ). note identical symbol to micro. A Micron is 1/1,000,000 metre or 10^{-6} metre. Can also be known as a micrometre.

Microprocessor the microprocessor is a central processing unit fabricated on a chip. It comprises, in general, an arithmetic and logic unit, control block and register array.

Microprocessor development systems ◊ DEVELOPMENT SYSTEMS.

Microprogram a program created from microcode. Used to write the instruction set of a particular programming language.

Microwave an electromagnetic wave which covers the frequencies between EHF (Extremely High Frequency) and VHF (Very High Frequency). Used for high speed data transmission.

Milestone ◊ SENTINEL.

Mill Babbage's term for the arithmetic unit in his design for an Analytical Engine, the first computer.

Milli (m) meaning divided by 1000 (1/1000th or 10^{-3}).

Minicomputer the distinctions between mini and mainframe have blurred with the acceleration in the development of new technologies. A mini is generally called a mini because its manufacturer calls it a mini. The differences between mini and micro are much more obvious because of size and, as yet, a limit on speed and performance of the micro; but with dramatically lower prices than a mini.

Mips Millions of instructions per second. A comparative processor speed measurement for the most powerful processors.

MKS system the accepted system for measurement and notation, based on the earlier metric version, cgs. MKS stands for Metre-Kilogram-Second.

Mnemonic Code a code designed to assist the programmer's memory. The binary code is assigned groups of letters that imply the definition of the instruction. It is a symbolic language used widely in programming languages, at high and low level.

Mode the state or style in which a machine or program has been set by programs or circuits for a specific task.

Modelling the simulation of events or systems using a computer and a variety of programming techniques. ◊ CYBERNETICS, STOCHASTIC, HEURISTIC.

Modem an acronym derived from MOdulation/DEModulation device. It enables computers or peripherals to communicate via telephone lines, or special dedicated data lines, by translating binary data signals to voice signals which can be carried over a telephone line, and then retranslating them to data signals at the other end of the line.

Module refers to a program component or system component that is discrete and can be separately identified and addressed.

Molecule a grouping of atoms for a particular material which is the smallest part of that material which can exist without loss of identity.

Monitor a commonly used term for the Cathode Ray Tube (CRT). Elements of some operating systems contain a monitor or executive suite of control programs.

Monolithic a system which is completely contained on one chip or substrate.

Move to 'copy the contents of'. Synonymous with load.

MSI ◊ MEDIUM-SCALE INTEGRATION.

MTBF Mean Time Between Failure. The average time, expressed in hundreds or thousands of hours, of the interval between device failures. This figure is used to calculate spares holding and service back up requirements.

MTTR Mean Time To Restore (Repair). The average time taken to bring a device, or system, back up to its normal operating performance level. Used by suppliers and the larger computer users, in conjunction with MTBF figures for maintenance planning and spares provisioning purposes.

Multilayer a sandwich or multiple layer printed circuit board. A device for fitting several boards, their components and connections into a confined space.

Multiplexing a process of transmitting more than one signal at a time over a single channel. A technique used to enable several devices to share a communications channel with a computer system or electronic system.

Multiplicand one half of a simple multiplication, the other being the multiplier.

Multiplier the hardware module which performs multiplication. ◊ MULTIPLICAND.

Multiprocessing the act of processing a number of programs or subroutines, at the same time. Actually the processor schedules tasks and takes them in order to service several users in a time-sharing environment.

Multiprogramming where several programs are being operated simultaneously by a single processor. Different programs are handled in separate partitions (e.g. background and foreground), each partition having different priorities. ◊ BACKGROUND and FOREGROUND.

Multi user a real time computer system, often designated as time-sharing which is established to serve a group of separate and otherwise unconnected users.

Multi-word instruction program instructions which require more than one line or location in the portion of memory occupied by a specific program.

Mylar a tradename for the most commonly used acetate in magnetic tape production and for general insulation purposes.

N

Naked a computer or electronics system composed of printed circuit boards and mounted in a chassis. A 'naked' system does not possess the industrially designed outer casing or customised input/output connections to enable it to appear unique to a particular OEM. The term applies to mini and microcomputer suppliers as well as electronic product and system suppliers.

NAND gate similar to the AND gate but producing an inverted signal. See appendix for LOGIC CIRCUITS.

Nano (n) meaning divided by 1,000,000,000 (1/1,000,000,000th or 10^{-9}). Note in US and French notation this is termed to be one billionth.

NC Numerical Control. An electronic method of controlling the tool movements in machine tools and various associated products, such as graph plotters and electronic design aids. The coordinates at the end of any given tool travel are converted by the program into numerical values. Programs and systems exist to simulate the movements of tools and other moving parts of machine tools in the three basic dimensions, x, y and z, together with combinations which can combine to machine a perfect spheroid shape, if necessary.

Negative feedback degeneration, or the inverse of feedback. ⇨ FEEDBACK.

Neon an inert gas which dispenses a red glow when ionised. Neon lamps are used in many forms of instrumentation as indicators or warning devices.

Nested (Loops and subroutines) software programs that use LOOPS within loops are said to be nested. Subroutines that use other subroutines are said to be nested. The nesting level is the number of times nesting can be repeated.

Network a term meaning an interconnecting series of processors, channels and peripheral devices. Also applied to project planning (PERT), a procedure to illustrate the interconnection and interdependence of tasks within an overall project. ⇨ PERT.

Neutron an elementary particle having zero charge.

Nibble (nybble) one half of a byte or a 4 bit word.

NIH Not Invented Here. A rather caustic acronym describing the attitudes of vested interests to new products or designs; the implication being that since it was not invented here, it is worthless.

nMOS or NMOS n channel MOS. A type of field-effect transistor (FET) structure in which the conducting channel is n-type (negative) semiconductor material. n-channel devices operate at higher speed than p-type (positive) devices. The current actually passes through silicon crystals.

Node one term for the terminal of any branch of a network having more than one branch.

Noise interference; electrical, acoustic or mechanical.

Non-linear a relationship between input and output that exhibits indirect or random characteristics. A polynominal relationship is deemed to be non-linear.

Non-volatile memory a memory which retains its contents even after power has been discontinued. Does not generally apply to semiconductor memory, fusible links and magnetic memories are non-volatile types.

Normalise to take a statistical mean, ignoring mathematical signs, in order to obtain a usable, normal numerical value.

NOT a logic operator. A circuit whose output is high if input is low. An inverter. See appendix for LOGIC CIRCUITS.

npn transistor a junction (or BIPOLAR) transistor fabricated with p-type semi-conductor base between two pieces of n-type semiconductor, the collector and emitter.

Nuclear referring to the massive central portion of an atom, the nucleus.

Nucleus the large central part of an atom.

Null mathematically and geometrically in balance at zero value; in equilibrium.

Numerical Control ⇨ NC.

O

Object program (Code) a source program produces an object program in binary code after it has been translated or assembled. Often referred to as object code, it is the only form in which a computer can read a program.

oc open circuit. A break in the current path or track of a PCB (printed circuit board), causing current leakage.

OCR Optical Character Recognition, or Optical Character Reader. A device which converts special typefaces into digital signals when scanned by the reading head. Can be an on-line device, or an off-line device producing paper tape or other media containing the data. Typefaces which make character identification easier for an optical scanner have been developed by several manufacturers.

Octal a number system constructed around the base 8.

Decimal	Binary	Octal
1	0001	1
2	0010	2
3	0011	3
4	0100	4
5	0101	5
6	0110	6
7	0111	7
8	1000	10
9	1001	11
10	1010	12
11	1011	13
12	1100	14
13	1101	15
14	1110	16
15	1111	17

See appendix for CODES

Odd-parity check (parity check) this is a popular programming technique to establish whether a number is odd or even. The computer adds up all the binary digits in a field (word, character, etc). The result is then compared with an established parity bit for that particular data field, to check whether the number of bits present is odd or even. After comparison the results determines whether the program will allow the contents of that field to be accepted as valid data for further processing by the computer.

OEM Original Equipment Manufacturer. A loosely applied term. It was originally applied to the major computer manufacturers. It is now increasingly being used to describe a company buying equipment, often from several different sources, assembling them into a unique configuration or with a unique function and then selling it on to a user, agent or distributor. The term now implies that the company adopting the description of OEM adds value to equipment before reselling it.

Off-line equipment that can function without necessarily being connected to a computer. For example, a card punch or an optical character reader which produces paper type from scanned input.

Off-line storage data stored in a media not contained in a device connected to the CPU, such as disk cartridges containing data but not loaded onto the disk drive, paper tape, punch cards, etc.

Ohms (Ω) a measure of the RESISTANCE or individual resistances in a circuit when the current flow is direct (DC).

OMR ◊ OPTICAL MARK READER.

On-board (In board) the generic term applied to electronic systems which are installed in moving vehicles, operating independently of mains power.

On-line the term that describes those computer peripherals that need to be connected to a central computer to function. Popularly refers to interactive terminals.

On-line storage the media, e.g. tapes and disks, which store data when connected to the CPU. ◊ AUXILIARY STORAGE.

On-line system a computer system where all input, processing and output is performed simultaneously. For example, an enquiry may be input through a terminal and the resultant data immediately displayed on that terminal, or a print out generated.

Operand the quantity on which a mathematic operation is performed. When two operands are employed, as in addition and subtraction for example, the first is called the source operand and the second is called the destination operand.

Operating Codes (Op code) SOURCE PROGRAM statements which generate machine codes after ASSEMBLY are referred to as operating codes, in particular that part of the source code which implies its function, i.e. describes what it does.

Operating system (OS) the main supervisor programs which are resident in memory and provided by the equipment supplier. Operating systems have certain basic functions in common between rival systems, e.g. disk handling, reading, writing and utilities such as disk to print dump, disk to disk write etc. However, the larger the computer the larger are the differences. It is claimed by many observers that the largest portion of computer companies development expenses these days is spent on software in general, and operating systems in particular.

Operation the task performed by a single computer instruction or simple subroutine.

Operational amplifier (op amp) a two stage (or more) amplifier constructed to perform arithmetic functions. Employed widely in analog computers.

Operators characters representing the basic mathematical functions such as +(plus), −(minus).

Optical Character Reader ⇨ OCR.

Optical Isolation a filter which only allows a voltage within specified limits to complete a circuit. Used to protect circuits from external overloads due to SPIKES, DROPOUTS, etc.

Optical Mark Reader (OMR) equipment which utilises marks or identification by special pencils or readable signs in special fields on an input document. Used particularly for creating computer-readable documents for applications which cannot justify an extra key punching operation from clerically created input documents. A rather specialised input method which is tending to be left behind as the cost of hardware declines and labour costs increase.

OR gate a discrete component which requires either (but not both) of two input signals to generate an output signal. See appendix for LOGIC CIRCUITS.

OS ⇨ OPERATING SYSTEM.

Oscillator a device to generate a periodic variation of electrical current or voltage. When applied to a microprocessor it is usually coupled with a crystal to provide very accurate time intervals for reading operations.

Oscilloscope (Scope) a widely used instrument. It can display an image of signal wave forms, either current or voltage, plotted against time.

Output the results of a computer program or run, in the form of any of the normally used computer media, e.g. printed output, output on disk, magnetic tape, punch card, paper tape or displayed output on a VDU.

Over specify to ask for, or define, an ideal system rather than a system capable of performing a specific task and no more. Over-specifying is a common occurence, especially by people or organisations specifying equipment for the first time.

Overlay the process of segmenting a program and calling segments into main memory as required. It is used to obtain efficient use of memory or to make memory process a program that is too large to fit into memory all at once. ◊ VIRTUAL MEMORY.

Overload the condition caused by loading an electrical component or device above its rated loading value. The amount of tolerance to overload is known as the overload capacity.

Oxidation the process of turning the surface of a silicon chip to silicon dioxide (silica). In this case the silicon dioxide is used as a barrier or insulator to the diffusion of the selected impurities used to create the various MOS devices. ◊ MOS (Metal Oxide Semiconductor).

P

Pack the process of combining data together into one location in order to save memory and speed up processing. Can be achieved by overwriting insignificant zeros contained before the significant digits in memory.

Package application package. A series of generalised programs written to perform well defined functions, e.g. payroll, accounting, etc. They are constructed in such a manner that the input and output format may be changed to suit an individual client's requirements. Also there may be options within the logic of the processing programs that allow alternate methods of calculation to be chosen. By the use of packages it is possible to share development costs between a number of users, even though the package may impose certain restrictions on the user.

Packaging the outer casing or package which surrounds an electronic device. Refers more particularly to the plastic insulating package which surrounds an integrated circuit, leaving only the connection pins exposed. ◊ CHIP.

Page a segment or block of contiguous memory which can be addressed by special means or by a specific field containing a complete address value. Used in overlaying and virtual memory control systems. ◊ VIRTUAL MEMORY.

Page printer a computer output device in which the output for a whole page of computer printing is accumulated either in the computer's main memory or in the printer's own buffer memory and then simultaneously released to drive the printer mechanism. The fastest computer output is achieved in this manner. Although very costly by comparison with other printer types it can achieve speeds in excess of 12,000 lines of print per minute.

Panel the precursor to the printed circuit board, it contained valves and accumulators and similar technology components. Also refers to an inspection hatch of a computer or electronic system and the central controlling console of an electronic system.

Paper tape similar to punch cards although the medium is a continuous reel of paper in this case. Uses a variety of different punch hole codes, from 5 channel (rows of holes) to 9 channel.

Parallel communications synonymous with PARALLEL OPERATION.

Parallel operation actioning all the digits of a word simultaneously by transmitting each one on a separate channel or bus-line. The technique is faster than serial or sequential operation but requires more equipment to control the process.

Parallel processing ◊ PARALLEL OPERATIONS. ◊ ANALOG COMPUTER.

Parallel run (Parallel running) two different systems operated simultaneously in order to verify results. Generally used to validate the output from a newly installed computer system against an older and more conventional method of achieving the same results.

Parameter constant or known values or known functions having variable values. The upper and lower figures between which a variable is considered valid.

Parity a single BIT extension to a field or word of binary data. It illustrates whether the field contains an odd or even number of ones (1). It enables a limited amount of editing, error detection and correction to take place. ◊ ODD PARITY CHECK.

Pascal a programming language finding rapidly growing acceptance in the field of industrial process control. To some extent replacing the more conventional languages, like FORTRAN. Pascal is also a unit of measure for force in the SI system.

Pass one complete cycle. In the compiling operation more than one pass may be required to complete a compilation.

Passive (Passive elements) any component or device which does not have more than one function or cannot vary its output is said to be passive. Components used for their main properties of resistance, inductance or capacitance are said to be passive. Components such as transistors which can amplify a signal and also act as a switch, in other words they can change their state, are known as active elements. ◊ ACTIVE ELEMENTS.

Patch a small modification to a computer program is often known as a patch. Used widely as the term denoting improvised modification, to either hardware or software.

Patch board (Patch panel) a device for temporarily modifying circuits or programs.

PC Programmable Controller. An electronics or microprocessor device used to control the sequence and duration of repetitive operations, for example, in automatic machine tools and domestic appliances. Earlier versions were known as sequential controllers or PLC. ⇨ PROGRAMMABLE LOGIC CONTROLLER.

pcb printed circuit board. The platter or board which contains the circuits and components for a whole system, or part of a system. The raw material is often an insulating layer of phenolic resin coated on one, or both sides, with a conducting film of, for example, copper. Photographic art work is used in a photolithographic process to etch away the unwanted conductive surface, leaving an interconnecting network of conductive paths. Components are then assembled and soldered in the correct position, after drilling the board to facilitate secure loading of components. Printed circuit boards can be loaded on both sides (double sided pcb).

PCM Plug Compatible Manufacturer. The term applied to a computer peripheral manufacturer whose products can replace those of the major systems manufacturer or OEM simply by plugging them in to the system. This implies perfect compatibility of interfaces, plugs, channels, buses, addressing methods and so on. A whole industry of plug-compatibles has grown up since the late 1960's. It has been stimulated by International Standards on interfacing, thus making it easier to simply replace other suppliers' equipment, by economies of scale and because of the pricing policies of some of the larger systems' suppliers. It has also been possible to develop a sizeable industry of special purpose peripheral suppliers, fulfilling needs that could not economically be satisfied by the larger companies.

Peripheral a device in a system which is not part of the central computer but is used for input or output purposes, for example, terminals and printers.

Peripheral (software) driver software which enables programs to control and communicate with peripheral devices.

Peripheral Interface Adaptor ⇨ PIA.

Personal computers (Homebrew) the basic, inexpensive microcomputer systems designed for the hobbyist for his own use in his own home. Inevitably these have been taken up by the small business and laboratory for the less demanding computing tasks. A supporting infra-structure is also beginning to develop such as computer shops, independent software houses, games for use with personal computers, suppliers of media, textbooks and the like. ⇨ HOME COMPUTER.

PERT Project Evaluation Review Technique. A sophisticated project planning and production control computer application package. Developed originally by the US Navy it is particularly appropriate for the planning, monitoring and control of large construction projects, such as bridge building and other major engineering projects.

Phoneme a grouping of signals which operate within the audible sound range. Selected groupings of phonemes can represent or simulate speech. ⇨ VAB (VOICE ANSWER BACK).

Photocurrent a phenomenon which occurs in semiconductors through the effect of incident electromagnetic radiation (incident light). The effect of the light is to free electrons from their normal position which generates current in proportion to the light intensity.

Photodiode a diode making use of photocurrent generated by incident light. Used in photographic applications (light measurement) and various tasks connected with infrared radiation and sound transmission, especially for remote control and light signal detection and measurement.

Photoetch the process of removing the current-carrying surface of a hybrid material used for printed circuits, generally a copper clad phenolic resin. ⇨ PHOTOLITHOGRAPHY.

Photolithography the process which is used to create printed circuits and various semiconductors and integrated circuits. Involves the use of photographic circuit masters (art work) and a version of chemical etching. ⇨ PCB.

Photomask a photographic plate which contains photographic images of circuits to be fabricated on a wafer of silicon (an integrated circuit). A photographic mask through photographic reduction techniques, can hold hundreds of circuit images, to be fabricated on a three or four inch diameter wafer.

Photoreceiver the materials and devices which convert light signals into current and voltage signals.

Photoresist a photosensitive material which forms a barrier when exposed to light. Thus, when a circuit is exposed onto a base material in the photolithographic process the negative photoresist resists the action of the photoetch process; the positive photoresist aids the photoetch process, thus a cohesive circuit remains on an insulating base at the completion of the photolithography process.

Phototransistor a transistor operating on photocurrent. Used in punch card and paper tape readers and photoelectric (optical) isolation devices.

Photovoltaic cell a cell in which voltage generated by incident light causes current to flow in an external circuit. Solar cells utilise this phenomenon.

PIA Peripheral Interface Adaptor. A universal interface for input and output, ensuring that a wide range of standard devices may be directly connected to a microprocessor board. The device handles the necessary intermediate control for harmonising input/output with the microprocessors requirements.

Pick-up (Pick-off) a TRANSDUCER that translates physical movement into a digital electrical signal, for example, a proximity switch.

Pico (p) Meaning divided by 1,000,000,000,000 (1/1,000,000,000,000, or 10^{-12}).

Pin one of the conductive connections to integrated circuits, enabling the chip to be connected into a circuit in position. ⇨ SIP, DIP.

Pin-out the term for a listing which describes the purpose for each pin on an integrated circuit or chip. In a memory chip for example, each pin would represent the input/output channel for a particular block of memory, whose location number would be sequential with the next pin.

Pizoelectric where certain materials such as silicon dioxide are placed under physical stress or strain, an electrical polarisation is created on the face of the material. The polarities are reversed if the stress or strain is reversed. Materials exhibiting this effect have obvious applications in strain gauges and other similar transducers. There are predictable relationships between deformation and field strength, which can be used as the gauging, or transducer element, in a gauge. Materials exhibiting the effect are said to have pizoelectric properties.

PL/1 Programming Language/One. Originally an effort to create a universal programming language as a single standard to replace all others. It has not been the universal success that its developers had hoped but it is widely used nevertheless. Various versions now exist including PL/M, a version for a microcomputer.

PLA Programmable Logic Array. An alternative to having either a standard or custom made circuit on a chip. A PLA enables the user to set his own switches and make his own circuits by selecting those he wants from a standard 'kit of parts' on a board. Can be a prerequisite to having a custom or special chip fabricated; a sort of BREADBOARD chip. Synonymous with ULA (Uncommitted Logic Array).

PLC ⇨ PROGRAMMABLE LOGIC CONTROLLER.

Plotter a full graphics (linedrawing) plotter or graph plotter. Converts analog signals from the computer into a graphical form on a special purpose printer.

Plugboard synonymous with PATCHBOARD.

Plug Compatible Manufacturer ⇨ PCM.

pMOS or PMOS p-channel MOS. A semiconductor (METAL OXIDE SEMICONDUCTOR) where current does not pass through silicon crystals but through small holes.

Pn junction ⇨ BIPOLAR.

Pointer any device which aids the central processing unit in finding data in memory. An ADDRESS can be regarded as 'pointing' to a particular location, or function.

Pointer register the register which stores memory address pointers.

Poles the two opposite parameters positive and negative, in a circuit, device or component.

Poll the process of a computer scanning each device connected to it in sequence to discover whether any data is waiting to be loaded or whether any messages require a response. Used in large interactive and multi-terminal systems.

Polynominal mathematical relationships that define the rate of change, as opposed to linear relationships which define a curve, or straight lines.

Port terminals which provide electrical access to or from a system or circuit.

Position independent code computer code that need not have a fixed or known location since it is to be found by RELATIVE ADDRESSING, or by a lookup table created by the program in memory.

Post-processor a device or program which orients computer results to a particular product or process. ◊ PROCESSOR.

Pot abbreviation for potentiometer. ◊ POTENTIOMETER.

Potential difference (pd) the difference in electric potential (voltage) measured between two terminals or points in a circuit.

Potentiometer (Pot) a variable resistor, having two or three terminals.

Power the energising force for a system or circuit. Usually refers to voltage.

Power fail detect a hardware technique to identify the absence of power and to store away all the important memory locations and component settings in battery backed up memory. This enables the computer to recognise where it was when power failed and thus to complete its cycle when power is restored. Part of HOT START and WARM START procedures.

Power supply a source of electrical power, either AC or DC, which is appropriate to a given circuit or system. In practice the power available from batteries or mains supply may require preliminary filtering or other treatment before it has reached the desired condition for the circuit under consideration. ◊ SIGNAL CONDITIONING.

Power surge ◊ SPIKE.

Power transformer a device for stepping down mains voltage to a lower, more precise, value. Part of the signal conditioning device in many microelectronics applications.

Preprocessor a conditioning program, used to set parameters for the main processor. ◊ PROCESSOR.

Pressure switch a series of switches designed to make and break contacts under pressure or weight rather than the normal lever action, or toggle switches in common use.

Print out the printed reports produced by a computer system or instrumentation device.

Printed circuit board ◊ PCB.

Printer the most common form of output from a computer system. Technologies of printers include impact, matrix, thermal, ink jet, laser and electrostatic.

Priority parameters which set the level of importance of a routine.

Priority interrupt a technique to ensure that a particular condition giving rise to a request to interrupt the normal running of a program in memory is given ascendancy over other types of interrupts. All interrupts can be assigned a priority level, or parameter.

Probe the sensitive end of a measuring instrument or transducer.

Problem-oriented language a high level language designed for the treatment of a particular task, e.g. COBOL for commercial work, FORTRAN for mathematical and scientific tasks, APL for time sharing and enquiry tasks, etc. Some authorities refer to these as 'procedure oriented languages'.

Processor either the actual hardware of the central processing unit or a language designed for a very specific problem.

A post-processor is a type of editing or conditioning program and is used in such things as numerical control programming languages in order to link the program statements into the physical characteristics of the machine tool for which the program has been written.

Another type of processor (a pre-processor) is an attached hardware processor, i.e. a support processor for the main CPU. Its function is to organise programs into the most efficient form for subsequent processing on the main processor. See also CENTRAL PROCESSING UNIT.

Program assembly of instructions which instruct the processor to perform a particular function. Note the spelling which is the internationally acknowledged standard although 'programme' is still widely used.

Program coding the process of writing down the lines of code or program statements, which comprise a computer program.

Program counter one of the registers in the central processing unit which holds all the addresses necessary to proceed through the program.

Program execution the process of running live data through a program to obtain usable output from a computer system.

Programmable Controller ⇨ PC.

Programmable Logic Array ⇨ PLA.

Programmable Logic Controllers (PLC) a microprocessor or minicomputer system able to accept digital inputs, which can be programmed to output digital outputs in a given sequence with given time delays. They are user programmable, utilising a fairly simple and straightforward programming language. Used in the automation of simple industrial processes, often to replace conventional switchgear or control equipment.

The newer versions of these PLC are almost completely solid state and are being referred to as Programmable Controllers (PC).

The first microprocessor devices were utilised as programmable controllers in such things as domestic appliances. They were used as replacements for conventional wired switches.

Another version of a programmable controller is a Sequential Controller, often using a plug-board to program the sequence of operating and timing delays.

Programmable Read Only Memory ◊ PROM.

Programmer the computer professional who codes problems into the appropriate computer language.

In another sense the term is used to describe the device which loads the binary data into PROM (a PROM 'blower').

Programming language a set of computer instructions organised in a coherent fashion to enable a programmer to fulfil a particular programming task. Languages may be low level (machine oriented) or high level (problem oriented). ◊ LOW LEVEL, LANGUAGE, HIGH LEVEL LANGUAGE, PROBLEM ORIENTED LANGUAGE.

Project Evaluation Review Technique ◊ PERT.

PROM Programmable Read Only Memory. A memory used to hold microprocessing instructions. It is a type of ROM which can be programmed, by the supplier, not the user. There are various technologies available including those that are ineradicable and unalterable, using a fusible link technology. Also available are EAROM, electrically alterable, either in part or whole and electrically programmable using short wave ultra violet rays. Hence the three, partially interchangeable terms: PROM (Programmable Read Only Memory); EPROM (Erasable Programmable Read Only Memory); EAROM (Electrically Alterable Read Only Memory).

PROM programmer the device which loads a PROM with a program. It is normally part of, or connected into, a development system. The program to be loaded into PROM is normally contained on the development systems' floppy disks. Current technology PROM programmers use an ultra violet source for writing the contents of PROM. Earlier programmers used programs contained on paper tape ('truth' tapes or 'personality' tapes) to enable the programmer to fuse links together to form a binary pattern in PROM. This device was often termed a PROM 'blower'. ⇨ PROGRAMMER.

Proposal the sales document presented to a prospective systems purchaser by the aspiring supplier.

Protective relay a device in a circuit used to protect that circuit against overload conditions.

Protocol an agreed set of rules. Serial data transmission must invariably rely on a defined protocol. There are several internationally agreed protocols. ⇨ CCITT.

Proximity switch a device that creates a magnetic field which can be broken by objects passing through it at fairly close range or proximity. It has similar uses to limit switches. ⇨ HALL EFFECT.

PRT Platinum Resistance Thermometer. A solid state method of determining temperature in which a resistor made from platinum registers changes of resistance due to temperature change. The resistance changes are converted by an instrument or computer system. A PRT is more robust than conventional thermometers and more tolerant, accurate and reliable than alternative methods of measuring temperature.

Pulse to energise a circuit digitally, using 'waves' of power such as AC. This contrasts with driving a circuit directly or in analog fashion.

Punch card a medium used for entering data into a computer. Data is represented by punched holes. Combinations of punched holes represent the full alphanumeric range plus a range of special characters.

Q

QC ◊ QUALITY CONTROL.

Quadrant a sector of circular movement, often used to describe the movement of an arm, fixed at a pivot.

Quality Control (QC) the application of inspection principles to determine acceptability. SQC (Statistical Quality Control) uses sampling and statistical techniques to maintain quality standards but avoid the necessity for 100% inspection.

Quantum (quantum jump) commonly used to denote a dramatic increase in an arithmetic value; a large step in a graph. A revolutionary jump rather than an evolutionary movement.

Quartz the crystal used in oscillators, silicon dioxide. The material exhibits the pizoelectric effect. ◊ PIZOELECTRIC.

Queue a stream of data, or mix of data and programs awaiting processing. Queues are not necessarily processed sequentially; they may be actioned selectively.

Queuing theory a study of queues. Uses various statistical analysis methods and the theory of probabilities.

Quiescent a term sometimes used to describe a state of inactivity in a circuit or system.

R

Rack a standard, basic metal enclosure to enable printed circuit boards to be directly mounted into one of a series of slots. There are many commercially available standard racks which facilitate standard mounting of microelectronic products. Racks and packaging can thus be selected from a range which conforms to the environment in which they are expected to operate thereby avoiding the time and expense of designing specials.

Radix the number or symbol for a system of numbering. In the decimal system the radix is 10, in octal 8, in binary 2, in quintal 5, and so on. ◊ BASE NUMBERS.

RAM Random Access Memory. A memory consisting of a variable number of RAM chips providing access to any storage location point by means of horizontal and vertical co-ordinates. Information may be written into or taken from RAM very rapidly, under computer control. RAM may be dynamic, i.e. the contents may have to be regularly rewritten (refreshed), or it may be static, in which case the storage cell is a FLIP-FLOP element, in one or two stable and electrically alterable states.

RAM loader Random Access Memory loader. A program, often a standard provided with the OPERATING SYSTEM, which reads data being entered through an input device and loads it into Random Access Memory (RAM).

Random Access Memory ◊ RAM.

Random logic design a design using separate and discrete logic units to create a circuit or product. An alternative to the more expensive custom-designed large scale integrated circuit (LSI) approach, which needs high volume for economic justification.

Rated voltage the datum, or design level, in voltage terms at which a device should be operated. There are generally safety margins built in and often overload protection techniques are also incorporated but the rated voltage is the key design criterion.

Reactance the combined effect of inductance and capacitance in an AC circuit. ◊ CAPACITANCE, INDUCTANCE.

Read to find and remove data from memory and then to place the data into a memory location where it can be used for comparison or processing purposes. The reading process can either destroy or remove the data, or it can be non-destructive of data. Data can also be rewritten immediately it has been read, in order to preserve it. The techniques depend upon the technology in use, the type of memory (main or peripheral) and the system architecture. The way in which the software is written can also determine whether data is destroyed on reading.

Read Only Memory ◊ ROM.

Read Out any presentation of output data from a computer system. Can be in hard copy (paper, card or tape), displayed on a screen or transmitted in magnetic form. ◊ PRINT OUT.

Read/write head ◊ RECORDING HEAD.

Read/Write Memory a memory or memory device which can be used to write into and read from. ◊ ROM.

Reader the device which acts as a primary input device for computer media, e.g. tape, card, magnetic tape, disk, optical media, etc. The term does not apply to data, or devices, in which information is keyed in directly via a keyboard or a video display unit in an on-line system.

Ready analogous to 'end of countdown'. The point at which all preparatory work has been completed where the computer is ready to receive data.

Real time a much misused term implying that the computer instantly performs the command the user has given and dedicates all of its resources to the completion of that one particular task. In practice the computer, when operating in real time mode, has to satisfy many such instantaneous requests. Thus, there are a wide variety of techniques designed to minimise response time by the computer to any user's request and to ensure a reasonably efficient use of computer resources. It requires a sophisticated operating system and inherently demands compromises by the user since the system must share its time and resources to near optimum levels.

Real time clock the timer device that enables a real time operating system to time and share operations rapidly and accurately. It is also used to provide normal time of day functions to 'time and date stamp' reports. Synonymous with 'Interval timer'.

Record format the design and layout of data or programs, generally relating to information to be held on file. The format must be well thought out since it will need to be regularly accessed for information and updating. A poorly thought out record format will impose a penalty on computer time and storage if it is to be accessed regularly.

Recording head (read/write head) the device employed on disks, floppy disks and magnetic tape drives. It converts electrical variations into magnetic variations and vice versa in order to read or write magnetic information on to a magnetic tape.

Rectifier the family of devices, or techniques, which converts alternating current (AC) into direct current (DC).

Recursive a software routine which is capable of calling and using itself with a nested routine. ◊ LOOPING, NESTED LOOPS AND SUBROUTINES.

Redundancy information in a system or signals in a circuit that are transmitted for verification purposes and are not critical to the function of the system. Thus they could be lost or dissipated without genuine adverse effects.

Reentrant code where a subroutine or program is common to several programs in current use there are two different techniques to ensure that the subroutine is available when needed. The first is to take a copy of it for every program which needs that subroutine and to store it with that program. The second is to form a single copy of reentrant code and locate it in an easily addressable area of memory. This latter technique ensures better utilisation of memory, and generally, faster processing since the programs are smaller. However, it does require a greater flexibility on the part of the OPERATING SYSTEM and programmers.

Refresh the process of rewriting data in memory or on a Cathode Ray Tube where data has to be dynamically restored or regenerated.

Register a register is a memory on a much smaller scale than RAM or ROM. It is used by the computer to store, on a temporary basis, arithmetic, logic or transferral operations.

Regulator a device which maintains voltage or current in a system at the desired value, no matter what the variation might be at the supply level.

Relative address an indirect address which points to the absolute or exact address of the data in question. When called up by the program the relative address is changed to the absolute address.

Relay a switch which operates with contacts made in the 'on' position on contacts open in the 'off' position, under voltage or current control. Preset limits determine the on and off positions. Relays can be used to indicate binary states of logical one and logical zero. Quite complex industrial logic systems are based on this principle.

Relocatable programs which can be located and reloaded anywhere in memory and still perform perfectly adequately.

Remote any location at which a peripheral or user may wish to use a system to which it is not directly connected by cable. In practice 'remote' means anything in excess of 300 metres (1000 feet) although this figure can be trebled if fibre optic cables are used. ◊ RJE.

Remote Job Entry ◊ RJE.

Repeatability the ability to perform the same operation or function to predefined parameters, or the number of times that the operation can be repeated. A comparative figure for instruments and components.

Requirements specification the document drawn up by a potential computer user. It lists all the main aims of the system, the facilities required and every identifiable factor which will influence the choice of system. Suppliers are then invited to tender against this requirements specification. The specification may be preceded by a feasibility study. ◊ FEASIBILITY STUDY.

Rerun the act of repeating a computer run due to a halt part-way through the process, or faulty output. To ensure valid reruns copies of all files, data and programs need to be maintained in the state that existed before the run commenced. Thus as a matter of good housekeeping the first step in a system is normally to take an up-to-date copy of any relevant input and file material. The maintenance of such data, performed on three successive generations of data is commonly referred to as 'grandfather', 'father' and 'son' maintenance.

Reset a facility which enables the microprocessor to be returned to a known state. The program will then start at address zero.

Resistance a material's tendency to resist the free flow of electric current. Resistance varies with physical makeup and environment. Resistance is measured in ohms (Ω).

Resistor a component having a known resistance.

Resonance when a small force creates a high amplitude oscillation it is known as being in a condition of resonance. ◊ DAMPED.

Reticle the photographic master pattern for a photomask, used in the fabrication of integrated circuits. A reticle is normally ten (10) times the size of the circuit to be fabricated.

Return programs, or subroutines, ending with a 'Return' instruction cause the program counter to be restored to the return address.

Reverse (voltage, current) a semiconductor can exhibit a greater resistance to current flow in one direction. Therefore a voltage applied in this direction is known as a reverse voltage, the resulting current as reverse current.

Reverse bias synonymous with REVERSE VOLTAGE.

Rheostat a variable resistor, exhibiting changeable values between known parameters. The changeable values can be physically controlled by an operator.

Ringing a jargon term for a signal exhibiting a damped oscillation wave form where it seeks stability. ◊ DAMPED.

RJE Remote Job Entry. The term given to the process of entering a job or stream of data in a device which is remote from the processor which is to process the data. Examples of use are where a small computer is used in one location for relatively light and uncomplicated tasks, it can also be used as an input device, by means of phone lines, to a much larger computer installation. In this way it is possible to use a small processor for all except the very largest tasks and then to 'buy time' on another processor for the more complex or higher volume work. A RJE device is used only for batch, or for periodic, volume jobs. It is not used for real time, on-line jobs.

Robotics an area of artificial or machine intelligence involving the use of computers, electronics, sensors and mechanical engineering. ◊ ARTIFICIAL INTELLIGENCE.

ROM Read Only Memory. A device containing information which cannot be changed under computer operation. It can only be read by a computer. ◊ EPROM, EAROM, PROM.

ROM bootstrap a small program enabling recreation of main memory if the contents of main memory have been lost or corrupted through program or systems error.

Rotary Potentiometer a version of the potentiometer having three terminals, the middle terminal being also known as a wiper. Since the wiper is able to change its position the resultant resistance measured between any two terminals will vary in relationship to the wiper position.

Rounding the process of abbreviating a numerical value to the most accurate figure within a given field length. Rounding can be an exact cut off, or up or down to different rules and to different numbers of decimal places.

Routine a small program. Can be used by many different programs. Written and stored separately, it can be called or NESTED, into other programs on command.

RPG Report Program Generator. A problem oriented programming language. A high level language, it enforces the discipline of documenting all aspects of the program before the actual program coding begins. It is aimed at the non-computer professional and is occasionally referred to as a program generator.

RS232C an international standard governing the transmittal of data or signals over cables. It applies to serial transmission, i.e. one bit at a time. Numerous international conventions aim to specify similar standards. ◊ CCITT.

Run-time the time taken by a discrete object program to complete its execution. ◊ PROGRAM EXECUTION.

Rugged a term used to describe the requirements of computer or electronics system in hostile or demanding environments. It includes the use of appropriate packaging, power supplies, vibration proofing, flame proofing, water proofing, and other requirements depending upon the precise environment to be encountered by the system.

S

S-100 bus an industry standard BUS meaning that there are 100 connections to circuits in the system available on that bus.

Sampling a technique or circuit in which only some signals or data are read. They can then be interpreted to form a much wider conclusion, based on statistical sampling techniques. ◊ QUALITY CONTROL (QC).

Satellite a preprocessor, or computer which serves another more important computer. Certain configurations are known as attached support processors. ◊ PROCESSOR.

Saturation the maximum capacity of a component, device, circuit or system.

Scaler a device used in counting systems where an output is produced for every predetermined number of inputs, e.g. a binary scaler requires two inputs for on output, a decade scaler ten, and so on. In these cases binary and decade are known as the 'scaling factors'.

Scan the process of continually reading all signals or data, either as presented (in the case of optical character recognition) or automatically on a regular basis, as in the case of a time sharing system in which each terminal is polled in turn. The process may involve converting analog to digital signals or digitising shapes or images. ◊ BAR CODE.

Scanner the device used for scanning purposes. ◊ SCAN.

Scatter the distribution of readings at a single point around the norm of the plot. Used in mathematical techniques like multiple regression analysis and statistical sampling methods.

Schematic a line drawing indicating function, size, main components, inputs and outputs. It is generally used to illustrate concepts, not for production purposes.

Schmitt trigger used in binary logic circuits it involves a BISTABLE circuit from which a binary voltage output level is produced, based on the magnitude of the input level. Thus output can be interpreted as a zero or a one.

Schottky effect a very fast switching diode can be created by substituting a metal barrier in place of a pn junction. The metal/semiconductor contacts acts as the barrier junction. ◊BARRIER EFFECT.

Scratchpad a term applied to a small fast computer memory, such as a register, which temporarily stores information, for example sub-totals which are required to be added together for a final total.

Screen the phosphor coated surface of a Cathode Ray Tube (CRT) in a video display unit or monitor.

Screen handling the software that enables a programmer to display data upon a screen and to tie several screens into a system, all capable of using the same program, inputting data into the same system running the same programs and enquiring on the same data base or files.

Second source an alternative, or one of a number of alternatives, for procurement of a critical component or device. For example, many of the most popular microprocessors are fabricated by second source suppliers, under licence from the original designers and prime suppliers.

Segment a cohesive and discrete part of a program which can be held in memory at one time but can be stored elsewhere separately from other segments of a program if neccessary. Segmenting is used to break up larger programs so that they can be stored conveniently, rather than in one large contiguous block of memory. ◊VIRTUAL MEMORY.

Select where a manufacturing process for discrete elements or sub assemblies produces products with a wide range of output characteristics a special inspection and quality control system is established to grade and select the products by performance. The ratio between price and performance for such selected components is more likely to increase on a geometric scale rather than a linear scale, due to the high proportion of reject devices necessary to produce one device to a satisfactory performance specification.

Selection an automatic process in systems work where, based on certain input parameters, variables may be identified and reported upon. Used in such things as enquiry programming languages where, for example, a user might want to list all occasions where a certain condition has been met or exceeded.

Semiconductor a material such as silicon or germanium in which the electrical conductivity lies between that of conductors and insulators. It also has a crystal structure whose atomic bonds allow the conduction of current by either positive or negative carriers when the appropriate dopants are added, in which the degree of electrical conductivity of the material is especially sensitive. The major categories or semiconductor memories are bipolar, n-channel MOS (nMOS or NMOS) and p-channel MOS, (pMOS or PMOS). ◊ TRANSISTOR, BIPOLAR, nMOS and pMOS.

Sense to read or examine an input to a circuit or system to determine presence or absence of signals or data. Can be applied to comparative values in which case only data falling within predefined limits (parameters) is accepted.

Sensor often a transducer, a device which converts physical data or phenomena into digital or analog signals. The signals are often capable of being read by a computer which in turn may produce an output signal or activate an output device, (an output transducer, for example). Any transducer or sensing element may be regarded as a sensor, often grandly known as sensory perceptors. ◊ TRANSDUCER.

Sensory perceptors ◊ SENSORS, TRANSDUCERS.

Sentinel (Milestone) a marker in a program or in a project management system symbolising a logical break point, or a sub-task completion.

Sequential a program, circuit or system in which the logic dictates that a known or predetermined sequence of events is to be followed, such as numeric, alphabetic, input/output, low/high, etc.

Sequential Controller ◊ PC, PROGRAMMABLE LOGIC CONTROLLERS.

Serial communication (serial input/output) describes the condition in which one bit of data at a time is transmitted over a line. ◊ RS232C.

Serial Input Output ◊ SIO.

Series (circuit) a combination of components connected end to end in a circuit so that current flows along one prescribed path.

Servo system ◊ FEEDBACK.

Shift in arithmetic or multiplication on output, the decimal point is shifted left or right to indicate changes in power.

Short a short circuit.

Shunt parallel connections to a pair of terminals enabling current to follow two routes (or more).

SI Système Internationale. ⇨ INTERNATIONAL SYSTEM.

Sign bit a binary digit (bit) which gives an arithmetic value its algebraic sign when held in binary form.

Signal in brief, any electrical pulse which can be interpreted as information.

Signal conditioning the process of filtering and purifying a signal; of protecting it from power surges and providing the exact signal strength to the circuit or system which requires the signal. ⇨ POWER SUPPLY, POWER TRANSFORMER.

Signal inverter a device for converting Direct Current (DC) into Alternating Current (AC). Another use of the term is for a logic system where a high input signal results in a low input signal, and vice versa.

Silicon (Si) a very common element. In the form of Dioxide (or Silica) it is widely used as a semiconductor material. ⇨ QUARTZ.

Silicon crystal the pure form of Silicon, reduced from Silicon Dioxide. The crystal is grown from the molten Silicon by inserting a perfect single crystal seed and slowly turning and withdrawing it from the melt. When the process is complete the crystal is ground to a standard cylinder size of 3 inches or 100 millimetres diameter. The crystal is then sliced into wafers upon which integrated circuits are fabricated.

Silicon on Sapphire ⇨ SOS.

SIL/SIP Single In Line/ Single In Line Package. Refers to the alignment of connection pins from the plastic or ceramic casing surrounding a chip or integrated circuit in its packaged form. ⇨ DIL/DIP.

Simulate to represent the behaviour of a system or process by a model. The model may be a hardware or a software device. The object is to obtain an evaluation of the behaviour of the system without the time, expense or risk inherent in the operation of the real system or process. For example, space launches may be simulated by a computer in order to test subsidiary systems.

Simulator the term given to the model that simulates something else. In the specific case of the microprocessor it is a special program that simulates the logical operations of another processor, thus enabling programs generated by a CROSS ASSEMBLER to be executed. Useful for validating programs prior to loading them into ROM.

Sine wave the wave form adopted by alternating current, following a known oscillation and amplitude, plotted against time. A sinusoidal curve.

Single board microcomputer the term given to a functioning microcomputer combined on a single printed circuit board. The board contains a central processor, memory, input/output interfaces and various other facilities, depending upon the sophistication of the board's specification.

Sink short for heat sink; a device to absorb unwanted thermal energy.

SIO Serial Input Output interface. A device for accepting serial input and converting to parallel output.

Slash ◊ BACKSLASH.

Small-scale Integration (SSI) a term applied to integrated circuits containing from one to twenty logic gates.

Smoothing a technique to flatten out peaks in a signal or data so that they fall within acceptable parameters.

Soak the process of submitting an electronic device or circuit to a continuous environmental loading. Can be applied to heat or power.

Software programs which can be changed and loaded at will. Software is the language used by the programmer to communicate with the computer. Software programs reside in Random Access Memory (RAM) and are entered from keyboard, paper or magnetic tape, disk or any other peripheral device. ◊ HARDWARE and FIRMWARE.

Software emulation to build a software model of another computer system. In this way programs written for another computer may be evaluated without the expense of buying a separate machine. ◊ MODELLING, SIMULATE.

Software House a computer business that obtains the major part of its income from the sale of software.

Software Instruction ◊ INSTRUCTION.

Software package ◊ APPLICATION PROGRAM.

Soldering the normal method of providing a secure conductive adhesion between a printed circuit board and a chip or component. In production the printed circuit boards are mounted with components, their pins being inserted into holes drilled in the pcb, placed in a fixture and then passed over a fountain of liquid solder to secure them in position. This process is known as flow-soldering; it ensures a good electrical connection and secure attachment to the printed circuit board.

Solenoid a current-carrying coil containing an iron core. A current is passed through the coil, generating a magnetic field which moves the core backwards or forwards. A solenoid is used as a switch. There is no proportional control of the movement of the core thus it can only be used as a binary device, either in the on or off position.

Solid state the areas of physics which deals with materials in their solid form, and having no moving parts. All silicon semiconductors are solid-state devices.

Solvent the liquid used to wash away the etched portion of circuits produced by the photolithography and photoetching process. ◊ PHOTOLITHOGRAPHY.

Sort the generic name for the family of computer programs which can read and rearrange data into a predetermined sequence. Sort programs can be highly specialised and specific to particular tasks. The majority of sorts involve reading and writing data onto peripheral devices, often disks but by no means exclusively. Some data can be held and sorted in memory but only on the largest mainframes is it possible selectively to undertake the efficient core-sort. This implies loading all the data to be sorted directly into memory and completing the sort in memory.

SOS Silicon on Sapphire. The use of sapphire as opposed to silicon as an insulating substrate in METAL OXIDE SEMICONDUCTOR technology (MOS).

Source a semiconductor's electrode. ◊ DRAIN.

Source code (Source program) the original programming statements as they exist in the language that the programmer has used to write the program, i.e. the high or low level programming language. It is generally taken to mean the program as its exists after all error correction and debugging has been completed. It can also include patches where the program has been in use and contains amendments. The source program is then compiled, or assembled, to produce an object program which the computer can then execute. The computer cannot execute a source program; it has to be translated by the use of a compiler, assembler or translator.

Specification the parameters and performance characteristics which accurately define a product, process, component or system. See also REQUIREMENTS SPECIFICATION.

Spike an occasional massive voltage surge which passes through a circuit. If overload protection has not been included in the basic circuit construction a spike could easily destroy a device, hence the need for optical isolation and other overload protection techniques. Power supplies which are capable of producing occasional spikes are sometimes referred to as 'dirty'.

SPOOL an acronym of arguable parentage. One definition is Simultaneous Peripheral Operations OverLap. It refers to one method of improving a multiprogramming computer's operation. For example, input will be organised on reading. It will not be processed but is written onto disk. This is undertaken in the BACKGROUND partition on a low priority. When sufficient FOREGROUND time becomes available processing takes place, output being written onto disk again. When a printer becomes available a disk-to-print program then transfers data from the disk to the printer.

Spooling attempts to optimise the efficient use of a peripheral device and the central processor, and is widely used in large and commercial data processing facilities. Unless a microcomputer has an array of microprocessors as the computing unit it is doubtful whether the speed of any of the microprocessor peripherals, or the processor would benefit from a spooling system – yet!

SQC Statistical Quality Control. ⇨ QC (QUALITY CONTROL), SAMPLING.

SSI ⇨ SMALL SCALE INTEGRATION.

Stable a condition where no unwanted variations of signal occur. A state of equilibrium.

Stack a block of successive memory locations which is accessible from one end, on a LIFO or FIFO basis. Some systems permit many stacks to reside in main memory, only two of them being capable of being used at one time.

Stack addressing ◊ ADDRESSING MODE.

Stack pointer the stack pointer keeps track of storage and retrieval of information in the stack; it is coordinated with the stack.

Stand alone self contained system that exists and performs as an autonomous unit. Many electronic and computer devices operate either in a stand alone mode or as a peripheral device for a larger system, for example, intelligent terminals.

Standardisation nationally and internationally agreed sets of rules for interfacing, dimensions, performance, measurement, limits and fits and interchangeability of parts.

Standby back up equipment or routines that enable a system to keep operating even though an important element may be temporarily out of operation.

Start-stop used in data communications. When transmitting data over a wire a signal is transmitted telling the receiver to receive data. At the end of transmission it sends a signal telling it to stop reading data. Effectively a logical on/off switch.

Statements lines of code in a computer program. The content of the statement depends upon the programming language being used. Generally speaking the high level languages need fewer statements to achieve a working program. ◊ SOURCE CODE.

Static either applied to a state of immobility or to electrical charges being present in a non moving conductor, i.e. static electricity, static discharge.

Static memory Static RAM (Random Access Memory) holds the contents of memory as long as power is being input. Contrast to DYNAMIC MEMORY.

Status codes indicators used to record the state of data in an accumulator, for example, zero, carry, minus and sum.

Step and repeat a software technique, often used to find a precise value or state. A subroutine is used on each value or in equal numeric steps, or in a file or array until it finds the required value.

Step function a mathematical term in which the number or function used has the effect of applying a dramatic increase in the calculated sum. Graphically, where the XY coordinate goes into a vertical line for a period before levelling off. ◊ QUANTUM JUMP.

Step counter used by the ARITHMETIC AND LOGIC UNIT (ALU) to keep track of the iterations or steps in arithmetic operations.

Stepper motor an electric motor in which speed can be regulated by a built-in gearbox. When connected to an external gearbox a proportionally controlled actuator may be constructed. Compare to SOLENOID.

Stochastic a programming term describing a learning process. In this case a discrete software model is created and the eventual totals in accumulaters or registers can be used to form conclusions. This is a random learning technique. It may be used for such tasks as statistical analysis over a wide range of samples. ◊ HEURISTIC.

Stop bit in data transmission, the bit (binary digit) that is used to describe end of character so that the receiving system then inserts an intercharacter space.

Storage a word used synonymously with memory. Is also applied to any medium or device which can store information.

Stored program a computer program retained in memory, as opposed to being held on tape, cards or in a plug-board.

Strain gauge an instrument employing a TRANSDUCER which converts the strain measured at the surface of an object into a digital or analog value, by means of appropriate circuitry and display devices.

String a stream of sequentially organised data.

Strobe (Strobe pulse) a pulse which defines a specific window in time during which data may be transferred to another device or part of the circuit.

Subroutine part of a master routine or program. The object of a BRANCH or jump command. It needs to be returned to its own location in memory after used. ◊ ROUTINE.

Subscript used in mathematics and the physical sciences to denote an iota or qualifying letter or numeral written below the main script. ◊ INFERIORS.

Subset a selection of the full complement of data or the full instruction set of a programming language.

Substrate the material on which a circuit is constructed or fabricated. Can perform insulation, separation and various other secondary functions. ◊ INTEGRATED CIRCUIT.

Sudden death dramatic failure of a component.

Superconductivity the theoretical condition that exists when a conductor is cooled to zero degrees absolute. At this temperature electrical resistance should not exist. Thus the lower the temperature in a circuit the better conductor that circuit becomes. At present a theoretical condition. ◊ JOSEPHSON MEMORY, GLASSY METAL.

Superiors ◊ SUBSCRIPT, INFERIORS.

Superscript Qualifying characters written above the main script. ◊ SUBSCRIPT.

Supersensitive devices that operate under minimal power or stimulae.

Supervisor one of the terms applied to the overall monitoring role of an OPERATING SYSTEM. That part of the operating system which enables an operator to 'talk' to the computer, via a console.

Support the generic term for the additional resources necessary to ensure the smooth and continuous operation of a computer installation. Generally referring to a supplier's staff and facilities, it includes programmers, education, maintenance, spares, etc.

Surge ◊ SPIKE, DROP OUT.

Switch any device, hardware or software which converts a system, device, product, process or program from an 'off' status to an 'on' status, or vice versa.

Switch delay the time taken from instructing a switch to perform its function to the resultant action.

Switching circuit a circuit which facilitates making, breaking or changing connections in a larger circuit. When combined together switching circuits can perform logical operations. See appendix for LOGIC CIRCUITS.

Symbolic name synonymous with LABEL.

Synchronous (sync., in sync) activities that take place in perfectly coordinated timing, often under the control of a clock or timer.

Synchronous transmission communication in which both sender and receiver are simultaneously open and operating in phase, with constant time intervals between messages.

Syntax the grammer or rules of a particular computer language. All languages have strict conventions and many will refuse to compile or assemble a SOURCE LANGUAGE statement that contains misplaced symbols. Remembering that a space is interpreted by the computer as a symbol, if a comma has been omitted and only a space is read, certain compilers will halt due to syntactic error. This type of compiler is known as an intolerant compiler, (often as something much coarser by programmers). Other compilers will continue but list out that statement as having a syntax error, for correction on a subsequent run. The compiler messages are called 'diagnostics'.

Systems analysis the process of analysing the best solution to a problem, either in terms of problem analysis or systems design prior to programming. It can include a clear problem definition, block diagrams of the steps involved in any solution and detailed instructions to programmers on logic, file design and program structure.

Systems design the outline construction of a computer system; a necessary prerequisite to programming.

Systems generation the process of assembling a complex program by locating and positioning all the subroutines, utilities and specially written programs prior to processing data.

Systems House a computer business which assembles computer hardware from various sources and writes unique software to enable that hardware to perform its unique function.

Systems Integrator Synonymous with SYSTEMS HOUSE.

Systems software the basic software tools provided by the supplier. Includes operating system, programming languages, text editors, diagnostic and debugging aids.

Systems test the running of a complete system, hardware, firmware and software, using data where known output and results are already available, for comparative purposes. A necessary state in evaluation before acceptance. ◊ PARALLEL RUN.

T

Table (Decision table) where a point in a program involves making a decision the action to be taken is either written into (embedded) the program logic or it can point to a decision table. This table is a matrix, or array, held in memory at the time of program execution. By referring to a decision table the program compares the conditions that exist, reads out the action to be taken and then inserts that action into the program being executed.

Another use of the same term can be a description of the programming problem during the systems analysis phase.

Tag connectors a range of standard connectors, generally for industrial purposes, which are designed to plug into edge connectors or to make other conveniently positioned electrical connections.

Tandem connecting two outputs from one circuit to two inputs of the next circuit.

Tap (Tapping) a conductor that connects with a point on a coil. Different positions can be selected on a coil to give different tappings, as in the case of a LINE TRANSFORMER.

Tape the media, either paper or magnetic, which is used to store coded information for a computer system.

Tape drive the device which powers and controls the movement of magnetic tape past the read/write head.

Target (machine) the intended (or host) processor for which software is designed.

Task a specific job that a computer or system has to perform. A computer can be dedicated to a particular task (single tasking) or can be shared for several purposes (multi-tasking). These definitions are more usually applied to computers in a process control environment.

TDM Time Division Multiplexing the technique for transmitting different signals over the same line by separating the signals with standard time intervals. Thus several different sources of signal could use a time divided multiplexer to input to a corresponding number of devices over a shared path or communications line.

Terminal a peripheral device to a computer providing input or output capability, or both. Generally applied to interactive devices, such as a video display unit but a more accurate interpretation is any device that terminates any input/output connection. In a specifically electronic sense a terminal is the connection point provided on a printed circuit board, electronic device or on wires and cables.

Test data the known data producing known results that provides the datum for testing a new or changed system. ⇨ SYSTEMS TEST.

Test gear inspection equipment aimed at proving or gauging certain key characteristics for an electronic device, especially where it may be concerned with control over mechanical products.

Test rig an improvised version of test gear, or inspection equipment. Used in the laboratory or the field test environment.

Text editor a program which enables input and correction of the SYNTAX and SOURCE CODE statements without necessarily addressing the logic of the program. A boon to programmers who tend to make more mistakes in inputting a program than in its writing.

Text processing the processing of variable length alphabetic information for the purpose of composition. Includes complex hyphenation rules, text editing, justification, area make up, page make up and many special processes unique to the printing and publishing industry. Output is generally through a typesetter which produces photographic output media, ready for printing. This term applies strictly to text in variable length FIELDS. Data processing is normally, but not exclusively, performed on a fixed field length, mainly numeric data.

Word processing is a subset of text processing, largely applied to the production of letters and standard typed material.

Thermistor a resistor which exhibits a high coefficient of resistance to temperature, thus its change in resistance due to changes in temperature is repeatable and reliable. Two main types are available; one in which resistance increases with temperature rise, and the inverse, one in which resistance decreases with temperature rise.

Thermocouple a type of transducer in which two dissimilar conductive metals are bonded together. The effect of temperature change results in an electrical reaction which can be translated to give a digital or analog readout.

Throughput a measure of the volume of work which a system can accommodate. Used for comparative purposes.

Time Division Multiplexing ◊ TDM.

Time sharing a system where any and all users can gain immediate access to and apparently obtain immediate use of all the facilities of a computer. The operating system organises sharing of facilities to provide an acceptable level of service to all users. ◊ REAL TIME.

Time slice a specific time interval during which a device has exclusive use (or priority use) of a systems resource, such as the processor. A technique used for polling (or interrogation) in some time-sharing systems.

Time switch a circuit making or breaking device with a built in timer, to enable breaking or completion of a circuit to take place at predictable times.

Timer ◊ REAL TIME CLOCK.

Timing and control circuits the synchronising elements of a system which ensure that control signals, read/write signals, etc. are sent to the appropriate device so that reading and writing take place when requested by the processor.

Timing loop a hardware or software ROUTINE which creates an exact timing delay, used for synchronisation, sampling, etc.

Toggle switch a two position switch with a convenient lever which only allows one of the two positions to be selected.

Trace (Edit trace) a record of previous states. For example, a trace containing an image of the register contents of the last few instructions provides a valuable diagnostic aid. When applied to text processing a trace of previous edited and sub-edited levels of text is a very useful aid to authors and editors.

Track a path along which data is written or read on a magnetic disk. A jargon term for the path of a current-carrying conductor in a printed circuit.

Transaction one coherent grouping of data which can update a file or record, or produce valid output from a program.

Transducer sensory perceptors, sensors. Devices that convert (transduce) one physical variable into another. Transducers are not restricted to electrical signal conversion techniques, but these predominate as electrical methods are the most widely applied. In effect a transducer employs an element that senses a physical change and converts that change into electrical energy which in turn activates mechanisms for recalling the display of the data, either in a digital or an analog form.

Transformer a device which accepts voltage and current at one value and outputs at different values, but at the same frequency. Line transformers can provide a variety of selectable output voltages.

Transient a random and infrequent surge, very brief, caused as the result of a sudden change in conditions.

Transistor an active semiconductor device with three electrodes (emitter, base and collector). Used as a switch or as an amplifier. The transistor is used as the basis for logic gates and memory fabrication. ◊ BIPOLAR, INTEGRATED CIRCUIT.

Transistor-Resistor Logic ◊ TRL.

Transistor-Transistor Logic ◊ TTL.

Translate to change from one computer language to another whilst retaining the original meaning.

Transmission sending signals or data along a known path or circuit.

Trap a software routine, or a special circuit, that seeks out and separates particular values.

Trickle charging the means by which a battery is kept at optimum performance by the main power supply. It is charged up at odd intervals or by very minute voltages during the process. Generally intended to maintain a battery back-up unit at optimum performance level over a very long period. Can also be used to recharge any battery unit.

Trigger an initiating signal or routine; can be applied to software or hardware.

TRL Transistor-Resistor Logic. A form of electronic-based logic which makes use of discrete components. Has now largely been superseded by Transistor-Transistor Logic. ◊ TTL.

Truncate to cut short.

Truth tables the arrays that display the switching conditions or logical relationship in BOOLEAN ALGEBRA for logic operations. ◊ KARNAUGH MAP. See appendix for LOGIC CIRCUITS.

TTL Transistor-Transistor Logic. A form of logic circuit design, common in logic integrated circuits. It requires +5 volt power supply to ±5% accuracy. TTL is the lowest cost approach to logic design but suffers as a result. It is relatively simple, is intolerant of NOISE, has high power dissipation (hence heat) and is among the slowest of available technologies. Schottky TTL has improved its speed, performance and cost. ◊ SCHOTTKY EFFECT.

TTY Teletype a family of products produced by the Teletype Corporation. TTY is a standard convention for communicators, originally based on paper tape code. TTY devices include consoles, punches, readers, printers and data communications equipment. TTY standard transmission rate is 110 baud.

Tuning (fine tuning) to adjust input or output levels to obtain the exact required responses.

Turnkey the provision by a supplier of a complete computer service, from design to installation. The supplier has total responsibility for hardware, software, installation and training.

Twisted pair a two wire cable. ◊ CABLE.

U

UART Universal Asynchronous Receive/Transmit. A standard technique for receiving parallel format data and transmitting serially.

ULA Uncommitted Logic Array. Synonymous with PLA (PROGRAMMABLE LOGIC ARRAY).

Ultrasonics signal frequencies which lie outside the range of human audibility. They commence at a 20 kHz frequency.

Unconditional jump synonymous with a BRANCH instruction; a software term.

Unipolar a transistor fabricated from a single type of semiconductor.

Unit record (equipment) punch card equipment, originally developed by Dr Herman Hollerith for analysing American census records at the end of the 19th century. The unit in question refered originally to data regarding one individual or family that could be contained in a single punch card.

United States of America Standards Institute ◊ USASI.

Universal development system a microprocessor development aid that is capable of programming all common types of microprocessors. Optionally they also include IN CIRCUIT EMULATION, analysis facilities and PROM (Programmable Read Only Memory) programming devices, all contained in a console, complete with data storage and printer.

Up time the time during which a machine is operational and available for use. Down time is the reverse. These terms describe a comparative measure of, or use of, machines. See also MTBF (MEAN TIME BETWEEN FAILURE), MTTR (MEAN TIME TO REPAIR).

Update the process of seeking out and amending a record, a FIELD, a file or a document.

USASI United States of America Standards Institute. An early standard-setting body. ◊ ANSI.

Useful life the duration of a component's or device's operational life, before replacement or repair. Measured in hours.

User a person, grouping or company which makes regular use of, or has access to, computer systems.

User group a special interest organisation, formed by, for example, users of a particular manufacturer's products. It functions as a forum for ideas, as an information exchange and as a pressure group.

Utility programs standard useful programs such as sorts, disk to print, etc. Software tools.

uv Ultraviolet radiation. Electromagnetic radiation which occurs between visible light and X-ray frequencies.

uv erasable PROMS/EPROMS Programmable Read Only Memory capable of being erased and rewritten using an ultraviolet radiation technique. ◊ EPROM.

V

V Volts. ◊ VOLTAGE.

VAB Voice Answer Back. An acoustic device which enables a telephone enquiry to generate a spoken response, assembled from digitised signals held in storage (phonemes).

Vacuum tube synonymous with VALVE.

Validate (validity checking) the process of auditing output or results from a circuit or system to ascertain whether they are reasonable and fall within the bounds of probability.

Valve the devices used to implement logic circuits in the first computers. They were designed as either gas filled glass tubes or an evacuated glass tube (a vacuum) in which two or more electrodes were present. Under these conditions current flowed only in one direction. Valves, or vacuum tubes, have now been superseded by other technologies for almost all applications.

Variable any data obtained from measurement which can be altered.

VDT Visual Display Terminal. Synonymous with VIDEO DISPLAY UNIT (VDU).

VDU Visual or video Display Unit. A device for writing programs, inputting data and obtaining the results on a television-type monitor screen. The principal device for communication with a computer user in a real time system. Comprises, at most basic level, screen, keyboard, enclosure, interfacing; it may contain some logic facilities and local storage. Some video display units include a light pen.

Vector (interrupt) in assembling a system, at commissioning time or during regular restart procedures, each peripheral device is given a discrete address or label (or vector). Thus on a peripheral fault condition the system reports a vector interrupt, thereby pointing to the offending device. This information is reported on the console log.

Verification the process of checking that data converted into a media for direct input to a system has been accurately transcribed. In some cases it is done by rekeying in the data on a system that compares the original and verified data and will pass on match, and halt on any mismatch. This enables fast on-line correction.

Vertical Integration ◊ INDUSTRY MARKETING.

Very Large Scale Integration ◊ VLSI.

Visual Display Terminal ◊ VDT.

Visual Display Unit/Video Display Unit ◊ VDU.

Visual Record Computer ◊ VRC.

Virtual memory a technique offered by many manufacturers which makes the memory size look larger to the program than it actually is. The virtual memory operating system scans programs for code that has already been used or has a low priority. It then moves these parts of the programs into a temporary storage area, unknown to the user or the programmer. It does not generally affect the speed of execution if the total size of programs to be executed does not exceed available memory by more than 25% or so. Thereafter there is an increasing degradation in performance.

VLSI Very Large Scale Integration. A term applied to integrated circuits containing a minimum of 5000 logic gates, or more than 16,000 memory bits.

VMOS, VeeMOS a METAL OXIDE SEMICONDUCTOR (MOS) where the silicon crystals are fabricated with vee shaped groves in addition to nMOS capability. It is even faster than nMOS.

Volatile memory a type of random access memory (RAM) which requires a constant refresh of contents. ◊ STATIC MEMORY.

Voltage (V) a measure of the potential difference, emf (electromotive force), or voltage in a circuit. For practical purposes, potential difference, emf and voltage all mean the same thing. ◊ EXCITE, ENERGISE.

Voltage inverter a device for converting AC or DC signals to a known or predetermined DC value. ◊ SIGNAL INVERTER.

Voltmeter an instrument to measure voltage.

VRC Visual Record Computer. Basically an accounting machine in which data is stored in a printed form or on stripes of magnetic material on record cards. Microcomputers are generally replacing these limited facility machines.

W

W Watts. ◊ WATTS.

Wafer a disk of semiconductor material, often silicon. Ground to either 3 inches diameter or 100 mm diameter, the semiconductor material is then sliced up into disks or wafers, about half a millimetre in thickness (0.020 inches). Semiconductor devices, packaged into integrated circuits, are then fabricated from this base material.

WAIT a software or operating system command which causes the computer to suspend processing until a certain condition has been met.

Warm Start a system restart after a fairly brief pause, normally for no longer than ten to twenty minutes. ◊ HOT START, COLD START.

Warm up a start period to ensure that a circuit or device has reached a thermal value consistent with normal operational requirements. The time taken to reach ambient temperature.

Watchdog (timer) a device which monitors execution times for instructions. It causes an error to be signalled if the normal time is exceeded.

Watts (W) a measure of the power developed by the flow of current through a circuit. One watt is the product of one amp and one volt.

Waveform the shape of a pulse, usually associated with alternating current. ◊ SINE WAVE.

Wiper the moving contact point on a rotary potentiometer. ◊ ROTARY POTENTIOMETER.

Wire gauge the standards determining wire sizes (diameter and cross sectional area).

Wire wrap making electrical contact with wire on metal as opposed to soldering.

Wired-in components which are soldered in place in a PCB as distinct from being plugged in.

Wish list an initial statement of requirements by a potential systems user to ensure that every possible facility which may be required of the system is documented in advance. ◊ REQUIREMENTS SPECIFICATION.

Word a group of characters treated as a unit and given a single location in a computer memory.

Word length the grouping of bits that correspond to the definition of a word by the supplier. This varies from 4 bits to 64 bits. In normal programming a word is the smallest unit of memory addressed by a high level programming language. At low level or machine level it is easier to address bytes and then to mask bytes and identify and shift bits. ◊ BYTE, HALF BYTE, MASK, BIT, DATA WORD SIZE.

Word processing the use of computer techniques to manipulate text rather than data. ◊ TEXT PROCESSING.

Wraparound an auomatic overflow on to the next available line of contiguous data or text.

Write to create a magnetic record of data in a computer system.

Write after read the process of automatically reading data and then writing it on a magnetic storage device to ensure that the process of reading does not destroy the data.

X

X axis the horizontal line, real or imaginary, which forms the axis for wave shape measurement against the vertical Y axis. Also used for alignment on graph plotters, Cathode Ray Tubes and other display devices.

X punch synonymous with the 11 punch in an 80 column punch card. Used to assign a minus value.

X ray electromagnetic radiation of a high frequency.

Xerography the principle involved in normal plain paper copying where a charge pattern is produced by exposing a master document to ultra violet light and applying appropriately charged carbon base powder to the copy. It adheres to the charged area to form a facsimile of the original.

X–Y plotter a graphical output device in which results are recorded by moving the writing pen across the paper in the direction of the X and Y coordinates.

Y

Y axis the vertical axis of a waveform. ⇨ X AXIS.

Y punch a punch in the 12 row of an 80 column punch card.

Yield a measure of the efficiency of the integrated circuit fabrication process, determined by the ratio of the number of acceptable dies completed to the number of circuits started in semiconductor manufacture.

Z

Z ⇨ IMPEDANCE.

Zener diode a DIODE using the principle of zener breakdown in which at a known voltage a sharp increase in current is observed. Used to regulate voltage.

Zero access store a very fast type of memory, or area of storage, which can provide the processor with data at speeds as fast as the central processor is able to process that data.

Zero potential earth (ground). ⇨ EARTH, VOLTAGE.

Zero suppress the suppression of printing or displaying zeros that occur before the first significant digit, to ease interpretation of data.

Zerofill filling in blanks with zeros within a defined FIELD, BYTE or WORD. This ensures that no old data remaining in memory can influence the contents of storage. It is also an alternative to shifting for decimal point alignment.

Zone an area of storage; the top two punch positions on an 80 column punch card.

APPENDIX

The Greek Alphabet

Upper case	Lower case	Name
Α	α	alpha
Β	β	beta
Γ	γ	gamma
Δ	δ	delta
Ε	ε	epsilon
Ζ	ζ	zeta
Η	η	eta
Θ	θ	theta
Ι	ι	iota
Κ	κ	kappa
Λ	λ	lambda
Μ	μ	mu
Ν	ν	nu
Ξ	ξ	xi
Ο	ο	omikron
Π	π	pi
Ρ	ϱ	rho
Σς	σς	sigma
Τ	τ	tau
Υ	υ	upsilon
Φ	φ	phi
Χ	χ	chi
Ψ	ψ	psi
Ω	ω	omega

Abbreviations and Acronyms

Many microprocessor, electronic and computer terms are conveniently referred to in their abbreviated or acronymic form. The following is a summary, taken from the Glossary, to act as a quick look-up. Industry-accepted conventions are used for the application of upper and lower case characters.

A	Amps
A to D	Analog to Digital
AC or ac	Alternating Current
ADP	Automatic Data Processing
ALGOL	ALGOrithmic Language
ALU	Arithmetic and Logic Unit
ANSI	American National Standards Institute
APL	A Programming Language
ASA	American Standards Association
ASCII	American Standard Code for Information Interchange
BAL	Basic Assembler Language
BASIC	Beginners All purpose Symbolic Instruction Code
BCD	Binary Coded Decimal
bit	*bi*nary dig*it*
bpi	bits per inch
bps	bits per second
BSI	British Standards Institute
CAD	Computer Aided Design
CAM	Computer Aided Manufacture
CCD	Charge Coupled Device
CCITT	Consultative Committee on International Telegraph and Telephone
cgs	centimetre gram second

CMOS	Complementary Metal Oxide Semiconductor
COBOL	COmmercial and Business Oriented Language
COM	Computer Output to Microfilm
cps	cycles per second
CPU	Central Processing Unit
CROM	Control Read Only Memory
CRT	Cathode Ray Tube
DAC	Digital to Analog Converter
DC or dc	Direct Current
DIP/DIL	Dual In Line Package
DMA	Direct Memory Access
DOS	Disk Operating System
DP	Data Processing
DTL	Diode Transistor Logic
EAROM	Electrically Alterable Read Only Memory
EBCDIC	Extended Binary Coded Decimal Interchange Code
EDP	Electronic Data Processing
EROM	Erasable Read Only Memory
EEROM	Electrically Erasable Read Only Memory
EIA	Electronic Industries Association
EPROM	Erasable Programmable Read Only Memory
F	Farads
FET	Field Effect Transistor
FIFO	First In First Out
FORTRAN	FORmula TRANslator
G^3	Gallium
Ge	Germanium
GIGO	Garbage In Garbage Out
H	Henrys
Hi	High
Hz	Hertz
IBM	International Business Machines Corporation
IEE	Institution of Electrical Engineers
IEEE	Institution of Electrical and Electronics Engineers

ic	integrated circuit
I^{2}L	Integrated Injection Logic
I/O	Input/Output
ISO	International Standards Organisation
JFET	Junction Field Effect Transistor
K	Kilo
KISS	Keep It Simple, Stupid
Laser	*L*ight *a*mplification by *s*timulated *e*mission of *r*adiation
LCD	Liquid Crystal Display
LED	Light Emitting Diode (or Display)
LIFO	Last In First Out
Lo	Low
LSI	Large Scale Integration
MAR	Memory Address Register
MOS	Metal Oxide Semiconductor
MOSFET	Metal Oxide Semiconductor Field Effect Transistor
mips	*m*illions of *i*nstructions *p*er *s*econd
MKS	Metre Kilogram Second
MTTR	Mean Time To Restore (Repair)
MSI	Medium Scale Integration
Modem	*Mo*dulation *dem*odulation
MTBF	Mean Time Between Failure
NC	Numerical Control
NIH	Not Invented Here
nMOS or NMOS	n (or N) Channel Metal Oxide Semiconductor
npn	negative positive negative
oc	open circuit
OMR	Optical Mark Reader (or Recognition)
OCR	Optical Character Reader (or Recognition)
OEM	Original Equipment Manufacturer
OS	Operating System
op amp	operational amplifier

pcb	printed circuit board
PCM	Plug Compatible Manufacturer
PC	Programmable Controller
PERT	Project Evaluation Review Technique
PIA	Peripheral Interface Adaptor
PLA	Programmable Logic Array
PLC	Programmable Logic Controller
PL/1	Programming Language/One
pMOS or PMOS	p (or P) channel Metal Oxide Semiconductor
pnp	positive negative positive
pot	potentiometer
PROM	Programmable Read Only Memory
PRT	Platinum Resistance Thermometer
pd	potential difference (drop)
QC	Quality Control
RAM	Random Access Memory
RJE	Remote Job Entry
ROM	Read Only Memory
RPG	Report Program Generator
SI	International System (of measurement)
SIL/SIP	Single In Line Packaging
Si	Silicon
SIO	Serial Input Output
SOS	Silicon On Sapphire
SPOOL	Simultaneous Peripheral Operations OverLap
SQC	Statistical Quality Control
SSI	Small Scale Integration
sync	Synchronised, synchronous
TDM	Time Division Multiplexing
TRL	Transistor-Resistor Logic
TTL	Transistor-Transistor Logic
TTY	Teletype
UART	Universal Asynchronous Receive/transmit
ULA	Uncommited Logic Array

USASI	United States of America Standards Institute
uv	ultraviolet radition
V	Volts
VAB	Voice Answer Back
VDT	Visual (Video) Display Terminal
VDU	Visual (Video) Display Unit
VRC	Visual Record Computer
VLSI	Very Large Scale Integration
VeeMOS or VMOS	Vee grooved Metal Oxide Semiconductor
W	Watts
Z	Impedance

Multipliers

In quoting very large or very small values standard multipliers are used to avoid writing out the value in full. The most commonly used multipliers quoted as a prefix to the value are:

Prefix	Symbol	Multiplier
atto	a	10^{-18}
femto	f	10^{-15}
pico	p	10^{-12}
nano	n	10^{-9}
micro	μ	10^{-6}
milli	m	10^{-3}
centi	c	10^{-2}
deci	d	10^{-1}
deka	da	10
hecto	h	10^{2}
kilo	K	10^{3}
mega	M	10^{6}
giga	G	10^{9}
tera	T	10^{12}

Codes

Codes are used by the programmer, the operator, the user and the computer system for the same reason, convenience. In the case of the computer it is convenient to hold and read data in a binary form but to display it in either octal or hexadecimal. For the purposes of different devices interacting with each other codes such as EBCIDIC and ASCII are the most widely used. The normal user of the computer system can only usefully read decimal and alphabetic script, depending on the language spoken.

The following table is a set of comparisons illustrating the coded representations used to represent the same characters for different purposes by different notations or conventions, from number systems to data communication systems.

Note that only standard alphabetic and numeric characters have been shown here. Special characters and normal typewriter characters have EBCDIC and ASCII notations but they have been deliberately excluded for the sake of clarity.

Binary (base 2)	Octal (base 8)	Decimal (base 10)	Hexadecimal (base 16)	ASCII (7 bit)	EBCDIC (8 bit)
0000	00	0	0		
0001	01	1	1		
0010	02	2	2		
0011	03	3	3		
0100	04	4	4		
0101	05	5	5		
0110	06	6	6		
0111	07	7	7		

Binary (base 2)	Octal (base 8)	Decimal (base 10)	Hexadecimal (base 16)	ASCII (7 bit)	EBCDIC (8 bit)
1000	10	8	8		
1001	11	9	9		
1010	12	10	A		
1011	13	11	B		
1100	14	12	C		
1101	15	13	D		
1110	16	14	E		
1111	17	15	F		
0001 0000	20	16	10		
0001 0001	21	17	11		
0001 0010	22	18	12		
0001 0011	23	19	13		
0001 0100	24	20	14		
0001 0101	25	21	15		
0001 0110	26	22	16		
0001 0111	27	23	17		
0001 1000	30	24	18		
0001 1001	31	25	19		
0001 1010	32	26	1A		
0001 1011	33	27	1B		
0001 1100	34	28	1C		
0001 1101	35	29	1D		
0001 1110	36	30	1E		
0001 1111	37	31	1F		
0010 0000	40	32	20		
0010 0001	41	33	21		
0010 0010	42	34	22		
0010 0011	43	35	23		
0010 0100	44	36	24		
0010 0101	45	37	25		
0010 0110	46	38	26		
0010 0111	47	39	27		

Binary (base 2)	Octal (base 8)	Decimal (base 10)	Hexadecimal (base 16)	ASCII (7 bit)	EBCDIC (8 bit)
0010 1000	50	40	28		
0010 1001	51	41	29		
0010 1010	52	42	2A		
0010 1011	53	43	2B		
0010 1100	54	44	2C		
0010 1101	55	45	2D		
0010 1110	56	46	2E		
0010 1111	57	47	2F		
0011 0000	60	48	30	0	
0011 0001	61	49	31	1	
0011 0010	62	50	32	2	
0011 0011	63	51	33	3	
0011 0100	64	52	34	4	
0011 0101	65	53	35	5	
0011 0110	66	54	36	6	
0011 0111	67	55	37	7	
0011 1000	70	56	38	8	
0011 1001	71	57	39	9	
0011 1010	72	58	3A		
0011 1011	73	59	3B		
0011 1100	74	60	3C		
0011 1101	75	61	3D		
0011 1110	76	62	3E		
0011 1111	77	63	3F		
0100 0000	100	64	40		blank
0100 0001	101	65	41	A	
0100 0010	102	66	42	B	
0100 0011	103	67	43	C	
0100 0100	104	68	44	D	
0100 0101	105	69	45	E	
0100 0110	106	70	46	F	
0100 0111	107	71	47	G	

Binary (base 2)	Octal (base 8)	Decimal (base 10)	Hexadecimal (base 16)	ASCII (7 bit)	EBCDIC (8 bit)
0100 1000	110	72	48	H	
0100 1001	111	73	49	I	
0100 1010	112	74	4A	J	
0100 1011	113	75	4B	K	
0100 1100	114	76	4C	L	
0100 1101	115	77	4D	M	
0100 1110	116	78	4E	N	
0100 1111	117	79	4F	O	
0101 0000	120	80	50	P	
0101 0001	121	81	51	Q	
0101 0010	122	82	52	R	
0101 0011	123	83	53	S	
0101 0100	124	84	54	T	
0101 0101	125	85	55	U	
0101 0110	126	86	56	V	
0101 0111	127	87	57	W	
0101 1000	130	88	58	X	
0101 1001	131	89	59	Y	
0101 1010	132	90	5A	Z	
0101 1011	133	91	5B		
0101 1100	134	92	5C		
0101 1101	135	93	5D		
0101 1110	136	94	5E		
0101 1111	137	95	5F		
0110 0000	140	96	60		
0110 0001	141	97	61	a	
0110 0010	142	98	62	b	
0110 0011	143	99	63	c	
0110 0100	144	100	64	d	
0110 0101	145	101	65	e	
0110 0110	146	102	66	f	
0110 0111	147	103	67	g	

Binary (base 2)	Octal (base 8)	Decimal (base 10)	Hexadecimal (base 16)	ASCII (7 bit)	EBCDIC (8 bit)
0110 1000	150	104	68	h	
0110 1001	151	105	69	i	
0110 1010	152	106	6A	j	
0110 1011	153	107	6B	k	
0110 1100	154	108	6C	l	
0110 1101	155	109	6D	m	
0110 1110	156	110	6E	n	
0110 1111	157	111	6F	o	
0111 0000	160	112	70	p	
0111 0001	161	113	71	q	
0111 0010	162	114	72	r	
0111 0011	163	115	73	s	
0111 0100	164	116	74	t	
0111 0101	165	117	75	u	
0111 0110	166	118	76	v	
0111 0111	167	119	77	w	
0111 1000	170	120	78	x	
0111 1001	171	121	79	y	
0111 1010	172	122	7A	z	
0111 1011	173	123	7B		
0111 1100	174	124	7C		
0111 1101	175	125	7D		
0111 1110	176	126	7E		
0111 1111	177	127	7F		
1000 0000	200	128	80		
1000 0001	201	129	81		a
1000 0010	202	130	82		b
1000 0011	203	131	83		c
1000 0100	204	132	84		d
1000 0101	205	133	85		e
1000 0110	206	134	86		f
1000 0111	207	135	87		g

Binary (base 2)	Octal (base 8)	Decimal (base 10)	Hexadecimal (base 16)	ASCII (7 bit)	EBCDIC (8 bit)
1000 1000	210	136	88		h
1000 1001	211	137	89		i
1000 1010	212	138	8A		
1000 1011	213	139	8B		
1000 1100	214	140	8C		
1000 1101	215	141	8D		
1000 1110	216	142	8E		
1000 1111	217	143	8F		
1001 0000	220	144	90		
1001 0001	221	145	91		j
1001 0010	222	146	92		k
1001 0011	223	147	93		l
1001 0100	224	148	94		m
1001 0101	225	149	95		n
1001 0110	226	150	96		o
1001 0111	227	151	97		p
1001 1000	230	152	98		q
1001 1001	231	153	99		r
1001 1010	232	154	9A		
1001 1011	233	155	9B		
1001 1100	234	156	9C		
1001 1101	235	157	9D		
1001 1110	236	158	9E		
1001 1111	237	159	9F		
1010 0000	240	160	A0		
1010 0001	241	161	A1		
1010 0010	242	162	A2		s
1010 0011	243	163	A3		t
1010 0100	244	164	A4		u
1010 0101	245	165	A5		v
1010 0110	246	166	A6		w
1010 0111	247	167	A7		x

Binary (base 2)	Octal (base 8)	Decimal (base 10)	Hexadecimal (base 16)	ASCII (7 bit)	EBCDIC (8 bit)
1010 1000	250	168	A8		y
1010 1001	251	169	A9		z
1010 1010	252	170	AA		
1010 1011	253	171	AB		
1010 1100	254	172	AC		
1010 1101	255	173	AD		
1010 1110	256	174	AE		
1010 1111	257	175	AF		
1011 0000	260	176	B0		
1011 0001	261	177	B1		
1011 0010	262	178	B2		
1011 0011	263	179	B3		
1011 0100	264	180	B4		
1011 0101	265	181	B5		
1011 0110	266	182	B6		
1011 0111	267	183	B7		
1011 1000	270	184	B8		
1011 1001	271	185	B9		
1011 1010	272	186	BA		
1011 1011	273	187	BB		
1011 1100	274	188	BC		
1011 1101	275	189	BD		
1011 1110	276	190	BE		
1011 1111	277	191	BF		
1100 0000	300	192	C0		
1100 0001	301	193	C1		A
1100 0010	302	194	C2		B
1100 0011	303	195	C3		C
1100 0100	304	196	C4		D
1100 0101	305	197	C5		E
1100 0110	306	198	C6		F
1100 0111	307	199	C7		G

Binary (base 2)	Octal (base 8)	Decimal (base 10)	Hexadecimal (base 16)	ASCII (7 bit)	EBCDIC (8 bit)
1100 1000	310	200	C8		H
1100 1001	311	201	C9		I
1100 1010	312	202	CA		
1100 1011	313	203	CB		
1100 1100	314	204	CC		
1100 1101	315	205	CD		
1100 1110	316	206	CE		
1100 1111	317	207	CF		
1101 0000	320	208	D0		
1101 0001	321	209	D1		J
1101 0010	322	210	D2		K
1101 0011	323	211	D3		L
1101 0100	324	212	D4		M
1101 0101	325	213	D5		N
1101 0110	326	214	D6		O
1101 0111	327	215	D7		P
1101 1000	330	215	D8		Q
1101 1001	331	217	D9		R
1101 1010	332	218	DA		
1101 1011	333	219	DB		
1101 1100	334	220	DC		
1101 1101	335	221	DD		
1101 1110	336	222	DE		
1101 1111	337	223	DF		
1110 0000	340	224	E0		
1110 0001	341	225	E1		
1110 0010	342	226	E2		S
1110 0011	343	227	E3		T
1110 0100	344	228	E4		U
1110 0101	345	229	E5		V
1110 0110	346	230	E6		W
1110 0111	347	231	E7		X

Binary (base 2)	Octal (base 8)	Decimal (base 10)	Hexadecimal (base 16)	ASCII (7 bit)	EBCDIC (8 bit)
1110 1000	350	232	E8		Y
1110 1001	351	233	E9		Z
1110 1010	352	234	EA		
1110 1011	353	235	EB		
1110 1100	354	236	EC		
1110 1101	355	237	ED		
1110 1110	356	238	EE		
1110 1111	357	239	EF		
1111 0000	360	240	F0		0
1111 0001	361	241	F1		1
1111 0010	362	242	F2		2
1111 0011	363	243	F3		3
1111 0100	364	244	F4		4
1111 0101	365	245	F5		5
1111 0110	366	246	F6		6
1111 0111	367	247	F7		7
1111 1000	370	248	F8		8
1111 1001	371	249	F9		9
1111 1010	372	250	FA		
1111 1011	373	251	FB		
1111 1100	374	252	FC		
1111 1101	375	253	FD		
1111 1110	376	254	FE		
1111 1111	377	255	FF		

Logic Circuits and Binary Arithmetic

The Glossary contains various references to binary systems and gates, or logic circuits. Since all digital systems can only work on signals, the signal being present or absent (logical one and logical zero) methods to translate these signals into usable numbering systems have to be provided, hence the section on codes.

The binary system is an obvious vehicle to handle digital inputs. The following is a brief outline concerning the use of binary signals (binary digits or bits) for arithmetic purposes. It then shows how the circuitry is constructed to enable a digital system to perform all the necessary logical operations.

Binary arithmetic

For the binary equivalents of decimal numbers, see the code tables.

Binary addition

i) Add 7 to 3:

	Decimal	Binary
	7	0111
	+ 3	+0011
TOTAL	10	1010

1010 is the binary equivalent of 10

Note that each individual bit in the binary total row is known as a 'sum bit'. A sum bit can only be 1 or 0, hence they can be very useful for a validity check on a result since an addition of two odd numbers or two even numbers will always result in a zero bit at the end of the sum. The opposite is true for the addition of odd and even numbers. Hence the use of similar techniques in parity checking.

ii) Add 10 to 6:

	10	1010
	+ 6	+0110
TOTAL	16	[1]0000

10000 is the binary equivalent of 16

The bit that is shifted left as the result of a binary addition is known as the 'carry bit', hence the binary 1 in the box is the carry bit.

Therefore, for any binary addition there are a number of sum bits, which equal the largest number of bits in the adding operation. There is also a single carry bit, which is not always present.

Binary subtraction:

Subtract 3 from 7:

	7	0111
	−3	−0011
TOTAL	4	0100

0100 is the binary equivalent of 4

Binary division

It is not possible to exactly reproduce the decimal method of division in a binary system, hence a technique to perform division has been developed. This involves the *addition* of a complement. See 'Complements' in the Glossary.

An example of the complements method is:
Subtract 3 from 7 by the complements method:

3 is binary 0011
7 is binary 0111

to arrive at the complement of binary 3:

a) reverse digits, thus 0011 becomes 1100
b) add a single bit (one) +0001

Therefore the complement of 0011 (3) is 1101

The answer can now be derived by adding the complement of 3 to 7, thus:

```
      7                   0111
+ complement of 3        +1101
                         ------
                         1 0100
```

Ignore the carry bit in this method: thus 0100 is the binary equivalent of 4.

To use this method for division is merely a case of repeating the subtraction process until the required number of sum bits have been obtained. Thus to divide 7 by 3:

```
3         = 0011
Reverse   = 1100              0111 = 7
+1        = 1101  ——→ + →     1101
               (Ignore     [1]0100 = 4  Remainder from
               carry bit)               1st subtraction
                              0100 = 4
                      +       1101
               (Ignore     [1]0001 = 1  Remainder from
               carry bit)               2nd subtraction
```

Therefore 7 ÷ 3 = 2 remainder 1

This process can obviously continue to as many positions of sum bits as the calculation or computer system requires.

Multiplication

Since the values of all digits are only 1 or zero, it is a simple task to shift the whole field left or right for power changes, rather than writing in zeros as in the decimal system.

Thus, to multiply 10 by 6

```
 10 =  1010
×6  =  0110
 —   ———————
 60     0000
 —     1010
      1010
     0000
     ———————
     0111100
     ———————
```

Binary answer is 111100, which is equivalent to 60

Binary logic

The preceding section on binary arithmetic was an illustration of the techniques used to find answers to any numerically expressed problem. In fact all problems are numerical to a digital system since, no matter what data is input, by the time it reaches the Arithmetic and Logic Unit (ALU) that data has been resolved into binary digits. Therefore the ability to make decisions is merely an ability to compare strings of binary digits and make the decision: Equal? High? Low?

In fact all computer decisions are reduced to this basic test, no matter what the instruction in the programming language actually implies. The program is decoded by microprograms until it reaches the pure binary form, capable of being handled by the ALU.

Thus a computer's logic depends on the speed, flexibility and sophistication with which it is able to make the fundamental binary decisions. Logic circuits, or gates are employed for this purpose. Individual gates will accept two binary input signals and produce one binary output signal. Logic circuits are built up from arrays of hundreds or even thousands of these logic gates to meet the specific demand for any particular computer system of binary word length, storage addressing requirements, register and accumulator size, processing speed and programming language facilities. Thus as a machine increases from 4 bit to 8 bit to 16 bit and ultimately to 32 bit complexity all of the other factors previously mentioned grow in complexity on the same scale. As a result the logic circuits become more sophisticated. In fact, the complexity of the logic circuits and their size are the real differences between the microcomputer, the minicomputer and the mainframe computer. This in turn underlines the reason why that difference is so difficult to explain to the layman, since to understand the answer requires knowledge that is generally only available to the specialist.

The remainder of this section describes the basic building blocks, gates, from which logic circuits are constructed.

Gates, or logical operators

There are six basic logic gates, which may be combined with each other, or permutated and multiplied to achieve a particular central processing unit specification. These are shown opposite.

There are various conventions and aids to understanding gates. There is a circuit diagram, of which a very simplified version is used in this text; there is a logic symbol which has already been illustrated and there is a table which itemises all inputs and outputs under every condition specified by the rules, or logic, of the gate. Various forms of this table, matrix or array are known as truth tables or a Karnaugh map.

NOTATION **SYMBOL**

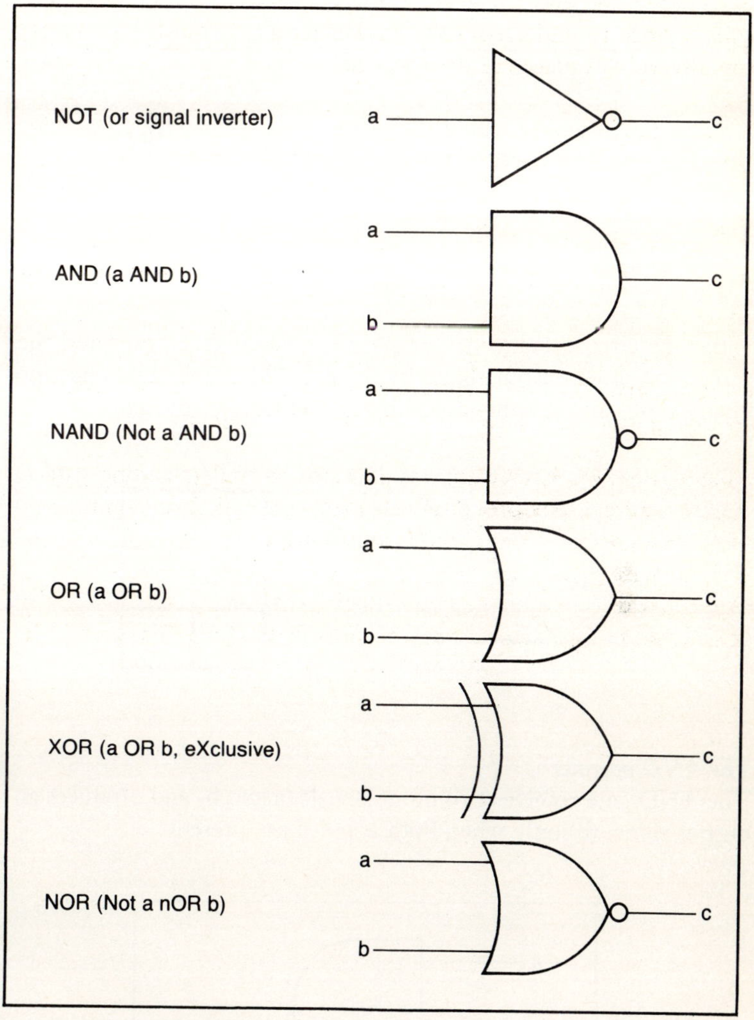

The NOT operator

Every digital signal which passes through the NOT gate is inverted and therefore interpreted by the NOT logic as the opposite signal. The NOT gate is also known as an inverter.

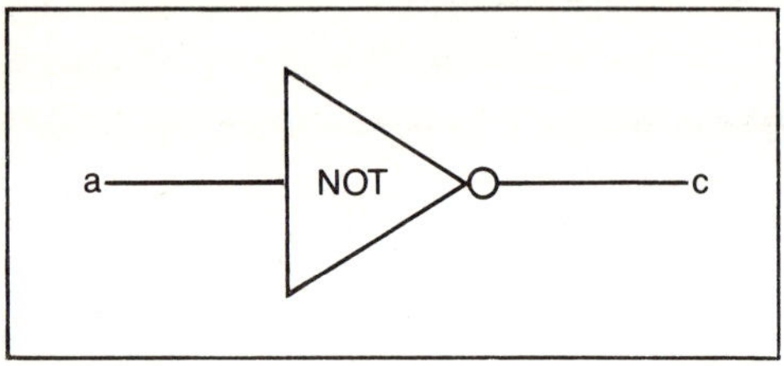

In the circuit below a completed straight line indicates the generation of an output signal by the gate. The table illustrates the binary input and outputs according to the logic of the gate.

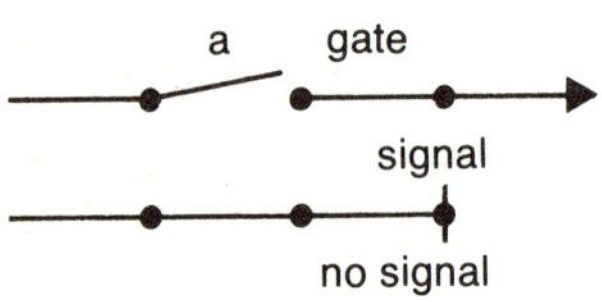

a	c
0	1
1	0

The AND operator

The AND gate receives two input signals (a and b) and produces an output signal (c) only when both a and b are present.

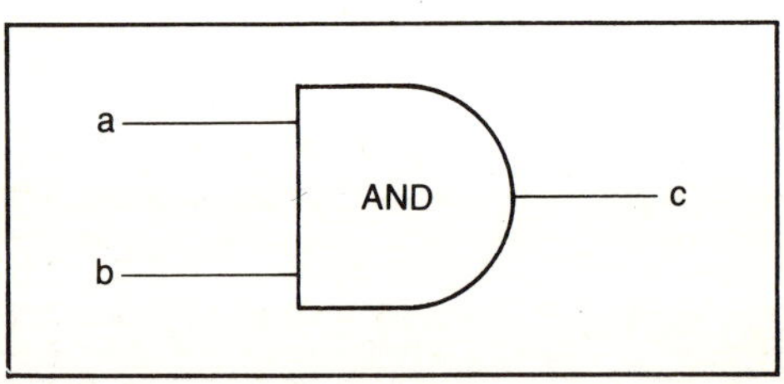

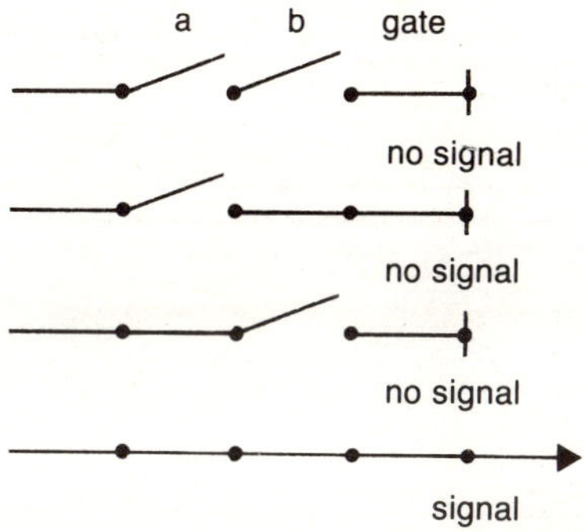

a	b	c
0	0	0
0	1	0
1	0	0
1	1	1

The NAND Operator
This is a negative AND. It says that if both inputs are present there is no resultant output, hence operationally it is an exact reversal of the AND operator, thus:

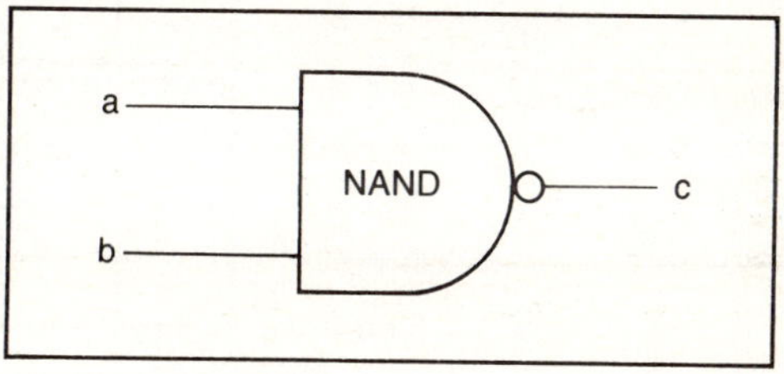

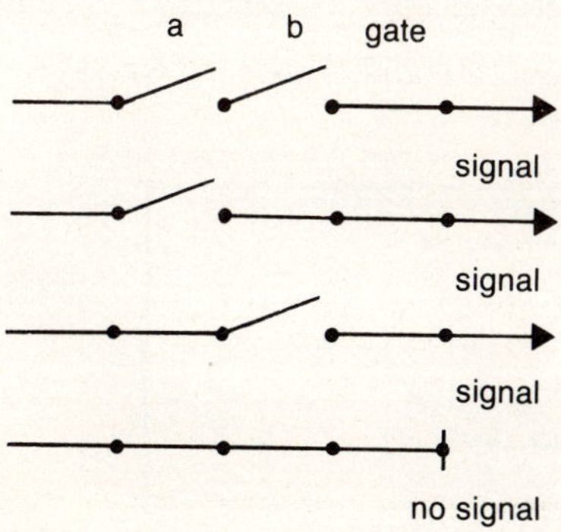

a	b	c
0	0	1
0	1	1
1	0	1
1	1	0

The OR Operator

The OR operator says that if either a or b signals are present the gate will generate an output signal. Only if neither a nor b are present will it fail to produce a resultant signal.

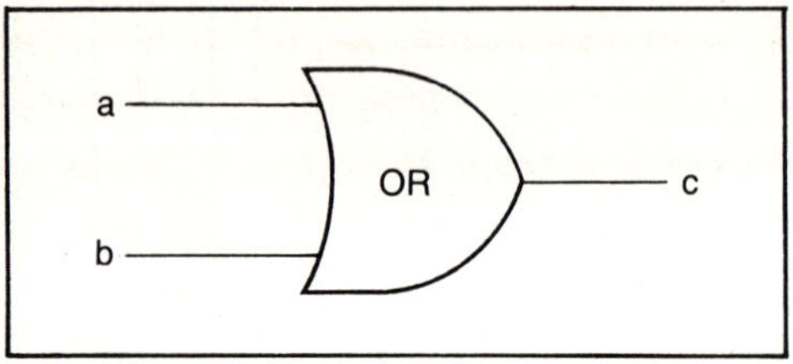

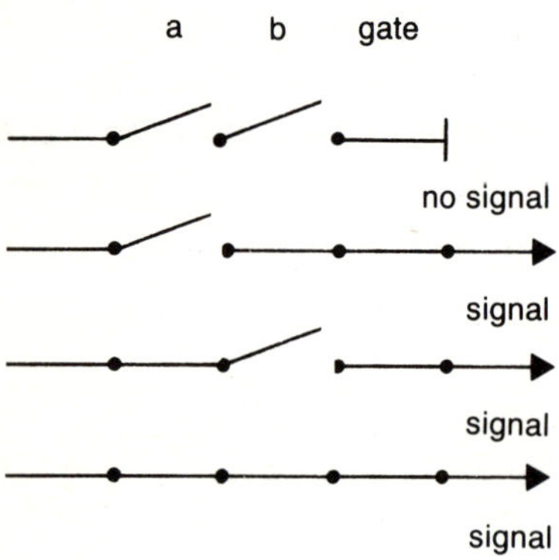

a	b	c
0	0	0
0	1	1
1	0	1
1	1	1

The exclusive OR Operator

The XOR gate says that if a is present it will generate a signal. If b is present it will generate a signal. If neither, or both are present it will not generate a signal.

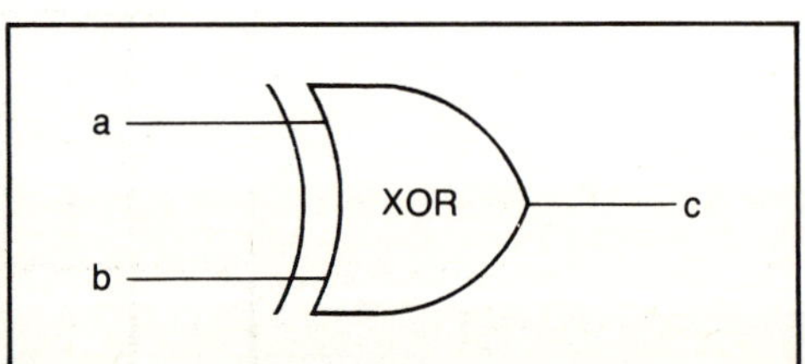

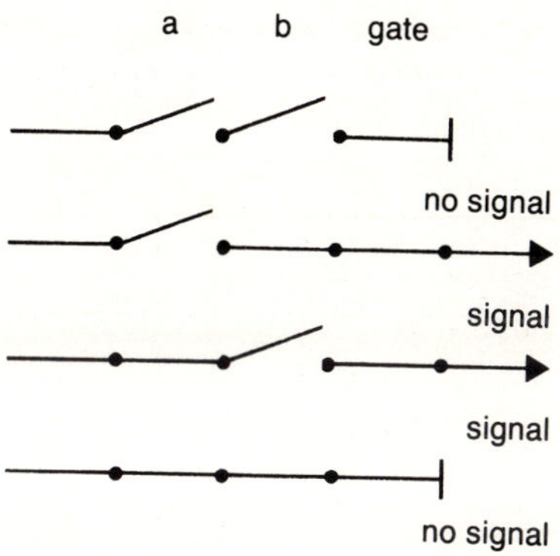

a	b	c
0	0	0
0	1	1
1	0	1
1	1	0

The NOR Operator
The NOR gate says that will not generate an output signal unless there is a total absence of input signals.

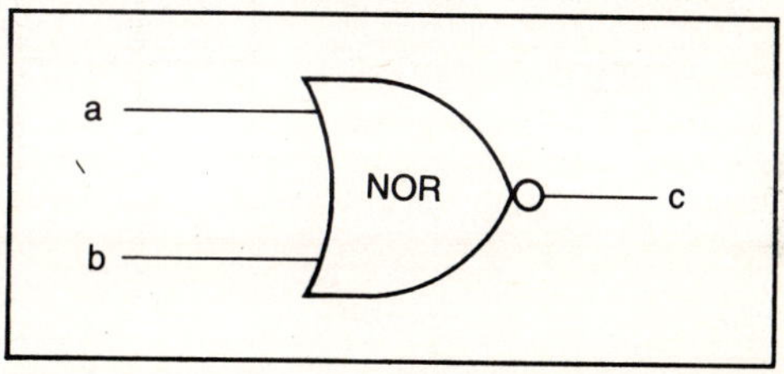

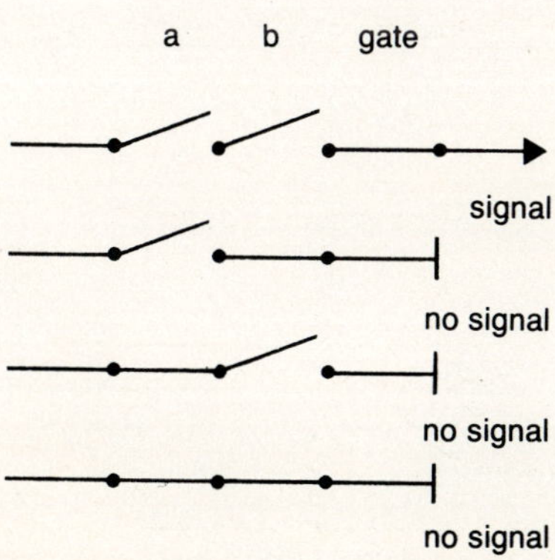

a	b	c
0	0	1
0	1	0
1	0	0
1	1	0

This brief appendix can do no more than introduce the reader to the principles of binary logic circuits. The bibliography lists several publications containing more detail on the design, construction and use of the principles briefly described here.

Bibliography

The following is a list of books providing a deeper coverage of one or more of the topics addressed by this book. The books which have been selected are the most recently published on the topic concerned. Unfortunately the book titles give very little guidance to the treatment of the subject matter. They vary from genuine introductions to in-depth treatments. However, the range listed should provide enough choice for readers of all levels.

General

F. Kinsman, *Impact of Microprocessors on British Business*, NCC, 1980

B. V. Bowden, *Faster Than Thought*, Pitman, 1953

Frank George, *Man the Machine*, Paladin, 1979

Peter Large, *The Micro Revolution*, Fontana, 1980

Christopher Evans, *The Mighty Micro*, Gollancz, 1979

G. L. Simons, *Uses of Microprocessors*, NCC, 1980

Electricity/Electronics

Martin Clifford, *Basic Electricity and Beginning Electronics*, TAB Books, 1973

Van Valkenburgh, Nooger and Neville, Inc., *Basic Electronics*, The Technical Press Ltd., 1969

Michael Deason and Terence L. Squires, *Beginners Guide to Electronics*, Newnes Technical Books, 1974

Ian McKenzie Smith, *Electrical and Electronic Principles*, Longman, 1979

J. T. Davies, J. Dutton and C. Grey Morgan, *Electricity and Electrons*, Penguin Books, 1973

Jacob Millman and Christos C. Halkios, *Electronic Fundamentals and Application*, McGraw-Hill, Kogakusha, 1976

J. M. Calvert and M. A. H. McCausland, *Electronics*, John Wiley and Sons, 1978

Noel Morris, *Industrial Electronics*, McGraw-Hill, 1978

George H. Olsen, *Modern Electronics Made Simple*, W. H. Allen, 1977

A. Morley and E. Hughes, *Principles of Electricity in SI Units*, Prentice-Hall, 1979

Philip Dahlen, *Semiconductors A–Z*, TAB Books, 1973

E. C. Young, *New Penguin Dictionary of Electronics*, Penguin Books, 1979

R. H. Waring, *Understanding Electronics*, Lutterworth Press, 1978

Microelectronics/Microprocessors

John D. Lenk, *Handbook of Microprocessors, Microcomputers and Minicomputers*, Prentice-Hall, 1979

Adam Osborne, *An Introduction to Microcomputers: Vol. O, The Beginners Book*, Osborne and Associates, 1977

Adam Osborne, *An Introduction to Microcomputers: Vol. I, Basic Concepts*, Osborne and Associates, 1976

Adam Osborne, *An Introduction to Microcomputers: Vol. II, Some Real Products*, Osborne and Associates, 1976

Charles M. Gilmore, *Beginners Guide To Microprocessors*, TAB Books, 1977

David F. Stout and Milton Kaufman, *Handbook of Microcircuit Design and Application*, McGraw-Hill, 1980

D. Aspinall and E. L. Dagless, *Introduction to Microelectronics*, Pitman, 1977

D. Roddy, *Introduction to Microelectronics*, Pergamon Press, 1978

Arpad Barna and Dan I. Porat, *Introduction to Microprocessors and Microcomputers*, John Wiley and Sons, 1976

G. L. Simons, *Introduction to Microprocessors*, NCC, 1979

Harry Garland, *Introduction to Microprocessor Systems Design*, McGraw-Hill, 1979

Donald D. Givone and Robert P. Roesser, *Microcomputers and Microprocessors: An Introduction*, McGraw-Hill 1980

Clayton L. Hallmak, *Microelectronics*, TAB Books, 1976

Jacob Millman, *Microelectronics: Digital and Analog Circuits and Systems*, McGraw-Hill, 1979

Edward V. Ramirez and Melvyn Weiss, *Microprocessing Fundamentals*, McGraw-Hill, 1980

Martin Whitbread, *Microprocessor Applications in Business and Industry,* Castle House Publications, 1979

Rodnay Zaks, *Microprocessors, from Chips to Systems*, Sybex, 1977

F. Halsall and P. F. Lister, *Microprocessor Fundamentals*, Pitman, 1980

Microprocessors, their Development and Application, ERA Technology Ltd., 1979

Martin Healey, *Minicomputers and Microcomputers*, Hodder and Stoughton, 1976

United Technical Publications, Inc., *Modern Guide to Digital Logic: Processors, Memories and Interfaces*, TAB Books, 1977

Robert Moody, *The First Book of Microcomputers*, Hayden Book Company, 1978

Computers/Data Processing

Anthony Chandor, *A Dictionary of Computers,* Penguin Books, 1977

M. G. Hartley, *An Introduction to Electronic Analogue Computers*, Methuen, 1962

Rodnay Zaks, *An Introduction to Personal and Business Computers*, Sybex, 1978

T. F. Fry, *Beginners Guide to Computers*, Newnes Technical Books, 1978

Judith Beer, *Choosing a Computer 1979*, Embankment Press, 1979

T. F. Fry, *Computer Appreciation*, Newnes-Butterworths, 1975

Edward G. Cluff, *Computerisation for the Small Business*, Input 29 1977

Martin R. Gore and John W. Stubbe, *Computers and Data Processing*, McGraw-Hill, 1979

Peter Haine and Ernest Haidon, *Computers in Business*, The Macmillan Press, 1979

T. F. Fry, *Further Computer Appreciation*, Newnes-Butterworths, 1977

Lou Frenzel, *Getting Acquainted with Microcomputers*, Howard W. Sams and Co., 1978

J. M. Eaton, *Introducing Data Processing*, NCC, 1980

Keith London, *Introduction to Computers*, Faber and Faber, 1979

Harry Katzan Jr., *Introduction to Computers and Data Processing*, D. Van Nostrand Company, 1979

Martin L. Harris, *Introduction to Data Processing*, John Wiley and Co., 1978

Glen A. Gibson and Yu-cheng Liu, *Microcomputers for Engineers and Scientists*, Prentice-Hall, 1980

Donald P. Kenney, *Minicomputers*, Amacom, 1978

M. Vardell Lines, *Minicomputer Systems*, Winthrop Publishing Inc., 1980

Steven L. Mandell, *Principles of Data Processing*, West Publishing Co., 1978

Brian L. Meck and Simon Fairthorne, *Using Computers*, Ellis Horwood Ltd., 1977

M. Peltu, *Using Computers – A Manager's Guide*, NCC, 1980

Transducers

P. H. Mansfield, *Electrical Transducers for Industrial Measurement*, Butterworths, 1973

The Bell and Howell Company, *The Bell and Howell Pressure Transducer Handbook*, CEC Division, 1974

Transducers 1: Temperature, Displacement, Force, Torque, Pressure, The Open University Press, 1975

Transducers 2: Acceleration, Vibration, Velocity, Flow, The Open University Press, 1975

G. A. Woolvet, *Transducers in Digital Systems*, Peter Peregrinus, on behalf of the Institution of Electrical Engineers, 1977

Peter H. Sydenham, *Transducers in Measurement and Control*, The University of New England Publishing Unit

Acknowledgements

The author and publishers wish to thank Ferranti Electronics Limited who generously supplied all the photographs used in this book, and *The Economist*, Motorola and *Business Week*, on whose published information figures 1, 2 and 5 have been based.

Catalog